THE
GREEN CARD
DOWRY PLAN

A TRIUMPHANT MEMOIR OF AN INDIAN IMMIGRANT'S
INGENIOUS PLAN TO BYPASS DOWRIES
FOR HIS FIVE SISTERS

THE
GREEN CARD
DOWRY PLAN

A TRIUMPHANT MEMOIR OF AN INDIAN IMMIGRANT'S
INGENIOUS PLAN TO BYPASS DOWRIES
FOR HIS FIVE SISTERS

T. R. COCA

Copyright © 2020 by T.R. Coca

All rights reserved. No part of this publication may be reproduced, stored in a retrieval system, or transmitted in any form or by any means, electronic, mechanical, photocopying, recording, scanning, or otherwise, without the prior written permission of the author.

Limit of Liability/Disclaimer of Warranty: This publication is designed for entertainment purposes only. It is sold with the understanding that neither the author nor the publisher is engaged in rendering legal, investment, accounting or other professional services. While the publisher and author have used their best efforts in preparing this book, they make no representations or warranties with respect to the accuracy or completeness of the contents of this book and specifically disclaim any implied warranties of merchantability or fitness for a particular purpose. No warranty may be created or extended by sales representatives or written sales materials. The advice and strategies contained herein may not be suitable for your situation. You should consult with a professional when appropriate. Neither the publisher nor the author shall be liable for any loss of profit or any other commercial damages, including but not limited to special, incidental, consequential, personal, or other damages.

Cover and interior design by The Book Cover Whisperer: ProfessionalBookCoverDesign.com

ISBN: 978-1-7345338-1-1 Paperback
ISBN: 978-1-7345338-0-4 Hardcover
ISBN: 978-1-7345338-2-8 eBook

Printed in the United States of America

FIRST EDITION

This book is dedicated to my loving wife.

CONTENTS

Preface		I
Prologue		III
1	Setting My Secret Goals	1
2	Arrival in America: New York City	46
3	Doctoral Dissertation	81
4	Job Reset	93
5	My Arranged Marriage	119
6	My Wife's Arrival in America	159
7	Transition: Teacher to Physicist to Lawyer	172
8	Dutiful Son, Benevolent Brother	227
9	Bar Examinations	234
10	Childbirth	255
11	Medical Residency	273
12	Triumph as Intellectual Property Attorney	317
13	Reflections	355
Author Bio		361

PREFACE

WHY DID I write this memoir? I wanted my memoir to document myself and my experiences. I wanted to keep my immigrant family's unique story immune from the ravages of time. I wanted to create memories and establish my family's traditions for generations to come. What follows is an account of the arc of my life, why I bent it to suit my life's goals.

    I always shielded and protected the privacy of my family. However, in writing this memoir, I had to close my eyes to peel back the curtain of my family's life, hoping it is the right thing to do. I only changed some names and identifying details.

PROLOGUE

AT A TIME when the immigration laws in the United States and their abuse is being hotly debated, I am telling the story of how I used the immigration laws for my family's benefit. Born into a middle-class family in India, I worked hard and earned an excellent education. With meticulous planning, I was lawfully admitted into this country as a student. I then used the U.S. immigration laws to help my father of ten children, who included five girls, from becoming destitute.

This book is about the dowry system which still prevails in India despite laws against it. The dowry is mandatory payment of wealth that is expected from the father in order to get his daughter married. The dowry is no small amount. Depending on the status, education and earning potential of the bridegroom the dowry could be astronomical. How does a father of five girls who is principled and proud to provide a good living for his family cope with the overly burdensome dowry?

I arrived under a university assistantship award to become a physicist. My original goal was to obtain my doctorate, earn money as a physicist in the U.S. and then return to India to settle down. My original expectation was that my earning potential combined with those of my four brothers who remained in India would help my father meet the dowry demands. However, this expectation soon collapsed. After earning my Ph.D., I was caught up in a U.S. recession and unable to find employment commensurate with my earning potential. This unexpected event reset my goal.

After working as a teacher and still unable to find employment as a physicist, I made a dramatic change in my career to become a lawyer. My study of law combined with my strong foundation in technology opened up a new vista to address my goal to solve the dowry problem that my father faced.

This book tells how I devised a clever solution to help my father by lawfully and judiciously using the generous immigration laws of the United States.

I qualified for my U.S. Green Card based on my scholastic accomplishments which paved the way to become an American citizen. I was able to sponsor my unmarried alien sisters to earn their Green Cards. I orchestrated their Green Cards as a currency for finding suitable husbands in India without paying dowry. The husbands then joined their new brides in the U.S. to live permanently and enrich the lives of these married couples.

In addition to looking at the hardships on India's dowry system, this book ponders on the question of whether family unification in the immigrant community still serves a vital purpose in the United States.

Do immigrants and the sponsor-host immigrant and other family already in the U.S. stay reunited? On balance, does the family unification bring in the right blend of immigrants to our country and enrich it with cultural, intellectual and economic vibrancy?

I invite you to read my story and decide for yourself.

SETTING MY SECRET GOALS

GOAL SETTING AND successfully meeting goals has always been a part of my life story. This started in my middle school years while I was playing soccer with my classmates during the lunch break and driving the ball across the goal post was that day's goal that I set for myself. Goal setting has seldom been for competitive reasons but to feel a sense of accomplishment when a goal was met. Perennial and systematic goal setting is a trait that remained with me in everything I did. My determination to achieve goals can be linked to where I am now positioned in my accomplished life.

I was born into a large and loving Hindu family. Although my father did not finish college, he had adequate education past secondary schooling to pass the administrative examinations to qualify as an Income Tax Inspector in the Federal government of India. He was excellent with numbers which was how I suppose he got into the tax business. He was also articulate in English. When his clients showed up at our home for consultation on tax matters, he always conducted business in English.

My father's job was solid, and it paid for the basic comforts of his large family. But he wasn't made of money. He was a hard-working man, as well as a disciplinarian and a stickler for principles. He admonished his children when they misbehaved or displayed unacceptable manners in the presence of others. He was by no means controlling but emphasized discipline in everything the children did. He never showed external love and affection. He seldom openly uttered, "I love you, son." However, such overt display was not common or expected in the Hindu culture. My father and I were close, and I admired him enormously.

My father believed in a higher being. Although he seldom went to Hindu temples to worship, he regularly prayed in front of Hindu gods and deities at home. Every day right after his bath, it was a ritual for him to go to the prayer area where pictures and idols of the different Hindu Gods and Goddesses were displayed over a shelf. He would pray for five minutes with his eyes focused on them.

I am not a devout Hindu. I have been a practicing Hindu when it was convenient to do so. I emulated my father in ritualistic prayer. I prayed for forgiveness and for grace and for the strength to be a good son and brother. I lived a life of faith and, eventually, scholarship.

My mother completed her secondary school and graduated with a Secondary School Leaving Certificate (SSLC). Telugu was her first language and English, her second. She was a caregiver and the one who held everything together. Every meal was freshly prepared. She named me after her father who passed away just before I was born. I did not like my name as it was old-fashioned. I thought of changing my name when I realized it was unpopular. However, such a change did not occur as I viewed it as a rejection of my mother's wish and the heritage that she wanted me to carry on. Later in life, I realized that popularity of one's name wasn't that consequential. What I wanted was to do something that mattered, to make a difference. I kept my given name and later just went by the initials TR.

To us children, my mother regularly read aloud stories from books and magazines written in Telugu. We loved hearing her read as she showed emotion in her voice in complete consonance with the happenings in the stories which rendered each one that much more vivid and real. My mother was my first coach. Her reading of stories coached me to read which endured my entire life.

Even though love was never overtly spoken, it was there always with both my parents. My siblings and I grew up knowing that our father and mother, different as they were from each other, and from us, cared. That's their legacy.

How large was our family? By the time I reached fifteen, my parents had a dozen children. I am the second with an older brother Avi of sixteen months preceding me. Two of my younger sisters (Sashi and Urmila) passed away due to health complications when they were less than five years old. Beyond those two sisters, the composition of the family was five sons and five daughters.

My parents' generation tended to have large families even though they were not agrarian. Further back, on my maternal side, my grandparents had two sons and eight daughters. My maternal grandfather was a school headmaster. My paternal grandparents had eight children, evenly split between the sexes. My paternal grandfather worked for the state government of Andhra Pradesh in an administrative capacity. It was common in those days that the women never worked, and the men were the breadwinners.

Male children were prized because of the age-old and still prevalent dowry practice in parts of India. Under this system, men commanded a huge payment of money and other assets from the bride's parents at marriage.

My parents and grandparents hailed from Kakinada in Andhra Pradesh where Telugu is spoken. Most of my parents' siblings lived around Kakinada, which was a large town on the southeastern coast of India by the Bay of Bengal. Being employed with the Federal government, my father was transferred regularly from place to place to meet the demands of tax collection from businesses. The towns and cities where each of my siblings was born provide a good roadmap of the places where my family lived. Four siblings were born in Kakinada, two were born in the rural town of Eluru, two were born in the city of Hyderabad and two in the city of Bangalore in the adjacent state of Mysore (now renamed as Karnataka). We did not live in Eluru, but two siblings were born there because my mother had older sisters who lived in that town; she chose to deliver the babies in their household utilizing their midwifery help.

I was proud to call Kakinada my place of birth. Coca (my last name) from Kakinada had a nice ring to it. I had a rare strain of the pioneer in me beginning in my childhood. I was precocious. I spent my first six years in Kakinada where I started elementary school. Soon after I entered school, my family moved to Hyderabad, which was then the capital of Andhra Pradesh. I continued two to three years of elementary-primary schooling in Hyderabad before settling down in the picture-perfect Bangalore.

It was the late summer before I just had turned ten when my father received orders that his job in Hyderabad was transferred to Bangalore. He came home very excited about the orders and showed off the transfer papers to my mother as the children attentively watched him. He raved about Bangalore and the cool climate it offered, being located at an elevation of 3,000 feet in the south-central peninsula of India. My mother asked, "Will you receive a higher salary?" He simply replied that he was promoted, without telling how much of a raise he was going to receive and added that Bangalore was a more expensive place to live.

My parents quickly identified that one of my mother's nieces (and my cousin), who was married to a Ph.D. chemist working for the Indian Dairy Institute, lived in Bangalore. My mother contacted them and asked them to line up a rental property for us in the neighborhood where they lived, which they did.

Within a month we were ready to move to Bangalore. I was excited about the move and the train journey from Hyderabad to Bangalore with my parents and seven siblings. It was my first trip anywhere. My father reserved essentially one of the train's compartments for our family, leaving four seats for other passengers. The open seats were situated across the berth from where he and my older brother and I were seated. The day's journey took nearly ten hours, from morning to dusk. Passengers got on and off at the various towns where the train stopped.

At midday at one of the train stops an English gentleman in his early thirties boarded the train and came into our compartment. He occupied a vacant seat in front of my father. The train soon roared into the cool wind and blew tiny bits of burnt charcoal from its engine into our compartment.

My father suddenly pointed to the outside and said, "Look, the woods on both sides of the train are moving backward," referring to the relative motion of the train and the surrounding woods.

The English gentleman smiled, and my father engaged with

him in a conversation in English. They discussed Indian politics it seemed, but I could not fathom what they were actually saying.

The English gentleman was holding a tiffin box and he opened it. It contained peeled hard-boiled eggs and pieces of fresh mango fruit. He offered the opened box to my father to share his lunch, and my father politely obliged by picking up an egg. The man then graciously offered tiny salt and pepper shakers, which had been tucked in the box. My father used them to sprinkle the contents on his egg.

As they enjoyed the shared lunch, I could not help admiring the Western habit of sharing food with a total stranger. This kind and generous gesture of sharing by the English gentleman was etched in my mind as a sign of human magnanimity and goodwill.

The rented house in Bangalore was small with only two bedrooms and a large indoor open space where we children played. However, it soon became apparent that its location was too far from where my father worked. He had to take three buses to get to work. He left home early and came home late, and we rarely had any time to spend with him. He started to look for a house closer to his place of work. With this uncertainty, his children's education became a casualty. None of the school-aged children were enrolled in schools and we just wasted our time exploring the neighborhood for several months until my father found a house in the High Grounds section of Bangalore.

The rented house in the High Grounds was less than half a mile from where my father worked, which made it convenient for him to walk to work. The address of 8 Miller Road became a landmark for our residence in this new city. The house was set back from the road and it had a large acreage of about 150 feet x 300 feet in the front. It was walled off from the neighbors who had equally spacious grounds. The front yard also was walled off with a set of large 10-foot-high dual gates.

The home had three bedrooms, a large veranda, a kitchen and a private bathroom. Adjacent to the house in a corridor there were two small dens and a private room for the toilet. We had complete plumbing–running water and an underground drainage system. The bathroom was fitted with an electric boiler which delivered hot water at any time of day or night at the flip of a switch. The bedrooms, kitchen and the veranda had electric power and good ventilation. Also abutting the house on the opposite side of the corridor was a spacious garage fitted with a set of large metal doors. As we did not have a car, the garage served as a bedroom for me and my older brother Avi. As the house was unfurnished, my father went to the local auction house and purchased beds, huge armoires, a large dining table that seated eight, wicker chairs, and desks. We were very comfortable in our new dwelling.

After all these moves, where my education was disrupted, I was glad that we settled down in Bangalore. The silver lining behind the disruptive moves was that I was able to skip two grades based on entrance tests that I took. I was placed in the same middle school class as Avi, who skipped one grade. I could declare that my formal education started in earnest in Bangalore.

Our next-door neighbor, who owned a large coffee plantation on the outskirts of Bangalore, invited our family to see their display of traditional dolls arranged in an aesthetic manner on nine steps during the Dasara festival. Being natives of the state, they filled us with useful information about Bangalore. I learned that the city had earned the reputation of the Garden City of India because of several public parks, freshwater lakes and such public buildings as the Vidhana Souda, the seat of the state's legislature, with its lofty landscaped gardens. Due to its high elevation Bangalore offed a moderate tropical savanna climate throughout the year with distinct wet and dry seasons. The rich diversity of flora and fauna that thrived in the city added to its reputation.

My father pursued his hobby of gardening and enlisted his older children to help with the digging of the fertile red soil that was characteristic of Bangalore and with planting seedlings or seeds for plants. He planted a variety of flowers, herbs, vegetables, fruits like tomatoes, and even crops like sugar cane, corn, peanuts and lentils. He engaged a tractor to till the acreage for planting crops. My father truly had a green thumb. Everything he planted yielded a bounty.

Books and magazines were aplenty in our house. Everyone who could read devoured them so much so that they all quickly grew dog ears. Despite the spacious quarters, living with ten siblings was a strain. I could feel the noise and chaos of a full household. A certain amount of rationing for food, use of hot water, and electricity when ironing clothes was a standard operating procedure. Sharing and working together among the family members became necessary. My siblings and I got along well. We developed a culture of comradery and accommodation. We taunted each other while doing everything whether eating papayas, *Banganapalli* mangoes, peeling and chewing on fresh sugar cane, or eating fresh peanuts boiled in saltwater. Some siblings had a sense of humor, a quality I attribute to my mother. She always preached with a smile for unity and cooperation among us children. The large dining table in the veranda where we often ate together became the center for our conversations.

My mom always sang while she was in the kitchen. She had

a melodious voice. At family gatherings during festivals and weddings, her sisters and other relatives always encouraged her to sing. After sufficient persuasion, she used to oblige and sing to the complete satisfaction of the audience. She sang like an angel, which amazed me.

My upbringing was rule-bound: unwritten rules like you must take care of yourself whether it was getting to school on your own, pressing your shirts and pants, and dealing with your injuries.

The sense of goal setting increased in me after an incident that took place soon after I graduated from high school in the spring of 1958. My older brother and I graduated from high school with our SSLC in the same year. My grade point average was excellent, and I was a few months shy of the age of fifteen then. The logical next step would have been to apply for admission to a one-year pre-university course at a college, completing it to pursue a bachelor's degree. However, my father had a different idea. He intended Avi and me to join the Indian Army.

Without any explanation, my father directed Avi and me to dress up. He ushered a bicycle rickshaw for us to ride. On his bike he led the way for the rickshaw driver. The air was crisp, the sky was blue, and we did not know where we were going. As we rode the rickshaw, I speculated that he was taking us to see a local college. We rode for well over 5 miles to the outer periphery of Mahatma Gandhi Road where we never had ventured.

Finally the rickshaw driver stopped at the entrance gate of the Army Recruiting Center on Mahatma Gandhi Road, which was guarded by two soldiers carrying army rifles. Large erected signs on both sides of the gate had pictures of such things as the tricolor Indian flag and of soldiers carrying rifles along with the words "Join the Indian Army" and "Protect India" in large letters.

My brother and I both got off the rickshaw. My father spoke to the gate guards and the three of us were let into the Army's facilities—many sprawling yellow-plastered buildings with Spartan furniture. We were led to the first building which had open doors and was airy. Large framed pictures of the Indian Prime Minister and the Indian President hung on the walls along with proclamations like "Protecting our country is our utmost duty" and "Contribute to India by joining the Indian Army." An array of the Indian Army Ranks and identifying badges in black and gold were affixed to a large wall. My father signed us in. Soon after, my brother and I were separated and escorted to different buildings.

I was orally quizzed on math, science and on my English-language reading and speaking abilities. The quizzing seemed to last for a long stretch and was grueling. Then I was led to another building with a large red-cross sign emblazoned on its outer wall. A physician clad in Army fatigues took over. He measured my height, weight and chest size. He checked my eyes for vision and ears for hearing. He checked me out thoroughly after asking me to undress. He poked my body at various places as part of the Army's physical examination and asked whether I felt any pain as he repeatedly poked me. I stammered and said, "No." He tested for my hand-to-eye coordination and reaction time. He asked me to stretch my hand out with the palm facing up. He then slammed my open palm with a cane to see whether I could avoid being hit. He looked bemused when I missed his slams all three times.

Then it was time for testing my physical skills and stamina. A different Army recruiter led me to an open sand and gravel field with planted markers separated by a distance of 100 feet and he commanded me to run four times between them. A posted sign in the field which stated, "No Pain, No Gain" only tormented my running.

The series of physical, stress and mental tests were grueling and lasted for three hours. At the end of it all, my father collected his sons and took us home. If we passed these tests, what remained would be a written test. If we also passed that, my brother and I would be ready to join the Army.

I felt disappointed that at the tender age of fifteen, my father was ready to send me off to the Army without knowing my true potential. I knew that I was capable of accomplishing far greater things in life than serving in the Army. However, my father's attempt to enroll me in the Army awakened my senses with a jolt. Later in life, I realized that between fathers and sons, it's always been the same, since the dawn of time. Fathers discouraged what their sons wanted to accomplish and directed them to meet their own wishes.

Two weeks later, we came to know by a letter received from the Army Recruitment Center that neither Avi nor I qualified for the Army. When I heard the news, I breathed a sigh of relief.

From my early childhood I kept a journal where I jotted down, before going to bed, the important happenings of that day. As I was getting ready to write down the revelation of rejection by the Army in my journal, it dawned on me that my father wanted his first two sons to be employed early, much before they reached adulthood. I kept thinking about this incident. It was his plan to receive financial support from his employed sons. He needed this support not for daily needs, which he could fully meet, but for the eventual time when he would have to pay dowries to marry off his daughters. The number of daughters had grown to five and equaled the number of sons.

Later I came to know that my father was following in the footsteps of his younger brother who persuaded his eldest son Govind to join the Army, perhaps for similar reason. Govind subsequently committed suspected suicide.

The majority of Hindus in India practiced a dowry system under which the bridegroom's family expected a large amount of wealth in the form of cash, gold and diamond jewelry, or even real estate, to accompany the bride. This sinister practice, even though outlawed on the books, was brazenly practiced by most, especially families with sons as it was a source of found wealth. The amount of the dowry was commensurate with the educational qualifications and economic well-being of the groom. Doctors, scientists, bankers and engineers commanded a much larger dowry than other grooms.

Many stories of atrocities regularly made the news when the dowry requirements were not met or reneged after the wedding. Even romantic and good marriage relationships were ensnared when the dowry was not satisfied. Sometimes the consequence of not honoring the promised dowry was fatal. Stories abounded including relegating the married bride to the menial work of a servant, physically and psychologically harassing her and even burning her alive.

I concluded that dowry payments for my sisters were inevitable and a plan for such payment must be addressed now.

What began as a chronicle of my rejection by the Army became something exorbitant. The rejection changed everything and launched my plan. It created a tension with my father but reinforced my determination to find a better and different avenue to financially help him.

Cerebrally I toyed with the thought that since there was five sons and five daughters in our family, my father could break even in the dowry gamble. He needed to offset the dowries he would receive from the families of brides for his sons with dowry payments to the families of grooms for his daughters. However, I set this thought aside as it seemed unpredictable and undependable to realize. I could not count on whether my brothers would voluntarily transfer the dowry that they would receive from their bride's family to my father so he could use that wealth to pay for my sisters' dowries. I wished, however, that my brothers would be so magnanimous.

Each of my four brothers was like a slice from different pies, each with a different perspective. Each brother was independent, and they seldom shared their thoughts with me.

I felt I needed to be pragmatic. I wanted a workable plan to address the dowry issue that my father would face. I made up my mind that I would not personally aid the sinister dowry machine. I would renounce the dowry from the parents of my would-be bride. I could not predict whether my independent-minded brothers would do the same. If they did, then my father could proclaim that, as a matter of principle, he would take no dowry for his sons nor pay dowry for his daughters to get them married. Under this principle, no money was needed for my father to marry off his children. Otherwise, my father would need a huge source of independent wealth to pay for the dowries of my five sisters. If he were to pay for the dowries of his daughters, he was bound to go bankrupt and become destitute.

It was then that I conceived a master plan, which was simple, I thought. I should go overseas to a wealthy country, establish myself as a professional, earn money and financially help my father to pay for the dowries for my sisters. The plan sounded ennobling for sure, but it depended on my accomplishing step-by-step the many challenging intermediate goals.

The challenges were many, burdensome and drawn out. The plan needed systematic attention, perseverance and eternal patience to work. Being goal-oriented from early on, I did have the beginning of a goal for my life—despite having fears about my future and doubts about myself. I wanted to earn an impeccable education. This was the cornerstone of my overall goal. Only impeccable academic accomplishments would open the doors to achieve my goal.

I was a precocious young man. My larger and long-term goal to financially help my father generated a number of short-term goals: I must get an impeccable higher education in India; I must decide which foreign country would be best for my further studies; I needed to apply to the foreign university, compete with applicants from around the world for admission, earn a scholarship and excel in my studies; I had to prepare myself to live in such a foreign country; and after graduating must professionally establish myself in that country, earn money and help my father.

I had to quickly decide what career path I should pursue. Since my major subjects in high school were physics and mathematics with a minor in chemistry, I was pretty much destined to pursue a career as a physicist or engineer. I regretted that I did not major in biology in high school. Otherwise, pursuing medicine would have probably been a logical and fitting career for my personality.

I applied for my undergraduate education in the most prestigious college in Bangalore—the St. Joseph's College which was an all-boys private school and run by Roman Catholic Jesuit priests. It was generally hard to get admission to this college, but my grades were good enough to apply. I was very lucky and received acceptance from St. Joseph's.

Fide et Labore (faith and labor) was the Latin motto of St Joseph's College, which perfectly matched my life governed by faith in hard work.

I had the benefit of competing with the crème de la crème of students from the city and got educated by some of the best professors, including many catholic priests. The Vice Principal of the college who was also the Head of the English Department, Father Lawrence, a slender man in white robes, took particular interest in me. He became my unofficial counsellor and a phenomenal mentor who listened to my thoughts and anxieties about attaining my goals. Father Lawrence guided me on how to think and what to think. Making informed, thoughtful choices in every area of student life was a learning experience that he stressed.

St Joseph's did not have a decent cafeteria, except for a small kitchen and an adjacent room under the same roof where simple Indian meals were served. It was always crowded, particularly at lunch time. This forced me every school day to dash home on my bicycle during the lunch break for a hot Indian meal. That ride refreshed me and split the day into two manageable segments.

My years at St Joseph's were also steeped in lessons about the value of conscience and compassion for others. Social service to benefit the poor and displaced was emphasized by Father Lawrence. He led small groups of us students on the weekends to nearby villages where people were suffering from poverty or affected by natural disasters like floods. We collected food and clothing donated by the Red Cross and distributed them to the villagers and assisted them in rebuilding their homes.

St. Joseph's promoted my critical thinking—not just having me embrace ideas but also encouraging me to challenge them. Because of this training, I was able to look at situations from a critical standpoint to be able to make the right decisions when presented with choices.

The diverse student body came together from many faiths including Hindu, Muslim, Christian and Jews and many different Indian languages were heard in the classroom, laboratory, and while participating in various academic competitions and social functions. Occasional entertainment where the students performed magic tricks or sang popular rock and roll songs with an organized band was something I looked forward to enjoying. I won essay competitions and was awarded prizes, including the books of Homer's *Iliad* and the *Bhagavad-Gita*.

I regularly volunteered to set up the annual event for parents on campus organized by the faculty. It had a white tablecloth reception where food was served, and the featured speakers presented topics of interest to them and about the academic accomplishments of the College. After one such event, in which my father participated without my mother, he cryptically commented that he did not care for the speech given by the British-educated English professor who taught me Shakespeare. My father said, "I did not care for the professor's attempted British accent. He appeared fake, particularly mixed with his bellowing laughter."

My determination to excel in the courses I took and the hard and disciplined work I applied paid me rich dividends. I pursued a double major in Physics and Mathematics with a minor in

Chemistry. I regularly supplemented my coursework by devouring books—English literature, fiction, mystery novels, and physics titles especially biographies of physicists. Competitive tennis after school with my college mates at St. Joseph's kept me physically fit and mentally alert.

At the end of completing my coursework came the statewide university examination. I was one of more than three thousand students who competed in the statewide university examination that year. Performance in this examination determined a student's overall academic capability and the university certified the achievement. I was blessed and did well in the examination. I earned the distinction of being placed in the First Class and ranked as one of the top 10 students in the university's award of Bachelor of Science degree that year.

After earning my B.Sc. degree, it was time to pursue my Master's in Physics. The university offered the graduate study program to only two colleges in the state—one was based in Bangalore and the other in Mysore. I obtained admission with the group based in the Central College, Bangalore. The best of the best graduates pursued graduate studies and I was among them. The professors who taught advanced courses in physics were excellent. Many of them received their doctorates from universities in Canada, U.K. or U.S.A. and developed interesting foreign accents which set them apart from the other professors who were educated in the Indian academia.

Choosing an area of specialization in Physics was the next decision that I faced.

Three years earlier I was inspired by an older cousin, Babu. He was the son of my father's older brother who lived in Kakinada. It is there that Babu completed his pre-engineering studies. My cousin came to spend a summer with my family while awaiting the decision for admission to an engineering school in Bangalore to which he had applied. Babu was four years older than me. He became a role model for me and my older brother Avi. He taught us mischief, such as dragging us to the Hollywood movies in local theaters. He made sure we always went to a matinee and returned home before my father did. (If we weren't home when my father returned from work, he would question our whereabouts.) On one occasion, he persuaded me to try smoking a cigarette which I did, but I thoroughly detested it and never smoked again after that experience. Babu treated us to afternoon snacks in fancy restaurants and to excellent coffee in the famous India Coffee House which subsequently became habit-forming for me.

Although Babu applied for admission to study engineering, he suggested that nuclear physics was an up and coming field for me to pursue. India just had inaugurated its Atomic Energy Commission and built the first nuclear reactor for its growing energy needs.

The thought of pursuing a career in nuclear physics stuck with me ever since. I thought it would offer good opportunities to further specialize in this field if I were to go overseas. A career in nuclear physics worked as a hedge if I were to remain in India because of the country's modernization by shifting from coal burning to nuclear power.

As expected, I chose nuclear physics as my specialty during my second year of the master's program.

SETTING MY SECRET GOALS

As my graduate study progressed, I concurrently engaged in activities which enhanced my chances to go abroad. One of them was my deep association with the people at the United States Information Services in Bangalore. The U.S.I.S. was run by the U.S. State Department and was headed by Bob Woods—an American national. Bob had a large staff of Indian nationals under him. The U.S.I.S. housed a large public library with many American books, magazines, newspapers for the general public to read and learn about America. The U.S.I.S. occasionally organized cultural performances by touring groups of professional American entertainers in local theaters and music halls.

I frequented the U.S.I.S. to read about America. One morning I decided to stop by Bob Woods' office to introduce myself and query about higher studies in America. I climbed up to Mr. Wood's lofty office. Bob was not in his office. His secretary, a charming American woman, directed me to speak with the deputy head at the U.S.I.S., George Thekekara, in an adjacent office. George was well-dressed in a white shirt and a necktie matching his pants. He rose up from his seat and greeted me with a firm handshake. From the very first moment I met George, he took special interest in helping me after I expressed my desire to go to the U.S. for higher studies. He was an Indian Christian from the state of Kerala and was very helpful with many aspects of the U.S. system of education which I did not know. It was easy and inspiring to talk with George as he came across as bubbly, gregarious, positive and encouraging. George and I instantly became good friends. He wanted to know all about me and when I mentioned that I graduated from St. Joseph's, his eyes lit up in admiration. Plus the fact that I was at Central College now pursuing to be a nuclear physicist impressed him even more.

Just then Bob Woods was entering his office, and George shouted at him, "Bob, come over here and meet this young man who wants to go to America for his doctoral studies."

Bob stopped in his tracks and came over and shook my hand. He commented, "Caltech and MIT are the best schools for a Ph.D. in physics."

I replied, "if only I could get admission and a scholarship from either of them."

An activity that I pursued with a passion was public speaking. I wanted to rid myself of my Indian accent, improve my vocabulary, and communicate with foreigners, particularly Americans, in a manner they could easily comprehend. I even trained my voice by going early in the mornings to the Bangalore Golf Course near our home and yelled to the wind cracking open my vocal cords on any topic that came to my mind. I wanted to train my voice to speak in a tone that appealed to listeners.

I listened to the Voice of America broadcasts not only to learn more about America but also to imitate the American accent, vocabulary and speech. By listening to the VOA programs, I got hooked on the American music and songs which the station regularly played and became familiar with the music scene in the U.S.

It was a period when the space race between the Americans and Russians had taken a feverish pitch. I was fascinated by this race and got immensely interested in the physics behind the mission to the moon and its unmanned rockets and satellites. I admired President John Kennedy's ambitious goal of sending American astronauts to the moon and safely returning them to the earth before the end of 1969. I rooted for the Americans to succeed.

The real platform for my public speaking was the Toastmaster's club at the local YMCA where college students participated to develop their speaking skills. I was a regular attendee of the club meetings as public speaking became an important and immediate objective for me.

It was time to narrow down the foreign countries to possibly go to for my higher studies. I immediately ruled out the United Kingdom as I was totally disillusioned by U.K.'s colonization and suppression of India for over two centuries. I was saddened by U.K.'s recalcitrance on the manner in which India was divided into two countries, which lead to bloodshed and forced migration of thousands of families. I gathered that this colonial power had plundered India and left it destitute, which bothered me quite a bit.

Then there was the old Soviet Union (U.S.S.R.) which ruled one-sixth of the planet's surface from Finland to Mongolia. The books authored by Russians on physics that I read sounded different from those that I used in college. While the principles of physics described in them were accurate, the names of physicists, like Isaac Newton, Albert Einstein and Max Plank, famous for their great discoveries and laws of physics, were replaced by Russian names which I never heard of. This raised suspicion of the books' authenticity and led to me to conclude that the Russians were faking the books for Communist propaganda and their country's aggrandizement. I sensed that the Russian government was flawed, as it did not seem to rest on values but on a set of malignant practices whose aim was to maintain power in the hands of dictators. In addition, the Indian leaders' close alignment with the Russian government for military and other aid bothered me. I thought it was not a good fit for democratic India to be aligned with Communist U.S.S.R. I strongly believed that India's alignment with the U.S. would have been a better fit.

I considered Germany as another country for my higher study. Earlier, I took courses in the German language at the local Max Muller Institute and picked up enough vocabulary to engage in simple conversational German. However, my interest in Germany for studies quickly waned because of the language barrier that I would have to deal with if I were to study there.

I was drawn toward the U.S. for my higher studies. The U.S. was founded on a set of democratic principles, such as the rule of law where the citizens were sovereign and were sources of power for the government. The free market economy based on capitalism that America established had been the envy of the world. America did not seek territorial expansion or attempt to impose its way of life on others. Instead, America helped build democratic institutions to defend sovereignty, security and prosperity. I was convinced that Americans were a people of deep faith and unsurpassed record of charity and fairness at home and around the world. I thought that the U.S. was an exceptional country. It was a beacon of hope and prosperity and I deeply admired its open society. My desire to go to America, as a key step toward my ultimate goal, got into my bones.

In my quest to establish friendships with Americans, using referrals by Father Lawrence at St. Joseph's, I developed two pen pals in the U.S. I also initiated letter writing with a third pal who lived in West Berlin, Germany. The American pals Sherry Derr and Ann-Judith Silverman were polar opposites in many ways. Sherry was from the rural town of Janesville, Wisconsin. She was fun-loving. She wrote about the Hollywood movie scene, particularly about stars like Elvis Presley. On the other hand, Ann was a city girl, an undergrad at the University of California, Berkeley. In the letters I exchanged with Ann, we regularly compared college life in the U.S. and India.

My German pen pal Heidi Claus was serious in her letters. I suspected that she wanted to write to me in order to improve her English vocabulary and writing skills. She lived in West Berlin near the Brandenburg Gate's rock wall which tragically separated her friends and relatives living in East Berlin. Heidi's occasional reference to the wall infuriated me over Russia's cruelty and disregard for human rights. It reinforced my decision not to go to U.S.S.R. for my higher studies.

Through the U.S.I.S., I came across two American scientists who had published papers on space-related topics and who interested me. I initiated corresponding with them on an intellectual level.

Dr. John O'Keefe was a geologist at NASA's Goddard Space Flight Center in Baltimore, Maryland. His research was on tektites, which were objects made of compressed minerals that fell to earth from outer space. The paper he published, which caught my attention and led me to correspond with him, speculated that tektites may be found in India. In our correspondence, he suggested that I should ask around and look for tektites in India. I did not do this as I was immersed in my studies and did not want to be distracted by the esoteric tektites.

Dr. Talbot Chubb was a physicist who worked at the U.S.

Naval Research Laboratory in Washington, D.C. He was a researcher who had separated uranium isotopes for the U.S. military's Manhattan Project which built the first atomic bomb during World War II. After the war he joined NRL where he performed upper-atmospheric research on solar flares. From his letters to me and from his published papers that I read at the U.S.I.S. library, I knew he was also involved in experiments to measure the temperature of certain stars, including the Sun.

Both Dr. O'Keefe and Dr. Chubb were gentlemanly and polite and took time to reply to my letters. We regularly corresponded for years. The scientific roles they held and the research they conducted inspired me and made me more determined to go to the U.S. and one day be like them.

As I was focusing on my goal to go abroad, my father was transferred again, this time to Ernakulum, a city in the adjacent state of Kerala. He had the wisdom not to move us to Ernakulum. Expecting that the transfer would be temporary, he decided to go there alone.

My brother Avi was unable to secure a seat at a local engineering college which he so desperately wanted to attend. Instead, he was forced to pursue engineering through correspondence which meant not having the benefit of live lectures and interaction with classmates. However, the free time gave him plenty of opportunities to play cricket which he loved. My three younger brothers—Ohan, Enku and Kash—were attending the same school in Bangalore as Avi and I had.

When it came to education for my sisters, particularly two of them, my parents did not encourage them like their sons. My first sister Jaya went to school on an irregular basis, partly because her education was interrupted by my father's frequent transfers and also because she was a much-needed help to my mother who was perennially pregnant. By default, Jaya was a surrogate mother for her sisters. She helped my mother with the cooking, cleaning and other household chores. She followed my mother in her Hindu religious beliefs. When my mother, who worshipped the Sun like the Greeks did, by directly facing the early morning Sun, Jaya followed suit. Whenever she got an opportunity, Jaya went to the temples with my mother as a way to escape the household chores. She was loyal and dependable, always subservient to the older males. Being the first of many daughters, she strived to be a strong role model to her younger sisters, despite lacking formal education. However, at the same time, she was secretive and never shared her thoughts.

My second sister Swati was feisty and wanted to be educated, starting from her early childhood days. She wanted her space and never let anyone invade it. She was to a certain extent a control freak. Swati was selfish, stubborn and angry. She disliked my father and avoided interacting with him as much as she could. She buried herself in her schoolbooks and worked hard enough to earn good grades in high school. This served her well as she gained admission to the Mount Carmel College for girls, which was the counterpart of the St. Joseph's College for boys.

My third sister Vitri was another neglected daughter. She never received formal education and essentially became a household sidekick like Jaya. She was docile, quiet and was satisfied with playing with her siblings when they were home. She never asked for anything and was content with the hand-me-down clothing from her older sisters. Even though she was neglected and abused, Vitri maintained a cheerful and positive demeanor.

My last two sisters, Mini and Mala, received a lot of attention from their older siblings. I remember their births. For the birth of Mini, the whole family, except my father who remained in Bangalore because of his job, went to my mother's older sister's (Aunt Satyam). Mother had her ninth child delivered there at my aunt's home in Eluru. A midwife assisted my mother and Aunt Satyam in the delivery of the new baby. Her delivery took place on a dark new moon night. A comment that my Aunt Satyam made that night stuck in my memory; she uttered the words "the devil has born." Perhaps, she was hoping the newborn would not be a girl in which case my father would not be burdened with a dowry payment. Or was she referring to Mini's birth on a new moon night, which was considered as inauspicious in the Hindu religion?

Mala came into this world unremarkably on a July evening in the Bowring Hospital in Bangalore. An incident that happened to me at home while my mother was admitted to the hospital for the delivery of Mala was literally etched in me. I was helping my sister Jaya with her household chores one morning after my father left for work. As was customary in India, milk was not refrigerated and sometimes was on the verge of spoilage when it was delivered. To kill bacteria and pasteurize it I wanted to boil the delivered milk. I put the milk in a large stainless-steel container. Then I placed that on the kitchen stovetop, which was well above my waist level, and turned the stove on. I was distracted and did not pay attention to the time I left the milk boiling. I suddenly noticed that the milk was bubbling over and spilling on the hot stove. In my haste, I grabbed the hot steel with my bare fingers to get it off the stovetop and the disaster stuck. The boiling milk spilled on my tummy and my skin was singed and an acrid smell emanated.

I received second degree burns. The servants rushed me to the

Bowring Hospital where I was admitted and treated for burns. After this incident when people asked whether I could cook, I would open up my shirt and show the scars on my stomach as evidence that I spent quality time in the kitchen!

Mini and Mala received a lot of personal interaction with their older siblings and flowered into cheerful girls. Adding to this, they commenced their nursery school early at St. Ann's Convent which was run by Catholic nuns and was conveniently located right across from our house. They regularly rehearsed many nursery rhymes at home and entertained the entire family. English was the only language used at St. Ann's to teach all subjects. Because of this early schooling and interaction with their older siblings, both sisters turned out to be outgoing, ebullient and displayed a sense of adventure. Mini was a dreamer with an innocent outlook on life and was also disorganized and undisciplined. Mala was vibrant, spirited, graceful and always fun-loving.

Of all my sisters, I was particularly concerned with the lack of formal education that my sisters Jaya and Vitri suffered from. I knew then that finding a good groom for them was going to be a challenge. This was not only because of their lack of education but also because while good-looking they were not beauty queens. It became apparent that in terms of dowry, my father would have to pay more than the normal amounts for these sisters to get them married.

As predicted, within a short period of over a year, my father was transferred back to Bangalore and we were so delighted to see him home. My father then faced the deadline for the big examination that he needed to take. By passing it, he would qualify for the prestigious job of Income Tax Officer which he so badly wanted. He studied with determination, mostly after six days of work at the office and on Sunday.

On the eve of the big exam, being the avid gardener that he was, my father wanted to trim the over-grown rose bushes in our garden. He was using a hand shear to trim them when his right thumb got caught in it and was smashed. My mother and we children worried whether—since he needed the thumb to hold a pen and write answers to the exam questions the next morning—he would be able to take the exam. Despite his injury, he did take the exam the next day.

Three weeks later, my father came home and broke the good news that he had passed. He was promoted to the rank of Income Tax Officer, which bought a sense of achievement to him and a raise in salary. He immediately had business cards printed with his name and the title of Income Tax Officer. This title, more than anything else, brought a sense of pride to him and he cherished it. He was at the peak of his job performance then and he was some six or seven five years away from the government-mandated retirement age.

My father's impending retirement added anxiety to my life. I wondered if I should soon step in to fund the family's necessities as he would not be able to support the family on his pension. I initiated my search of U.S. universities that I should consider for applying for my higher studies, particularly institutions which were willing to grant financial aid to foreign students.

I kept up with my correspondence with my pen pals Sherry and Heidi. However, I lost touch with Ann-Judith for more than six months until I received an airmailed letter. When I read her letter, I could not believe the profound changes in her life that had taken place. She was caught up in the student protests against the war in Vietnam on the campus of the UC Berkeley. She was arrested and faced expulsion from the university. She fled to Germany and abruptly got married to a German sailor. I was startled by these changes in her life. Meanwhile I admired her tenacity to protest for causes that she believed in. I wrote back conveying my feelings and wishing her well.

My sister Jaya, who had reached her high teen years, finally began to receive my parents' attention to make her eligible for marriage. As a way of compensating for her lack of formal education, my parents decided to provide her with music lessons and engaged a music tutor. The tutor turned out to be one of my high-school classmates who performed at the high-school shows by singing popular songs. I was not sure whether he had received formal music education as I had lost touch with him after high school. Nevertheless, he brought a portable harmonium instrument and played it as an accompaniment while teaching Jaya to sing traditional songs from classical Indian music.

The music teacher came once a week and taught Jaya for an hour. Jaya's way of getting ready for the music teacher was to look in the mirror and apply another coat of mascara. My mother would ask why she was getting dolled up for her music teacher. "Don't you think you should be practicing music instead of putting on makeup?" I overheard mother ask once. Several months of tutoring did not seem to bring out Jaya's artistic talents and my parents ended the lessons.

Months later when I was home, the music teacher appeared at our house dressed in pure white and sitting atop a motorcycle that made a thunderous vroom, vroom sound. I greeted him after he turned off the roaring bike and asked, "What brings you to our house, now that you are no longer providing music lessons?"

He glanced at his motorcycle.

I asked, "Is the bike new?"

He made an affirmative nod. He asked, "Is Jaya home? Could I see her?"

I replied, "Yes" but confronted him with the question of "why?"

He touched the black-leather passenger seat and said, "I would like to take her for a ride on my new bike."

Knowing the music teacher from my high-school days as a classmate, I did not think much of him. I suspected his motives were sinister. I was convinced that he would not be a good provider if he were to develop a romantic relationship and marry Jaya with the elders' approval. This prompted my abrupt action against his overtures toward my sister. I told him, "Buzz off, my friend." He roared off, creating a dust storm in his wake.

Concurrent with the tutoring in music, there appeared another young man on the scene who took a sudden and special interest in our family. He was Raj, a distant relative who was completing his Ph.D. in biochemistry at the prestigious local Indian Institute of Science. Raj had recently married my cousin Shini (the daughter of the brother-in-law of one of my mother's older sisters). The newly married Shini remained with her parents in Kakinada following the wedding while her new groom returned to Bangalore to finish his dissertation. I knew Shini well because of our periodic summer visits with my maternal family in Kakinada. I thought that she fell short when it came to being feminine in her looks, mannerism and speech. I could only surmise that Raj was enticed by Shini's parents with a huge dowry payment because he was tall, handsome and on the verge of earning his Ph.D. This degree assured that he would find a good job and would provide a good life for his bride.

Whenever Raj arrived at our home, he first would meet with Avi and me. On one such occasion, he came to our open garage and asked what my plans were after I completed my Master's. He noticed on my desk the Directory of U.S. Universities that I had borrowed from the library.

I responded, "I might apply for a job with the Atomic Energy Commission."

He queried whether I would apply for the Ph.D. program at the Indian Institute of Science where he was finishing his Ph.D. I expressed no such interest and I volunteered, "I might try to go abroad, instead."

It turned out that Raj and I had similar interests. I wanted to go abroad to earn my Ph.D. He wanted to go abroad for his post-doctoral fellowship. We both discussed and arrived at the conclusion that North America should be our destination for higher learning. He leaned toward Canada, whereas I leaned toward the USA. This commonality of purpose bonded us somewhat.

Months later, I asked Raj to join me in the hosting of a young American Peace Corps volunteer who I had invited to visit my family. Over cups of tea and crunchy biscuits we discussed many topics with the volunteer, including American politics particularly America's deep involvement in the war in Vietnam and my desire to go America. I shared my wild dream with her of studying at Caltech while Raj shared his dream of doing research at the University of British Columbia. I had photos taken with the American girl, Raj, Jaya and me.

Raj would regularly visit my family on Sunday afternoons and spent time with Jaya listening to broadcasted shows for teens on All India Radio. In fact, all of my siblings congregated to listen. On some occasions, Raj took my sisters Jaya and Swati to local parks to spend private time with them, despite the fact that he was married. My parents probably thought that because Raj was married and was a part of our family, his motive to spend time with my sisters was harmless.

In my graduate studies, I used many books in different fields of physics. One book stood out as my bible for specialization in nuclear physics. This was a book authored by Rob Evans titled *The Atomic Nucleus*. It was recommended by a professor at Central. I could not find it in local bookstores. However, my father managed to get it for me. *The Atomic Nucleus* was a classic text on the experimentalist's approach to the understanding of nuclear physics. Being a pragmatist, I was driven to the side of the experimentalist (ideas based on experiments) versus theory and adored this book. I loved studying nuclear physics.

Having successfully completed my course work and experimental research in nuclear physics, it was time to take the university examination for my master's degree. The university examination was given to graduate students in many disciplines including physics. Nearly two hundred students in these various disciplines across the university took this examination and vied for their class and rank. Of the sixteen students in my class, three male students including me stood out as the best. The desire to make a name among us was intense. Some of our professors quietly identified their favorite candidate and rooted for him to come out on the top. I knew that at least one professor was rooting for me.

The university examination consisted of three parts: theory, practical and *viva voce* (oral exams), where each component required a minimum score of 35% and an aggregate score of 40% in these components to be earned for passing. I earned an aggregate of over 69% and passed the examination in First Class. Crowing this accomplishment, I was ranked #7 in the university. I knew then that this was a good omen–of being the lucky seven!

I was three months shy of twenty-one then. I briefly looked back at my life and felt good about achieving my perfect report card though my will and hard work. I was on track to reach my goals.

Energized by the success in my education, I compiled a list of U.S. universities to apply to for admission to a Ph.D. program. George T. at the U.S.I.S. was a great resource in winnowing my list. He gave me some commonsense advice like "Don't apply to Caltech or MIT." He gave me some confounding recommendations: "Apply to less well-known schools like Case Western, Lehigh, Lincoln, Purdue, Stevens and Temple. These schools have a proven record of granting admission to Indian grads." He reinforced my goal of applying to schools which had the financial ability to grant a scholarship. "Getting into any university in the U.S. which offers financial assistance is an important first step," George preached. "You can always change schools once you are in the U.S." The short list that I winnowed down with George's help included Temple University in Philadelphia, Pennsylvania.

I graduated with my master's degree in late spring. It would be perfect if I could start my Ph.D. study that fall. Although my filing of the applications was quick, the selection by the universities' faculty committees and approval of the financial aid packages took many months. I filed my applications and patiently waited for approval.

While waiting, I wanted to be gainfully employed. I applied to an entry-level physicist position at the newly opened Tata Institute of Fundamental Research in Bombay. Based on my credentials, I was invited for an in-person interview in Bombay. I travelled by train and attended the interview, which was conducted by a committee of four scientists sitting across a large conference table from me. They pelted in rapid fire a variety of questions from the simplest to most complexes on all aspects of physics, particularly nuclear physics. Some questions were abstract and were designed to test the way I tackle problems on the spot. I provided thoughtful answers as best as I could and came away thinking that I did well in my interview. However, a few weeks later I received a letter of regret that I was not selected for the post. Perhaps I did not show a burning interest in working for any of the interviewers as they appeared humorless and stiff. I did not care for such personality types. Also, my heart was already set to go to America and this position, even if I was selected, would have been temporary.

I applied for an Assistant Professor position at the Government Arts & Science College in Bangalore to teach physics beginning that fall season. I was spontaneously hired. I taught freshmen physics and supervised laboratory experiments conducted by the students as part of their required curriculum.

My desire to go to America intensified. I kept looking for students who had returned from the U.S. to learn about life in there as a student. Conversing with them helped further to rid my Indian accent and I learned the American accent and jargon. I continued my participation in the Toastmaster's club and frequented the U.S.I.S. library to read more.

To supplement my thirst for reading, my pen pal Sherry regularly mailed me the past issues of *Life* and *Readers Digest* which I devoured as soon at the postman delivered them. I continued my correspondence with Dr. O'Keefe and Dr. Talbot by peppering them with questions on space exploration to which they promptly replied and additionally sent articles related to my queries. Delivery of airmail envelopes and neatly packaged bundles of magazines bearing American postage stamps was a special service that our mailman took pride in.

As part of my preparation to go abroad, I frequented Hollywood movies which played in theaters. I adored Alfred Hitchcock thrillers like *Psycho* and *North by Northwest* and James Bond movies with Sean Connery like *From Russia with Love*, and other classics like *The Sound of Music*.

Unlike my father, education was everything to me. I believed that the best investment anyone could make was in good education. I believed that there were no limits to what I could do in life with a good education. Earning a Ph.D. from the U.S. was going to be the next investment in my life.

Meanwhile, my parents and siblings had no clue that I was planning to go abroad to pursue my Ph.D. In fact, going overseas, particularly to America, was unheard of in my own as well as in my extended family. It was such an esoteric idea that they never gave any thought to it. Even though they knew that I was corresponding with people in foreign countries, that I occasionally invited young visiting Americans to our house and of my strong attachment to the U.S.I.S., they did not conjecture that I planned to go abroad. I did not tell my parents of my overseas plan for two reasons. I did not want them to be disappointed if I did not succeed. Second, I wanted to pleasantly surprise them when I did succeed.

Even in the large cosmopolitan city of Bangalore, going overseas was such a rare event that when such sojourn happened it was actually proclaimed by the family in the local newspaper by a paid advertisement under the heading of Going Abroad. A photo of the person and a description of the purpose of the travel and particulars of the destination city and country were part of the announcement.

Nearly a year had passed by since I had graduated with my master's degree. In late spring my teaching job was extended for the second year. While I was mulling over whether to accept the extension, I started to receive letters of decision from the universities in the U.S. that I had applied to for admission. Almost all of them granted me admission to graduate school and touted in flowery language how good their doctoral program was. However, they fell short in offering me the financial assistance.

I breathlessly awaited a decision from Temple. I was aware that Temple previously had awarded financial aid to at least one alumni of Central College who had a master's degree in physics.

One a fine morning in May, I was home reading Homer's *Iliad* that I had received as a prize at St. Joseph's. I heard the footsteps in the gravel road leading to our house and saw the postman walk toward our house with the mailbag on his shoulder. I walked toward the postman with eager anticipation that I might get the good news of admission to Temple. He placed the letter from Temple in my hand. It was in a distinct airmail envelope with a red, white and blue border and lettering in bright red which read Temple University. I nervously looked at the envelope and sized up the number of pages inside the envelope by feeling it. I dreaded that it was a single page like all of the previous decision letters I had received which did not award me the financial assistance. I fretted that the decision letter from Temple would fall in the same camp. However, when I mustered courage and opened the envelope, the single page letter from the Dean of Admissions contained astonishing news. It stated that the university not only granted me admission to the Ph.D. program starting in the fall of that year but also awarded free tuition for up to 15 semester credits and a teaching assistantship as long as I remained in good standing as a Ph.D. candidate at Temple University.

I clutched the letter in my hand and prayed to God in thanks for His blessing and the unbelievable gift He had handed me. I was excited. I hooted and hollered at the top of my lungs, racing to give a tip of gratitude to the postman who had just delivered such wonderful news, but he had disappeared. I kept my new knowledge to myself for a few minutes that morning, reflecting at my amazing accomplishment.

Then I went to my mother who was in the kitchen cooking. I could smell the fresh coriander leaves that she had used to garnish the eggplant dish that she just had prepared. I could also smell the fresh mint that she was blending in a mortar and pistol to probably make mint chutney. I interrupted her and shared with great excitement the news of my admission and the financial aid I just had received from Temple. The letter was still in my hand.

At that moment she did not fully comprehend my accomplishment. She said nothing except that I should wait until my father arrived to share the news with him. She rarely responded to unexpected news. However, there was something different about her silence this time. She noticed the excitement in my voice and appeared to take pride at my achievement, whatever it was.

I was ecstatic for many reasons. For one, the admission letter from Temple opened up an immensely vast horizon for my study abroad. Also, I felt that I had pioneered an event that no one in my family, either on the maternal or paternal side, had ever accomplished. Or even dreamed of. Now, too, I was firmly on the track to go to America. I was a step closer to realization of my goal of helping my father with the dowries that he would have to pay to marry off my five sisters. I was ecstatic that I was on the path to helping my siblings to follow my footsteps to go to the U.S. in one capacity or another, although not in the same capacity in which I was destined to head. All the different levers that I had pulled to make myself prepared for life in the U.S.—like cultivating pen pals, corresponding with well-placed U.S. scientists, ridding my Indian accent though speaking at the Toastmaster's club, keeping abreast of the American news, music and Hollywood movies—seemed to neatly fit together and position me well for a new life in the USA.

That evening when my father came home, he changed and went into the garden to check out the plants. It was a cool dry evening with a gentle breeze blowing to the east. I approached him in front of the rose bushes as he bent over to smell the roses. I showed him the letter I had received from Temple. He quietly read it and was perplexed.

I said, "Dad, I am going to America." I filled him in on my plan to go abroad for higher studies. I explained the long and meticulous effort that I had put in to secure my admission and financial aid from an American university. I did not share my grand plan underlying my move to go to America to earn money, as I did not want to raise his expectations. I wanted to keep my goals to myself and then surprise him when I executed them, like I did now with my application and admission to Temple.

He asked, "How much of a stipend will you be paid?"

I explained the free tuition cost that I would receive and the dollar amount of cash I would be paid monthly. I converted the stipend of $350/per month that I would be paid into Indian rupees, which was five times the salary I was receiving in my job as an Instructor. His eyes lit up when he heard this huge stipend.

He then asked, "Will Temple University pay for your travel to America?"

I realized that this was a financial concern for him as it would cost a huge amount to purchase a plane ticket to America. Luckily, I had saved some money.

I explained to my father: "My savings will take care of most of the expenses associated with my preparation to go overseas."

However, the cost of international airfare remained an important item to be addressed. He told me, "I may have to borrow money for your plane ticket. Perhaps, I can borrow from my Provident Fund?"

I responded, "Dad, please do not borrow from your pension plan. You'll need those funds when you retire."

Silence befell us. A gentle breeze kept the bougainvillea in the garden moving at a distance. A faint fragrance of jasmine was leaking from a nearby creeper.

I continued after a long pause. "Maybe, one of your business clients could loan you the money? I would try to periodically send you money from my stipend. You can pay back the loan."

My father continued his silence.

Like my mother, my father did not fully comprehend my accomplishment and its profound ramifications. As expected, paying for my travel remained an issue for him.

My aspirations to go abroad may have seemed outlandish to my parents and siblings, but they were real to me. Besides my parents, there were no others whose approval I craved for more. While I considered that my admission to Temple with the financial assistance was a monumental achievement, my father or mother did not say "nice job" or "great accomplishment." They said nothing. My father was worried about the money for my travel. But in their hearts, they were giving me their blessings to go to America and succeed.

The timing to focus on my move to America was perfect. The academic year at the Government Arts & Science College where I was teaching just had ended. I notified the college of my intention not to return to this post in the following academic year. I had plenty of time that I could devote to my preparation to go abroad.

A few days later I received additional documents from Temple which formalized my admission and included the specifics of the financial aid and for applying for my student visa with the Immigration & Naturalization Service (which is now called the U.S. Citizen & Immigration Service or U.S.C.I.S.) at a U.S. Embassy in India.

I never had obtained a passport before. Now the passport became the first item that I needed to procure which I did using the local travel agency of Thomas Cook. After my passport arrived, I travelled by train to the U.S. Embassy in Madras to obtain my student visa to the United States. The next morning, I walked into the gated American Embassy which was guarded by two Marines. I explained to one of the guards that "I am here to obtain my student visa to go to the United States." I was led to a spacious room with high ceilings where fans were whirring to cool the room from the oppressive humid heat outside.

A Consular Officer soon appeared in the room and after I presented the papers I had received from Temple and my passport, he quipped, "Are you ready for the mighty visa interview?" He was friendly and pleasant and behaved like a host whose house I was invited to as a guest. He politely asked me to move to an open desk where we sat across from each other to start the interview.

He glanced over the visa application I had filled out and the associated documents I presented. He cordially said, "The America government likes to invite bright young scientists like you to my country." He admired my ability to have received admission for doctoral studies from Temple with the financial assistance to boot. After that, receiving the official authorization for my student visa was a cinch. The Officer gently explained that "you are not permitted to work in the U.S. under the student visa. Except, you can perform jobs that Temple University will authorize you to carry out such as teaching or research on the campus."

I replied, "I understand the limitations associated with my student visa."

He handed me an envelope to present to the immigration agent at my first port of entry to the U.S.

The next two months revolved around receiving titbits from George T. and others employed at the U.S.I.S. as well as visiting Americans that I frequently met there. U.S.I.S. organized an orientation session for students like me who are going to the U.S.

to study. The session was chaired by a panel of Indian students who had visited or completed study in America and returned. Their down-to-earth advice starting from campus life, activities, weather, clothing, food, etc. was very helpful. I distinctly remember one student asking them what a hamburger was! This session also provided me with an opportunity to meet two graduate students from Bangalore who were also headed to Temple that fall semester.

I left the orientation session believing more strongly than ever that America upholds with conviction that ordinary individuals could speak, worship and live as they please so long as those actions did not infringe upon the fundamental rights of others.

I updated my wardrobe with new tailor-made suits, shirts, neckties, pairs of shoes, and all other clothing I needed.

I just had turned twenty-two when the time for my sojourn arrived. My father had raised enough cash for my plane ticket from one of his clients who was a saree merchant. By raising this cash, he was giving me his blessing to go to America. I also needed to obtain enough U.S. currency to wade through my initial expenses in America until I received my first stipend from Temple. My travel agent sold me the U.S. currency and airplane tickets for going from Bangalore to Bombay on Indian Airlines and from Bombay to New York City on TWA.

The travel date was set for the Thursday before the U.S. Labor Day of 1965. As expected, in that morning's newspaper was my photo along with my and my father's name as well as the university, city and country where I was headed. This was published under the caption of "Going Abroad."

The departure time for my flight from Bangalore to Bombay

was in the late afternoon. I packed my belongings in a new leather suitcase. I placed all travel documents and a letter from Temple and the visa authorization from the Immigration & Naturalization Service in my attaché case to hand carry.

As was customary at the time for travelers on airplanes, I was dressed in one of my new suits and a tie. My entire family travelled to the Bangalore Airport for my sendoff.

The departing scene was very moving. This was the first time for me and my family members to bid each other good-bye, not knowing when we were going to see each other again. We had lived all our lives under the same roof. We had laughed and played and had our own moments of happiness together. My parents were proud of me and supportive.

Just then friends of my father's adorned me with white garlands of fresh and fragrant flowers. Flash cubes popped to capture my photo with the garlands on my chest. Perhaps those photos were intended for publication in the next day's newspaper, I speculated.

I was bombarded with questions: "Got your passport?" "Got everything you need?" "Will this plane take you to New York?" I politely answered them.

I approached my father and asked whether I could exchange my new Bulova wristwatch with his old watch which he had used for as long as I could remember. Without waiting for his reply, I unbuckled the strap of his watch and slid my watch onto his wrist.

I told him, "I will keep your watch as an heirloom."

To this, he replied, "It may break down any day."

"Then I will buy a new watch in America," I said.

My flight was called in. Hugging was not practiced in Hindu culture. I muttered to my family that I would return soon, which was a lie as I would not return for years. I touched the hands of my youngest sisters Mini and Mala and whispered, "Someday, you will be in America." I was not sure why I uttered those words to them as my plan was to return to India after I achieved my goal.

Head down, passport and boarding pass in hand, I took a deep breath and made my turn toward the open gate. I walked on the concrete pavement to the plane parked 50 feet away from the terminal. I pushed back tears which I did not wish my family to see and decided not to look back until I was well on the stairs leading up to the plane. From there I waved them good-bye.

As I sat by the window of the airplane, I could see at a distance my entire family who had moved to the rooftop balcony of the airport to see my plane take off. A sense of sadness crept into me, while simultaneously I was thrilled at the many firsts that I was about to experience—including my first plane journey. I departed with a heavy heart. I knew that many challenges lay ahead and I was determined to meet them successfully, no matter what. At the same time, I felt courageous and was comfortable with my journey to the new world. I told myself that I was set to go to America with a sense of powerful purpose. The plane soon ascended into the clouds.

Three hours later, the plane touched down in Bombay's domestic airport. A representative of TWA met me at the airport and transported me to the Taj Mahal Hotel across from the landmark of the Gateway of India on the Arabian Sea with hundreds of pigeons flocking around the monument. The Taj was spectacular from the outside and I was mesmerized by how luxurious the hotel was inside with my well-appointed room. The lavish bathtub in my room attracted my attention. I filled the tub with warm water, sprinkled it with fragrant salt crystals, and enjoyed a relaxing bath.

After a few hours of rest and relaxation at the hotel, it was time to head to the Bombay International Airport. There I took a Boeing 707 jet emblazoned with the red lettering of TWA on the outer body and was transported to New York's Idyllwild Airport.

Things were happening that would alter the course of my life. I felt elated at the possibilities.

2

ARRIVAL IN AMERICA: NEW YORK CITY

IT WAS FRIDAY afternoon and the start of the Labor Day Weekend of 1965 in America. The Statue of Liberty stood alone on little Ellis Island, with a torch held high for everyone to see and the needy to flock toward. It appeared to beckon me as the TWA jet that I flew on touched down in Idyllwild (now LaGuardia) Airport in New York City. I knew the purpose for my journey to America. It was simple, yet ambitious. I would earn my Ph.D. in physics, and then earn enough money to assist my father so he could pay for the dowries for my younger sisters that I had left behind in Bangalore. I believed that I was chosen to fulfil this important duty to my parents. It was this call that propelled me to achieve what I had already initiated and then land in America to achieve the rest.

I walked up to the immigration counter where an agent sitting in a glass-enclosed booth asked for my passport and immigration papers. I produced my Indian passport and provided the visa authorization document that I had received from the U.S. Consulate in Madras. The agent was a middle-aged man with a smile on his face and a lapel on his shirt marked "U.S. Immigration."

He perused my documents and asked, "What are you going to be studying?"

I blurted, "Ph.D. in nuclear physics," pointing to the book, *The Atomic Nucleus*, that was in my hand.

He asked, "How long will it take?"

I replied, "Not sure. May be four to five years?"

He appeared satisfied with my answers and applied a stamp to my passport specifying the grant of my student visa with the day's date. He formally welcomed me to the United States and wished, "The best of luck to you in your studies."

After the immigration check, which I thought was friendly, I collected my suitcase from the baggage carousel and moved to the zone which read "Nothing to Declare." The Customs agents who stood in that zone simply waved me to move on to the exit door.

As I was instructed before I left Bangalore, I carried my luggage to the designated public bus stop within the airport and asked the driver whether the bus would be going to midtown Manhattan. He nodded in agreement. After I got in, I produced a dollar bill and he returned the change. I got off near 47th Street and 3rd Avenue and lugged my belongings to the Vanderbilt YMCA.

The desk clerk at the Y was a young man who asked how many days I planned to stay. I replied three days. I volunteered that "This is my first stay in America. What kind of room do you recommend?"

He robotically replied, "Single for $3 per night or a double for $5."

I opted for a single room with a private bathroom but no tub or a shower to bathe.

The next morning when I went to take a shower, I noticed

that it was a communal shower. A number of the men taking showers were stark naked. I quickly showered and avoided drawing anyone's attention to me.

The Y was centrally located close to Grand Central Station, Times Square and all major New York City attractions. With a street map of Manhattan in my hand, I ventured out to explore the city on the quiet Saturday of the Labor Day Weekend as far down as the southernmost part of the island where Battery Park was situated. Everyone on the street was white except for a few blacks who were making deliveries to various establishments. I was exhilarated to be walking on the streets of New York and looked for any Indians or Indian establishments. At the end of one of the buildings I noticed the red neon sign of Air India and the airline's iconic bowing statute of the Maharaja on it. The sign gave me a lump in my throat, but I felt comfortable knowing that my countrymen were present there.

I crisscrossed Manhattan for miles until I was exhausted and felt hungry for lunch. I stepped into a Horn & Hardart cafeteria, grabbed a tray, and proceeded to the designated line to pick up cooked food of my choice. I looked for food that appeared somewhat familiar to me. When I approached a dish that looked like meat curry, I asked the woman who was serving what it was.

"It's a stew with meat and variety of vegetables," she told me.

I asked for a serving. I also selected a hard roll of bread and cut pieces of fresh fruit.

I paid for the food at the end of the counter and ate at a table by a window facing a Manhattan avenue. The stew was bland but edible. I regularly ate lamb back home, mostly as a curry along with plain cooked rice. This is what I had expected. However, the meat was tough to chew. Then it occurred to me that I was eating beef—for the first time in my life! The thought of eating beef repelled me. This was not because I had any religious compunction against eating beef, but the thought of eating a cut-up cow was unsettling to my stomach. I almost threw up, but I controlled myself. However, within a few days after this incident, eating hamburgers became not so repelling.

After spending the Labor Day Weekend in Manhattan, I took the Greyhound bus to reach my destination city of brotherly love, Philadelphia. I camped out for a couple days at the International House for foreign students, located in downtown Philadelphia, while I explored permanent housing on the Temple University campus. I met a number of foreign students from many countries including from India who were temporarily living at the house. The students included those slated for Temple but also University of Pennsylvania, Drexel University, Hahnemann Medical Center, and other schools in Philadelphia. From my conversations with these students, I was impressed with their caliber, intelligence, enthusiasm and friendliness. They were the crème de la crème of the countries from which they hailed. All of the Indian students were undoubtedly the best and the brightest.

Soon I took the subway on Broad Street and headed northward to Temple University. When I got off the subway and entered the university grounds, I was impressed by the sprawling campus and its varied architecture of historical buildings interspersed with modern structures.

On this Wednesday morning after Labor Day, the campus was buzzing with students who were mostly white males and females. I went to Mitten Hall to meet with my Foreign Student Advisor,

Dr. Caroline Hanson, in her well-appointed office. Dr. Hansen was a pleasant and cheerful woman in her early thirties. She stood up and extended her hand with the words "Welcome to the USA. Welcome to Temple." She exuded enthusiasm and an intense interest in what I had to say. She listened attentively and made a spontaneous connection with me. Dr. Hansen appeared approachable and easy to talk with. I instantly admired her incredible patience to listen despite my remaining foreign accent and somewhat limited vocabulary.

I expressed to her my priority of finding suitable housing on campus.

She explained, "The dormitories are generally reserved for incoming freshmen students. There are no dorms for graduate students. It is best to find housing off campus." In fact, I eventually did opt to share an off-campus apartment with other graduate students.

Dr. Hansen took note of my desire and indicated, "This is a perfect time as many graduate students are looking to team with other incoming students." She told me that a number of events had been planned for incoming foreign students in the next week before classes started. "Perhaps you will find your roommate then," she remarked.

She introduced me to her staff and the student volunteers who happened to stop by looking for things to do. I met many wonderful students, mostly female. Marylyn, Judy and Michelle were friendly and showed genuine interest in helping me with my needs. They made me aware of the available resources at Temple, such as the post office, bank, bookstore, cafeteria and infirmary. At my request, Marylyn took me on an unofficial tour of the sprawling campus and showed me Barton Hall, a modern building where the Physics Department was located. Barton Hall was going to be my place of confinement for the next several years.

The neighborhood where Temple's campus was located was not impressive. It quickly became apparent that the neighborhood was a slum where mostly black Americans lived in dilapidated rows of buildings.

I remembered that I had not communicated with my family in more than seven days. I stopped at the campus post office and purchased an international aerogram for 19 cents. That evening, I wrote a detailed letter addressed to my family explaining my initial impressions of America and the places in Manhattan that I visited.

I told them: *"I am so thrilled to be in America and am excited about reaching my destination. I met a number of helpful people at Temple. While a great distance now separates us, my thoughts are with you. I miss you all dearly and, particularly, Mom's home-cooked meals."* I added, *"I am going to miss the birthdays and memories we make and laughter we share in our family, but soon I will return after I have completed my Ph.D. We can catch up on what I missed."* I ended with a P.S. addressed to my parents: *"Without your silent love, I would not be the person I am. I promise to make you proud of me."*

I returned to the International House and continued to look for potential roommates, focusing on graduate students from Temple. One such potential was Arun Wagh who was staying at the House. It turned out that he was also admitted to the Ph.D. program in Physics at Temple. Arun was from Bombay and spoke a different language (Marathi). We conversed in English as was customary with many from India when not knowing the regional language.

The following day, a young, skinny student by the name of Krishnan appeared at the House looking for graduate students of Temple to share a two-bedroom apartment with him. Kris was a third-year grad student pursuing his Ph.D. in Chemistry at Temple. He spoke yet another Indian language (Malayalam) which is spoken in the state of Kerala.

Kris explained, "My previous roommates—my older brother and a friend of my brother—just graduated with their Ph.D.'s and moved on to their newfound jobs. I'm looking for one or two roommates. The rent is affordable for two and cheap for three to share." I grabbed Arun and introduced him to Kris.

The apartment was located on the 2000 block of North Broad Street right across the street from many Temple buildings including the undergrad dormitory. The apartment was conveniently located at the corner block on the top floor of a three-story row house. The rent for the three of us, including all utilities, was $100 total. Arun and I agreed to room with Kris and moved in the following day.

As it turned out, Kris monopolized a small bedroom for himself and Arun and I shared a larger bedroom with two beds. The apartment was spacious and furnished, and it had a large living room, large kitchen, and a single bathroom. What impressed me the most was its ideal location. I just needed to walk a couple of blocks to be at the center of Temple campus.

Just before I left the International House, I received a formal invitation from a host family. Mr. Leonard Lovitz and Mrs. Ann Lovitz in King of Prussian, Pennsylvania, which is a suburb of Philadelphia, were asking whether I would be interested in meeting with them. The house manager explained that it was a common practice for host families to reach out to foreign students who had left their parents and siblings overseas. The hosts tried to make the students comfortable by inviting them to visit their family and sharing family events like special dinners or visits to local places of interest. I accepted the invitation and promised to take up on their wonderful offer at a later date after I settled down.

When I first visited a supermarket to purchase food for our apartment, I was astounded by the variety and abundance of food that was available. Fruit of different kinds were neatly arranged in pyramid-like stacks. Fresh cut meat of all kinds was nicely wrapped in cellophane and placed in open refrigerators. Rows of breakfast cereals were meticulously stacked on shelves. A variety of coffee, tea, hot chocolate mixes, fruit juices and carbonated beverages abounded. I was just fascinated by the immense quantity of different kinds of food all available in a single store. This was something I had never seen before. I also could not believe the posted incredibly low prices for common food items. Coming from India where food was scarce, this scene reinforced my belief that the U.S. is truly blessed with abundance.

I relished in a sense of comradery with my new roommates. We all hailed from the same country. We all had a common purpose—to earn our Ph.D.

My roommates and I took turns cooking dinner, which was the main meal we ate together before attending evening courses. We stuck to vegetarian dishes to cook as Kris was a vegetarian by choice, although he occasionally gobbled up hamburgers for lunch at the Temple cafeteria. Each of us prepared food that we knew.

Kris prepared dishes from Kerala, heavily into lentils like dahl mixed with vegetables such as okra, pumpkin and sweet potato. Arun invariably cooked strange leafy dishes. When questioned about his prepared food, Arun always said, "It is a special dish from Maharashtra" (the state where he came from). Neither Kris nor I believed his statement.

When it was my turn to cook, they quickly found out that I knew how. I had learned cooking in Bangalore when my mother was away in the hospital delivering my little siblings. I showed them the scars on my tummy resulting from the accidental spilling of boiling milk, which was further evidence that I could cook.

Strong emotional food memories of my mother's cooking drove me to try to recreate similar types of food every time I was parked in front of our kitchen stove. Even her humblest food items, like cabbage, carried a lifetime of meaning. I cooked dishes based on eggplant, squash and potatoes, spicing them with turmeric, cayenne and masala. I cooked fresh green beans and carrots in tamarind juice with a soft base of yellow lentils imported from India.

However, my way of cooking soon became transgressive and revolutionary—at least I thought so. I took liberty to experiment with different spices without realizing that I was creating Indian fusion food. My roommates unwittingly became guinea pigs for the dishes I concocted.

After I settled down in my apartment, a series of orientation sessions followed which I attended. There I gathered useful information about life on campus. These sessions were also enjoyable social events. The orientation ended with a dinner session organized by the departments of physics, chemistry, biology and pharmacology for the new foreign graduate students.

At one orientation session, I met my advisor, Dr. Robert Intemann, who was an Assistant Professor of Physics. He looked young and was charismatic. I asked him about the initial set of courses I should register for.

He told me, "You should sign up for three courses to start, although there is no restriction on enrolling in more." He added that I would be expected to handle ten to fifteen hours per week of lab classes, which would keep me occupied. "You should enroll in a master's and Ph.D. combined program in which the coursework during the first two academic years will be common for both degrees," he advised.

I reminded him, "I already earned my master's. Receiving another master's would be redundant, isn't it?"

He did not respond. Nevertheless, I did not protest Dr. Intemann's advice beyond that.

I decided to enroll in three courses which carried three semester hours each. These would serve as a forerunner for advanced courses like the Theory of Relativity, Quantum Mechanics, Solid State Physics, Statistical Mechanics, Low Temperature Physics, etc.

Some professors taught the courses during the morning or early afternoon. Others taught them in the evening to accommodate part-time students who worked during the day and pursued graduate study in the evening. Actually, keeping awake and being attentive particularly right after lunch or an early dinner was a challenge. Some professors knew about this problem we faced and made it a point to call on students to keep us alert during the class lectures.

The core group in my Ph.D. program composed of eighteen full-time students. More than half of them were foreign students from China, India, South Korea, and Taiwan and the rest were Americans. All the Ph.D. students were men. Some of the American students were pursuing graduate study as a way to be sheltered from the mandatory U.S. military draft that was prevalent then at the height of war in Vietnam.

The foreign students, especially the Chinese, hardly spoke a word of English, but they were fiercely competitive. They paid intense attention to the notes that the professors chalked on the board, especially the equations that governed the physical principles. They seemed to grasp the complex equations much more than the rest of the class. One Chinese student from the Mainland, De Ching Chen, was particularly impressive with his grasp of advanced mathematical principles of physics. He seldom spoke, incessantly drank tea, smoked like a chimney and listened to classical Western music as he pondered over physics problems. When he smiled, which was rare, I could see brown and black stains from tea and smoke on his teeth.

I developed friendships with three American classmates—Frank Ryan, Tim Lambarski and Bill Klein. Frank was from Upstate New York and lived in a rented apartment. Tim lived with his parents in northeast Philly. Bill also was a Philadelphian and he lived with his wife Susan. All three had a sense of humor. Ryan talked about his girlfriend in Seneca, New York and Tim, about a local girl that he was dating.

All of the first- and second-year grad students were assigned a personal desk in the basement of Barton Hall, an area which became a meeting ground and facilitated interaction among us.

Most American students left after attending the evening courses, but I lingered at my desk along with my foreign classmates to prepare for my next day's course homework or for teaching lab.

Even though I had received an impeccable education and was considered smart as measured by my high ranking in my university examinations, I was unsure of myself when I started at Temple. American education was different from the system that had made me a success in India. Analytical thinking and acute problem-solving through rigorously applying the principles of physics was the root of the teaching methods used by my American professors. The pace of teaching was fast. My new education was exciting and daunting, too. I attacked academic life at Temple which sparked my mind. I could feel new principles of physics fire in my brain as the professors lectured.

There was a regular dose of homework, mostly physics problems, which the professors used to grade us. Some students formed study groups to collectively solve the assigned problems. Sometimes, after completing a class, late into the night Arun, De Ching and I brainstormed together to solve the homework. At other times I spent the wee hours of the night at my desk alone and struggled to find acceptable solutions to the problems and readied them for turning in the next day.

In addition to turning in homework, the professors kept us busy with mid-semester and final exams—all of which helped determine the grade for the semester for the course. Some students dropped out of some difficult or demanding courses in the middle of the semester for reasons that others did not know.

My teaching of laboratory physics to the undergrad students was always during the day and was easy and enjoyable. In fact, it was a pleasant distraction from the hard problem-solving and intense lectures that I faced. The lab experiments were creative and interesting and were conducted by the students to reinforce basic principles of physics, like Newton's laws of motion, principles of conservation of energy, transfer of momentum, projectile motion, etc., that the students were taught in the lecture hall. I could see that making them understand the physics behind the experiments opened their minds to the concepts.

My years of public speaking at the Toastmaster's club in Bangalore came handy while I taught lab physics at Temple. My Indian accent was substantially eliminated—although when I uttered some words while teaching, I received quizzical stares from my students. I then quickly spelled out the word on the chalk board, which immediately made them realize what word I was uttering. The same was not true when some fellow foreign graduate students taught.

The accents of the Chinese and Korean students were so different, and their English vocabulary was very limited. Some undergraduate students openly complained to their professors that they were unable to comprehend the lab instructions given by those foreigner instructors.

Days after I settled down, I remembered the invitation from host parents, Mr. and Mrs. Lovitz, and I telephoned them. They suggested that we meet at a restaurant in China Town in Philadelphia, which was just a few subway stops away from my apartment. We met for dinner at their favorite Chinese restaurant. Ann was in her late thirties and Leonard in his early forties. They told me that they had hosted a student from Thailand before and found out how wonderful the experience could be. Len was a pharmacist and Ann worked as a helper in the same pharmacy in King of Prussia near where their family lived. We exchanged information about our respective families, and I talked about the purpose of my coming to America. They sympathized with my lonely life and promised to invite me for the Thanksgiving dinner at their home.

It was late fall and time to get warm clothing. The monthly stipend that I received from Temple was only about $350. Still, the sharing of rent and the monthly expenses for food and eating out in the school cafeteria at lunchtime did not require more than $100 per month. I felt rich as I was easily saving over $200 of my stipend every month. I splurged and bought myself a long overcoat, sweaters, neck scarfs, wool socks and leather gloves.

As promised, days before Thanksgiving, I received a call from Ann Lovitz inviting me to join them for Thanksgiving dinner. I accepted, as this was the first festival and feast that I would be experiencing in America. What better place could I expect to spend this festive day other than with a family that celebrated it as a tradition?

King of Prussia was more than 25 miles away from where I lived, and I received instructions to catch a train from North Philadelphia which took me to the suburbs. Len was waiting for me at the designated suburban train station where I got off and he drove me to his house.

When I entered their house, it was filled with people. Besides Ann and Len and their teenage son David and daughter Ellen, the guests included the parents of Ann and two of their close friends and their families. The friends were the Fred and Rose Goldman and Ed and Shirley Pennis. Fred was a dentist and Ed was a physician. The Goldmans had four young children and Ed and Shirley had two. Ann explained that it had become a tradition for them to take turns and host the three families at Thanksgiving. The house was festive with mirth and merriment.

Right from the start, it became apparent that the adults were interested in politics. They peppered me with questions on Indian politics including about the Prime Minister Mr. Nehru and the boisterous Indian ambassador to the United Nations, Mr. Krishna Menon. Mr. Menon had made provocative statements against the United States in a speech before the U.N. General Assembly. I expressed my disdain for Mr. Nehru as he was a socialist and aligned with the Soviet Union, even though he took the public stance that India was a non-aligned country. I liked India's five-year plan, which emphasized education in science, engineering and medicine, but disliked Mr. Nehru for rejecting America as a defense partner. This rejection led the U.S. to persuade Pakistan to join a treaty called the South East Asia Treaty Organization that was previously established. SEATO served as a source of the collective defense of Southeast Asia against Communists. I reasoned that India, which had just fought a war with China on the Himalayan border to re-establish its territorial rights and suffered a humiliating defeat, should have joined SEATO. Despite this humiliating defeat, Mr. Nehru refused to join SEATO because he had aligned with the Soviet Union.

I explained, "Krishna Menon hails from the state of Kerala, which has been a strong Communist state since India gained independence from the British in 1947. Like Mr. Nehru, Mr. Menon is sympathetic to Communist Russia. He publicly spoke in support of Russia even if it meant speaking against the United States."

The dinner was served on three tables and the youngsters, teens and adults, respectably, were seated at designated seats. Ann took the cooked turkey out of the oven and Len did the carving and served it on individual dinner plates. This was followed by servings of stuffing, mashed potatoes, boiled yams and freshly cut and cooked green beans and heaps of cranberries in an accompanying sauce. The meal was accompanied by small servings of beer for the adults.

The meal and the conversation were memorable. I expressed my sincerely thanks to Ann and Len for inviting me. Time flew at the dinner table and soon it was near midnight and time for me to catch the last train back to Philadelphia. Len dropped me at the train station. After getting off the train, it felt spooky to walk alone past midnight in the ghettos of North Philadelphia to my apartment.

Although the American classmates in my graduate school worked hard, they also enjoyed a social life. Some were already married, and others were in intimate relationships close to calling their better half a fiancée. In stark contrast, we foreign students did not have a social life. We were smart and ferociously competitive.

As for me, I dedicated myself to my studies as if nothing else mattered other than earning a good grade in every course I took. I came to the U.S. with a singular quest: to earn my Ph.D. so I could get a good job after graduation and monetarily help my father with the dowry payments for my sisters in India. I never lost sight of this goal. I dedicated every minute of every day to my studies, spending early mornings, late nights and all weekends on it. No social life, no physical exercise. The concept of "all work and no play" did not bother me. I was married to my studies and was happy with my marriage. Still, I did socialize once in a while.

Periodically my American classmates Frank and Tim invited me to parties that they held at their homes. They were low key BYOB (bring your own bottle) get togethers where most of the other invitees were paired with a person of the opposite sex. I went alone and had spirited discussions of life in India with the guests, especially the wives or girlfriends of my classmates who were curious about it.

I also attended large parties hosted by the International Student House where foreign students attending the various local colleges in the Philadelphia area were invited. I recall a lavish party held on the top floor of the building where the Philadelphia Savings Fund Society was located. I happened to have a savings account at that bank. The party had an open bar and a variety of exotic finger foods to enjoy. I compared notes with students who were studying for their Ph.D. at the University of Pennsylvania and Drexel to see what we were missing at Temple which was a state college. I sensed a snobbish air of superiority from the students at the Ivy League school University of Pennsylvania.

Occasionally the volunteers, mostly undergraduate girls, who assisted Dr. Hansen in the foreign student affairs felt compelled to take us around to the cultural attractions in Philadelphia. On one Saturday afternoon I was persuaded by a beautiful girl named Michele Ziskind to go with her to the Philadelphia Museum of Art. Michele was an undergraduate at Temple. The Museum was a magnificent showcase of arts from all over the world including a full-sized replica of a Hindu temple that was constructed inside a large wing. The physical setting of the Museum offered a panoramic view of the skyline of Philadelphia.

Some Temple girls were looking to date foreign students. The girls confessed it was an exotic experience for them. In fact, weeks after our visit to the Museum, I came to know that Michele was by then going steady with an undergraduate student Nalin Jugran from Katmandu, Nepal, whom she subsequently married.

Christmas was generally uneventful as I was not a Christian, but I knew about Christ from my years at St. Joseph's. One Christmas Eve, Tim and his girlfriend Maryann dragged me with them to go for Christmas caroling on a cold December night. With a booklet of Christmas carols in my gloved hand, I sang along with the others in the group in front of many suburban homes of Philadelphia. We received small tokens of thanks like cookies and warm milk. It was simple fun.

I looked forward to the day after Christmas when the local department stores like John Wanamaker offered many clothing and other personal and household items for sale at discounted prices. The scene at these sales was pandemic with buyers grabbing items without even looking at the price. I picked up most of my clothing and other necessities at these special sales events.

During the first two years, almost all of my classmates signed up for the same required courses. We felt comfortable enrolling in the same courses and commiserating over the homework assignments that we struggled through. Mid-semester exams and the finals were always stressful because of the intense competition.

During my second year, after I had completed essentially all required courses, I needed to make a decision of whether I should opt for a master's degree from Temple or continue to plough through for my Ph.D. To earn the M.A. degree, I needed to take an additional six semester hours of non-thesis experimental research. As most of my classmates opted to receive the M.A. degree, I followed them. The research that I wanted to pursue was a topic in nuclear physics, but no professor conducted research in this specialty. *The Atomic Nucleus* book that I had hand-carried from India was never put to use again. I settled on working in optical physics with Dr. Howard Poss who was then carrying out research on a double-star using lunar occultation.

Dr. Poss was a shy gentleman but had a never-ending smile or at least that is how he appeared all the time to me. He was soft-spoken and approachable, qualities that prompted me to consider him as my advisor.

With the clear understanding that I did not have to write a thesis for my research, I discussed with Dr. Poss the nature of the research he was involved in and a research problem that he could suggest for me. He wanted me to measure the diameter of a double star Alpha Centauri, which was a star system closest to our solar system, being 4.4 light years from the Sun. It actually consisted of three stars: Alpha Centauri A and Alpha Centauri B, which form the binary star with a nearby third star. His interest was directed to the double star, per se.

I asked, "Are you proposing to solve a problem in astronomy?"

He explained, "No. The topic I am proposing is based on a measurement I made at the Kitt Peak National Observatory in Arizona. That measurement is based on a diffraction pattern of light from the double star when it was occulted by the passing moon in its geocentric orbit." In other words, he brought with him photographs recorded by the telescope at the Observatory of the light pattern emitted by the dual star when the leading edge of our Moon passed by them.

The research problem centered on my ability to reproduce in the laboratory the exact diffraction pattern that Dr. Poss had recorded by using the Observatory's telescope and to derive the best estimate for the diameter of each part of the double star.

Then he added this: "I would like you to also estimate the mutual separation of the double star."

I accepted the topic for my research.

Being an experimentalist, I took this challenge on in my stride and worked for countless hours by applying my knowledge in optical physics and mechanical motion. I collaborated with the technicians in Barton Hall's basement workshop to conduct numerous trial and error experiments. I was able to simulate a slowly revolving razor blade mounted in front of a pair of pin holes perfectly bored with precise diameters on a metal diaphragm. I illuminated the pin holes from behind by a bright light source. The illuminated pin holes represented the double star and the rotating edge of the razor represented the leading edge of the moon. I darkened the lab and recorded the optical diffraction pattern as the razor slowly rotated past the light emitted from the illuminated pin holes.

It took many weeks to tweak three variables under my control: adjust the size of the pin holes and their mutual separation on the metal diaphragm; adjust the revolving speed of the razor blade; and adjust the intensity of illumination of the pin holes. I made these adjustments and recorded the resulting diffraction patterns. Finally, close to the end of the semester, I was able to reproduce Dr. Poss's occultation pattern. Armed with this close match of patterns, I was able to calculate the diameter of each of the double stars and the distance of separation between their centers. Dr. Poss was pleased with my research and graded me very highly.

By the end of my second year, I had satisfied all of the requirements for my M.A. degree. However, I neglected to apply in time for graduation thinking that I did not need a second master's degree, as I considered it a redundant degree.

Because of the intense competition in the courses we took, it was a challenge to maintain a B average grade for most students in my class. After six semesters of facing such stiff competition as well as for personal reasons, a few of my classmates opted to settle for a master's degree. Frank Ryan, who got married, and whose wedding I had attended in Seneca, New York six months earlier, decided to take a full-time job with a military establishment in Baltimore, Maryland. Tim Lambarski opted for a job with the Sandia Lab in Albuquerque, NM. I felt sorry that Frank and Tim moved on. My other classmates, like Bill Klein and Bruce Taggert, marched forward with me to follow the footsteps of senior American graduate students like Angelo Armenti, Alex Vargas, Alfred Foote and Dan McFarland to earn doctorates. In fact, I monitored the progress of these senior students and discussed with them the issues they faced so as to learn from their mistakes. Based on their advice, I applied for my M.A. degree for which I already had completed the required coursework. I received my M.A. from Temple in the spring of 1968.

One of Temple's requirements for students enrolled in the Ph.D. program was the ability to possess sufficient knowledge in two foreign languages so as to be able to read scientific literature written in those languages. Typically, the foreign languages were French, German or Russian. Given my previous exposure to German, I opted for German as one of the languages. The test was to translate a thousand-word German document into English in an hour. I passed the German language test in the spring, followed by similar success with French in the fall of the same year.

It was the end of summer when Raj (who regularly visited my family in Bangalore, particularly my sister Jaya) appeared at my apartment. I was surprised by his unexpected visit, as I had lost touch of his whereabouts after I left home. Raj explained that he had been living in Vancouver, Canada for the past year and working as a post-doctoral fellow with one of his Ph. D. thesis advisors at the University of British Columbia in Vancouver. He said he wanted to spend time with me and to take me to Expo '67 that was taking place in Montreal, Canada. I was taken aback by his unexpected visit but was glad to see him.

My roommate Arun talked to a friend who owned a car and the friend agreed to drive us to Montreal. The driver was motivated because his girlfriend needed a ride to visit with her family in Ithaca, New York. Five men and the girl crammed our bodies into the car and drove up north toward Canada. The first night, the girlfriend's parents magnanimously let us sleep in their house. We spread out on the living room sofas and on the carpeted floor which was covered with a flat cotton sheet.

The next morning on the way to Montreal we made a detour. We visited Niagara Falls at the U.S.-Canada border, both sides of it. The thunderous and roaring waterfall was beyond anything I had seen before. We did the touristy stuff. Took the Maid of the Mist tour and stood under the Horseshoe Falls. It was wonderful. Then we drove up on the Trans-Pacific Highway heading westward toward Montreal.

The 1967 International and Universal Exposition or Expo 67, as it was commonly known, was the largest exhibition I ever went to where sixty-two countries participated by setting up their own pavilions. The American pavilion was a magnificent geodesic dome with a built-in set of monorails. The exhibition, an impressive collection of majestic waterfalls and spectacular minarets, was a feast for the eye and left a lasting impression on me.

On the last day of our trip to the Expo, when we were alone, Raj revealed the real reason he came to see me. He popped this question: "Are you agreeable to my marriage to Jaya?"

I was startled by his proposal, which felt like a bolt from the blue since I was aware that he was married to my cousin Shini.

I asked, "What happened to your wife Shini"?

He replied, "I stopped seeing her for years now."

I asked whether he had any children with her to which he replied in the negative. As I listened, he added, "My marriage with Shini was never consummated." I asked whether he had discussed his proposed with my father. He demurred and later said, "Jaya and I want your consent before I discuss this with your father."

I was pleased that he sought my support and interpreted it as a sign of respect for me. I pondered the idea a bit. Since I am not one who minces words, I told him that he needed to meet two conditions to marry my sister: "First end your marriage with Shini by seeking a divorce; and second obtain my father's permission to marry Jaya."

He agreed and appeared satisfied. We returned to our respective abodes.

I felt good about the proposal that Raj had made. I concluded that he would be beyond an excellent match for Jaya, considering that Jaya did not have the benefit of a formal education and that Raj was highly educated and an established scientist with a good job.

The conditions that I had laid out for her marriage with Raj were important. I wanted Jaya, being the first daughter in our large family, to be a role model to her younger sisters. She must establish high standards for the professional stature, appearance and character of the man she would marry so her younger sisters could emulate her when their turn came. The approval of my parents, particularly my father, was imperative as he was principled and a proud man. Family honor was important to him. I figured that giving his first daughter in marriage to a divorced man might be objectionable, as his family and friends might not readily embrace such an alliance.

The idea of a dowry to Raj never entered in my short discussion with him in Montreal or subsequently. I assumed that he would not ask for a dowry for several reasons. First, I presumed that he was in love with my sister. Most young men who fell in love in a natural and voluntary way and without family coercion tended not to expect a dowry. Such men were independent-minded, self-assured that they could make a living on their own without depending on the dowry. Second, Raj may have already received a dowry from his current in-laws. Third, he would be divorced. It was unheard of for widowers and divorced men in Hindu families to demand a dowry. All of these factors neatly came together, and I assumed that my father would be relieved that he did not have to shell out a dowry to marry off his first daughter.

During my third academic year, I enrolled in advanced courses such as Solid State Physics, Statistical Physics, Introduction to Functions in Complex Variables, and Problems in Experimental Physics. Completing these courses would essentially round up the basic coursework required for my Ph.D. The next hurdle I would face was passing my Ph.D. preliminary examination, offered once a year in the fall.

As I was pondering whether to take the prelims, I received a letter from my father. It was a disturbing letter. It stated that my sister Jaya disappeared from home. My family scrambled to find out her whereabouts. They tried to locate Raj at the Indian Institute of Science where he was supposedly employed as a post-doctoral fellow after his return from Vancouver, but he also had disappeared. My family reached the inevitable conclusion that Jaya had eloped with Raj. I was sick to my stomach at this news.

In the letter my father explained that a few months earlier after returning from Vancouver Raj had asked him whether he could marry Jaya. My father, as I correctly predicted, told him that he would allow the marriage only if he first divorced his wife and completely severed all ties with her. My father did not know whether Raj had made an effort to seek the divorce as he never reopened his earlier discussion with Raj about Jaya. No doubt, the news had shaken him and my entire family.

I immediately replied to my father expressing my anger at

what my sister did, more than what Raj put her through. I sympathized with my family's sudden predicament. I explained in my letter about the conversation I'd had with Raj months earlier when we were together in Montreal and the two pre-conditions that I had laid down—namely that Raj should end his first marriage by a divorce and seek my father's express permission to marry Jaya. I urged my father to remain calm and collected until Jaya was found.

I viewed my sister's decision to go off with Raj as an act of defiance and rebellion. I began to have second thoughts on what might have happened when Raj asked my father for my sister's hand. Perhaps my father outright refused. Perhaps my father did not want his first daughter to marry a divorced man, and so even if Raj obtained a divorce from his wife Shini, he and Jaya would not have my father's blessing.

Two days later I received another letter from my father. It stated that the family received a letter from Raj which he enclosed for my reading. The enclosed letter from Raj was short and was counter-signed by Jaya. It read, "Raj decided to convert to the Muslim religion. He and I exchanged our wedding vows in a temple before Hindu Gods." My father's latest letter still did not disclose the whereabouts of Jaya and Raj.

In India, like in most other countries, Muslim males were allowed to practice polygamy. My father surmised that Raj for some reason was unable to divorce Shini. A formal divorce in India was rare and if one wanted annulment the process was slow. Raj found a quick way to marry my sister by changing his religion to Muslim. Jaya was a low-hanging fruit for him to grab. Unwittingly, my sister became his second wife. With this fiat accomplished, Raj officially became my first brother-in-law and parent's first son-in-law!

I could sense the shame and humiliation that my father faced by this unforeseen event. Elopement has a stigma attached to it. It connoted a major disagreement between the parents and the eloped child on a matter involving marriage. Compounding this, my sister Jaya, though being the first daughter in our family, seemed to have ignored the ramifications of her disgraced behavior on the rest of the family members, particularly her younger sisters. Her acquiescence to elope puzzled me as she was a caring person. Certainly, it raised the suspicion of an unexpected pregnancy for Jaya. "Has she become deceitful?" I wondered.

After this incident I questioned whether any young men would step forward to marry my other sisters when they found out that the first sister eloped with a married man. I felt that my first sister and Raj threw a monkey wrench in my grand plan to help my father find suitable husbands for the remaining unmarried sisters. I sensed that my father would now need a lot more money for the dowry to satisfy the grooms for my unmarried sisters because of the unexpected stigma that was created.

Still, Raj was not stupid, and he did not abandon his well-paying and prestigious job. Sometime after the temple wedding, he returned to his job at the Indian Institute in Bangalore and moved into an apartment with Jaya. It was my mother who conveyed this additional news in a letter to me. I valued and believed my mother's letters. She wrote that "a blame game between your father and Raj has broken out. Your father feels betrayed. He took to pen and wrote to Raj making various allegations to provoke him. Raj responded in kind. Unfortunately, Raj and Jaya have now become pariahs in our family."

My father was not a planner. He did not seem to have a plan for his children's future. He certainly did not set expectations for his children in terms of accomplishments and career goals. He took life as it was delivered, believing in karma. He also did not seem to exercise care in cultivating harmonious relationships with friends and relatives. Most of the friends and relatives who visited our family did so because of the gentle and kind feelings that my mother engendered.

It was early spring of 1968 when a terrible event happened in the United States. Martin Luther King, Jr., who was leading the U.S. civil rights movement, was shot and killed in Memphis, Tennessee. King's death led to the black community's anger and disillusionment. Riots broke out. I feared that the blacks who lived in the ghettos surrounding the Temple campus would resort to violence against the students. I was terrified of walking at night immediately after King's assassination, but luckily the campus was spared.

I barely had recovered from King's assassination when another tragedy gripped the country. On June 5, 1968, Robert Kennedy, who just had won the California primaries and was slated to be nominated by the Democratic Party as the presidential candidate, was assassinated.

The violent assassination of these prominent leaders in rapid succession and the war that was engulfing Vietnam raised doubt in my mind whether the United States was a peaceful country. I had a long conversation with Ann and Len about this violence. Ann, who had participated in a civil rights march in Washington, D.C. that was led by King, was more saddened by his assassination. They assured me that "the country is bedrock of democracy.

Liberty and freedom are fundamental rights upon which the United States was founded, and the society is continuing to fight for them." Ann added, "Despite the latest setbacks, there is no need to panic."

Sending money home out of the small stipend I received under my student assistantship had become a habit. Generally, I sent international bank drafts in U.S. dollars to my father who cashed them in the local Indian bank and received the equivalent money in Indian rupees.

In late spring of 1968, I sat with my advisor Dr. Intemann to review the progress I had made toward my Ph.D. I had completed my required coursework, earned a good GPA and satisfied the foreign language proficiency requirements. I questioned the need for the preliminary examination.

Dr. Intemann stood up and gave a mini-lecture as if he was teaching in front of a class: "The purpose of the prelims is to assess a student's competency, knowledge and potential for independent research in physics. The examination will provide the faculty with an opportunity to evaluate the student's problem-solving, written communication skills, mastery of physics and the ability to tackle unfamiliar problems in real time."

He added that "passing the prelims is determinative to take the next step of conducting basic research toward the Ph.D. thesis. People who fail the prelims have another opportunity to take them again, but the Graduate Committee ultimately decides whether the student should be advised to end the Ph.D. program and settle for receiving only a master's degree."

After hearing this sermon, I requested that he allow me to take the prelims in the fall, which he OK'd.

My anxiety over getting ready for the prelims set in. I studied during the entire summer of 1968 for the prelims scheduled for November.

My classmates who had started with me in the doctoral program also took the prelims. The exam took place in a classroom where I had taught the lab for undergrads. We sat on backless chairs in front of polished granite tables. The atmosphere in the room was informal but tense.

The proctor distributed copies of an official stapled book with a blue cover. On this cover we wrote our name. Then a mimeographed question sheet, which contained the physics problems to be solved, was distributed. Some questions included a diagram related to the problem. While studying the question, I had a lot of butterflies in my stomach.

I studied each question as calmly as I could, formulating the solution in my mind before I put my pen to the paper. The proctor left us alone except for brief appearances to check whether we needed anything. I craved strong coffee to stimulate my brain, but I could not have asked for it.

The preliminary exam lasted for three consecutive days. We were tested in topics including fluid mechanics, heat transfer, properties of materials, analytical and quantum mechanics, thermodynamics, statistical physics and the general theory of relativity. The examination was grueling and at the end of the third day my energy was completely drained.

Two weeks after the prelims were held, the results were communicated to us by individual letters. I and most of my fellow students passed, except my roommate Arun who had to settle for the M.A. degree. He subsequently transferred to the State University of New York, Buffalo to continue his Ph.D. studies there.

I was so thrilled with my passing. Immediately I called Western Union and dictated a telegram to my family to convey the good news. It cryptically read, "Passed the Ph.D. preliminary examination." My folks did not know what my message meant and the ramifications of passing the prelims until I explained in a follow-up letter to them. I explained that passing the prelims was a milestone toward earning my Ph.D.

With Arun's departure, I did not room any longer with Kris. Temple had just built a brand-new apartment complex for graduate students. It was located a couple of blocks from the main campus. I teamed up with a new roommate Kumar who I knew from Bangalore and he had been my classmate throughout my graduate school at Temple. He just had passed the Ph.D. prelims with me.

We rented a two-bedroom apartment, and each had the privacy of a bedroom. Kumar was five years older than me. He was a ladies' man. He never missed an opportunity to invite girls to our apartment. He purchased a new car which accelerated his dating of more girls.

It was a huge relief that I had succeeded in the prelims. I was inching closer to my goal of earning my Ph.D. What remained now was to select a dissertation topic in consultation with a faculty member who agreed to serve as my thesis advisor. I needed to conduct research and write the dissertation. I was also required to defend it in an oral examination. Upon successfully defending my thesis, I would be awarded my Ph.D.

The area of research I selected for my thesis would determine my career opportunities. Being a hands-on person, I looked for professors who were experimentalists. I was left with a choice between two professors: Dr. Ted Mihalisin, who had moved from another university and was just starting his research in condensed-matter physics, and Dr. Leroy Dubeck, who was active in superconducting-materials physics. I talked with both and opted to work with Dr. Dubeck, as his lab was established, and he had a student who was finishing his Ph.D. dissertation.

Before I delved into my dissertation, I thought it was time to visit my parents and siblings. Even though we regularly corresponded, the desire to see them became intense. It was May of 1969 and nearly four years since I had left home. It was an appropriate time to visit them as I would be preoccupied for the next couple of years with my research.

Since I would be visiting home for the first time after a long absence, I went overboard and purchased many presents including portable shortwave and AM/FM transistor radios, a portable tape recorder, a portable typewriter, clothes for my sisters and brothers, expensive fountain pens, and many other luxury items that my family could use.

I purchased an airplane ticket for a flight from New York City to Bangalore with a stopover in West Berlin to buy more presents in Berlin's duty-free shops and meet my pen pal Heidi. Heidi and her boyfriend met me at the Berlin airport and drove to their apartment. Heidi was a serious person. Nevertheless, the couple was gracious and took me around Berlin which appeared grey and gloomy. They took me to Checkpoint Charlie where frozen-faced Russian guards in topcoats were guarding the gates to East Berlin. We then went to the shops where I purchased the presents on my list to take to my family.

The reunion with my parents and siblings was emotional. My parents looked a bit aged but still in great shape. My siblings—particularly, my last two sisters who were eight and nine, respectively, when I left India—had grown into full-bodied individuals.

After I showered and rested, my siblings and parents gathered in my parents' bedroom. They had no clue what my luggage contained. When I opened the suitcases containing the presents, they were so surprised to see what I brought. I took out a gold wristwatch first and handed it to my father. He opened the box and instantly liked it. He wanted the expensive wristwatch not for himself but to repay, in the form of a gift from overseas, the saree merchant who had loaned the money for my plane ticket four years earlier. I gave the SLR camera to my youngest brother Kash; an electric shaver to my younger brother Ohan; a portable typewriter to my brother Enku; a second portable typewriter to my father to facilitate typing his letters; an AM/FM transistor radio to my sister Vitri; binoculars to my sister Mini; a portable tape recorder to my sister Swati; a pantsuit to my sister Mala; and lastly Swiss chocolates to my mother. Many other electronic items were intended for the entire family to use. I felt like Santa Claus handing out presents at Christmas. They were thrilled with the presents. The pantsuit that I delivered to Mala fitted her so perfectly that she beamed and wore it on a regular basis to show off to her girlfriends.

Many of my friends in Bangalore were still there and now held good jobs. Some were married and settled down. Meeting with them was not the same as when they were bachelors. Their tastes and responsibilities had changed so much that I could not persuade them to join me for a meal in a restaurant, which used to be a common practice before I went to the U.S.

Jaya and Raj were not living in Bangalore at that time and I did not encounter them as a married couple. My sister Swati was in her final year of a bachelor's degree program in biology and chemistry. Sister Vitri continued to remain at home and not receive any formal education. Sisters Mini and Mala were now in middle school at St. Ann's School. St Ann's Convent, where they started elementary schooling, had now expanded to offer middle and high school education at the same convenient location across the street from 8 Miller Road where my family lived.

My older brother Avi, who was studying engineering through correspondence school, passed his competitive examinations and earned his diploma of Associate Member of the Institution of Engineers. AMIE was considered to be on par with the degree of Bachelor of Engineering. He found a good position with the Electronics & Radar Development Establishment in Bangalore, which was part of India's Defense Ministry.

My younger brother Ohan was in the middle of his study to earn a Bachelor of Engineering degree in a local College of Engineering. Brother Enku had completed his pre-university course and was unable to obtain admission in a college that offered an undergraduate degree. My last bother Kash was enrolled in a local college to earn his Bachelor of Commerce degree.

All in all, I felt that most of my siblings were making strident progress in their studies. I continued to worry about my sister Vitri, however. She was not receiving formal education. She had a kind and generous heart. The satisfaction that she displayed with her simple life astounded me. I used to worry about my first sister Jaya because she had been in the same situation as Vitri was in now. However, Jaya's life now seemed so much better than I had anticipated with Raj marrying her. My parents never brought up the incident of elopement by Jaya, but my father continued to harbor a feud with Raj, despite the fact that the elopement solved his first dowry problem.

DOCTORAL DISSERTATION

AFTER I RETURNED to Temple from a satisfying visit with my family in India, I plunged into what remained to be accomplished to earn my Ph.D. Selecting a topic and a specific problem in that topic to be solved by experimental research was next. I was fascinated by superconductivity which is a phenomenon by which below a certain temperature, known as the critical temperature, materials lose their resistance for the passage of electrical current. This means that an electrical current can pass through the material without dissipation of energy. Most of the known superconductors then were metals or alloys when chilled below 254 degree Celsius (or 19 degrees Kelvin). Physicists were looking for superconductors which exhibited zero electrical resistance at room temperature.

I was carried away by the thought of looking for a material that exhibited superconductivity at a temperature higher than known at that time, hopefully at the liquid nitrogen temperature of minus 196 degrees Celsius (or 77 degrees Kelvin). Dr. Dubeck, who was an avid player of chess, encouraged me to take the gamble. That was how my dissertation topic was established. My thesis topic was bold and read, "Material research to identify new types of superconductors which have a high critical temperature—preferably room temperature." I felt that I was working on something highly significant.

I wondered about the profound effect a room temperature superconductor could have on the energy industry. It would revolutionize the world like the invention of the steam engine had two centuries earlier.

It was July 20, 1969—a warm summer day. As I was driving on the streets of Philadelphia, the news broke on my car radio that Apollo 11 just had landed on the surface of the Moon. American astronauts Neil Armstrong and Buzz Aldrin had successfully landed the lunar module. Armstrong became the first person to step on to the lunar surface. Aldrin joined him minutes later. This was an accomplishment that President John Kennedy had set as a goal for America earlier in the decade. These astronauts, with strong leadership and support from NASA, fulfilled the Moon Mission and attained the nation's goal. I felt good about this accomplishment—that the United States had once again taken leadership in science and technology and accomplished something that had never been achieved by man. It was an amazing feat and a triumph for America and the humans living on earth.

I was excited and quickly rushed to my apartment and spent the next several hours glued to the color TV in our complex's social room. The astronauts spent about two and half hours together outside the spacecraft, hoisted the American flag, hit a golf ball that they carried, collected lunar rocks and headed back to Earth. By talking with my fellow graduate students at the complex, I sensed that the Moon-landing had rekindled a sense of patriotic American intrepidness.

After brainstorming with Dr. Dubeck, I reached the decision to target organic materials to determine their superconductivity. Around this same time, Dr. Dubeck was made the Assistant Chairman of the Physics Department at Temple, and this signaled that he would soon become the Chairman of the department.

I procured different organic powders in their purest form and compressed them by applying a high pressure into narrow, inch-long samples. I inserted the sample into the test chamber of a vibrating sample magnetometer. I chilled the chamber first by using liquid nitrogen, followed by injecting liquid helium and then suddenly caused the liquid helium to expand inside the chamber so the ultimate chamber temperature reached close to absolute zero. In these conditions, by applying a small and controlled magnetic field to the sample as it vibrated in this field, I tested the critical temperature at which it exhibited superconductivity. I catalogued the results.

Some samples were duds and did not exhibit superconductivity at all. I discarded such specimens from further research. Other samples exhibited superconductivity but not at the high temperature I was hoping for. My search for the high-temperature superconductor was like an alchemist looking to discover gold by combining cheap metals.

In parallel with doing my research, I continued to take advanced physics courses to earn credits. While the bulk of the courses I enrolled in were on Problems in Experimental Physics or my Ph.D. dissertation, I also took courses in Low Temperature Physics to gain a better theoretical understanding of materials when chilled to near absolute zero.

On the personal front, my roommate Kumar decided to move into his own apartment off campus. I suspected that he wanted more privacy to continue his dalliance with girls. Luckily, I was able to find a substitute roommate almost immediately. He was Mohammed Khuddus (Mo, as he was called).

Mo was in the same boat as I was, doing his thesis work in Chemistry. He was a Muslim from India, but his religious affiliation did not matter to me as neither of us practiced religion in the U.S. He occupied the larger bedroom that Kumar had vacated.

Mo was short, about 5 feet 3 inches in height. He also was fond of girls, not as much as Kumar. He brought beautiful girls to our apartment to impress me. He was also a party guy. He arranged a number of BYOB parties in our apartment to which we invited our classmates and their better halves to join us. After he had a few drinks, Mo would show off his skills in dancing to Indian tunes by imitating the Bollywood movie scenes and entertained the crowd.

Like me, Mo was a pragmatist. Occasionally we met for lunch at Temple's cafeteria for hamburgers and talked. On one such occasion, he asked what I would like to do after obtaining my Ph.D. I replied that the choices I had would be to either return home or to find a job in the U.S. I added that I must make money first and then decide whether to return home, without telling Mo of my plan to raise money for my sisters' dowries. Mo also ruled out returning to India right away. We both wanted to find high industrial jobs.

However, since we were in the country on student visas, by law we were prohibited from employment other than small campus jobs. Besides, we could not justify remaining on our student visa once we completed our doctorate. We decided to do research on the U.S. immigration policy and talk with foreign students who preceded us and were now gainfully employed in the U.S. We found an answer to our quest. The answer lay in the Immigration & Nationality Act of 1965 that was enacted by President Johnson that year.

Under the Act, the Immigration & Naturalization Service offered a special merit-based preference for foreigners of extraordinary ability in sciences to become permanent residents of the U.S. As a foreign student on visa and pursuing my doctorate in physics, I was eligible for this preference. The permanent visa, also known as the Green Card—as the card that was issued by INS was green in color, offered many benefits. The Green Card holder could remain in the U.S. permanently and could work here. The Green Card holder could petition to the INS and obtain the same status for his/her foreign spouse or children under the age of twenty-one years. The Green Card enabled the holder to become a U.S. citizen after living in this country for five years by a process known as naturalization. Once naturalized, the new citizen could apply for sensitive jobs with the government and industry which required security clearance. The citizen could sponsor his foreign parents, brothers and sisters for Green Cards. The latter was known as chain migration.

The political climate in the country was such that the government encouraged skilled professionals like me to live permanently in the U.S. and contribute to the American society.

Mo and I paid a visit to the branch of the Philadelphia-based INS office and picked up the official petition form to apply for a change of our visa status.

On February 3, 1970, I typed up the petition requesting an adjustment of status from student visa to that of a permanent resident under the third preference category or 203(a)(3) of the Immigration & Nationality Act. I supplemented the petition with an official letter written on Temple University letterhead by Dr. Dubeck under the dual title of Assistant Chairman of the Physics Department and Thesis Advisor. In the letter Dr. Dubeck certified that I was working on my Ph.D. dissertation in the field of low-temperature solid-state physics. It further stated that I was exceptionally qualified in electronics and low-temperature techniques.

Armed with these documents, I returned to the INS Office. A female officer dressed in a blue suit met me at a counter in the office. She wore a lapel pin featuring the words "U.S. Immigration."

She greeted me with: "Hello! And what can I do for you?" and smiled.

I explained, "I'm here to have my present student visa converted to Green Card." After a short pause, I added, "I am petitioning for the granting of a Green Card based on my technical skills under the third preference."

I presented the documents I brought with me, including my Indian passport which contained my student visa stamped inside.

The receiving immigration officer thumbed through my documents. She smiled at me again and commented, "Everything seems to be all right."

She made a copy of the relevant pages from my passport and returned it to me. She ended our brief meeting with: "You will hear from the Office in due course after your petition is processed."

Two weeks later, I received official notification from the INS that I was placed in the queue for my Green Card. I was excited about the prospect of having my temporary student visa converted to a permanent resident visa which allowed me to live in the U.S. indefinitely and seek employment outside the university campus and all of the other extraordinary benefits that the Green Card conferred on me.

By now, I had spent six months doing intensive experimental research in my lab and countless hours of time to find the elusive high-temperature superconductor. I was starting to have second thoughts on continuing with my research problem.

I met with my thesis advisor and said, "Dr. Dubeck, I've had no luck in finding the high temperature superconductor. It has been more than six months now."

After taking a deep breath, I continued, "I would like to graduate within the next fifteen months, or so, which would then be six years after I enrolled in my Ph.D. program at Temple. However, the discovery of a high-T superconductor may take longer. Perhaps the discovery of high-temperature superconductor should be pursued by a post-doctoral fellow?"

My advisor sympathized with my timetable to graduate and agreed. He said, "Let's settle for a more realistic, boots on the ground type of research to tackle." He and I chose a new topic of research: Magnetization Studies of certain Type-II Superconductors. I quickly got into action.

I selected alloys of lead-thallium, indium-thallium, niobium-thallium, and lead-tin to study their magnetization properties as they were cooled below their critical temperature and returned to their normal state. I prepared dozens of these alloys from high purity metals and studied them by using the vibrating sample magnetometer and generated hundreds of plots of their magnetic hysteresis patterns. My study demonstrated that these superconductors tolerated local penetration of the magnetic field, which enabled them to preserve their superconducting properties in the presence of intense applied magnetic fields. My thesis attributed this behavior to the existence of a mixed state where superconducting and non-superconducting areas coexist within the material.

In March 1971, I received a letter from the Philadelphia-based District Director of the Immigration & Naturalization Service responding to the petition I had filed more than a year earlier for my Green Card. It mentioned a "Medical Examination and Immigration Interview" and provided instructions for a medical examination with a physician of the U.S. Public Health Service at a local address on a designated date, which I followed up. The physician turned out to be Dr. John H. Kolmer who had treated me months earlier for a mild case of influenza at Temple University Health Services.

At the exam, I reminded him that we had met before at Temple's infirmary

This he acknowledged by saying, "You were the skinny vegetarian, isn't it?"

I responded, "Yes, it was convenient to be a vegan because of my roommates, but I do eat meat."

Dr. Kolmer performed a thorough medical examination including a serology test for syphilis and took an x-ray of my chest, possibly to determine whether I had tuberculosis.

After the medical examination, the doctor gave me a sealed envelope, presumably containing the large chest x-ray he took and a report on my blood test. He asked me to deliver it to the immigration officer.

Immediately after the medical exam, I went to another location in Philadelphia for the scheduled interview with the immigration officer. The interview was merely to deliver the package from Dr. Kolmer. The final outcome depended on the results of my just completed medical examination.

A month later on April 22, 1971 I received notification of lawful admission for permanent residence in the United States. I went back to the INS office and collected a wallet-sized card with my designated Alien Registration number printed on it. This was my Green Card. This was a big step in my life. By earning my Green Card, I officially became a permanent resident of the U.S. It bestowed me all other rights, benefits and privileges. I now could work anywhere in the country, travel abroad and return, and petition for certain close family members, such as my future wife, to also receive Green Cards. Eventually, I could become a citizen of the U.S. which conferred more privileges and benefits.

My doctoral research was nearing completion after fourteen months of work. It was now my sixth academic year at Temple. I did not apply for a renewal of my research assistantship for the following academic year, which meant that I needed a job outside Temple to make a living after that academic year. It was in late spring of 1971 that I requested my thesis advisor to schedule my final Ph.D. examination to defend my thesis.

Because of the complex equations and numerous graphical plots of the data that I generated which was integral to my thesis, I decided to type up my thesis rather than engage a professional typist. I was able to continuously pound the typewriter over weeks after which I neatly copied the complex equations using India ink and completed my thesis document in a record time.

I made copies of my thesis and submitted them to the Physics Graduate Committee which scheduled my oral examination to defend it. I felt confident that for the first time I was in control of answering any question on my dissertation. I knew my research more than anyone on the Committee, including my thesis advisor.

Three faculty members participated in the oral hearing—Dr. Dubeck, Dr. Mihalisin and Dr. Peter Havas. Dr. Havas had taught two courses on the Special and General Theory of Relativity, respectively, early in my Ph.D. coursework. He was from Austria and had a heavy combination of German and Austrian accents. I did well in his courses, nevertheless. He was a theoretician and I was puzzled that he showed up to question an experimentalist on a topic that he may not fully be in tune with.

I was greeted by the three professors as I prepared for the oral. I stood in front of them without the aid of any tools for visualization of my research. The examiners and I relied on the copies of my thesis that were in their possession.

Dr. Dubeck remarked, "This is the final stretch for you, Mr. Coca." I nodded in agreement.

Most of the substantive questioning was done by the two experimental physicists. I fully answered Dr. Mihalisin's many pointed questions, which were designed to gain a genuine understanding of my research. They both were cordial in their questioning.

Dr. Havas focused on nitpicking my thesis topic. He insinuated that the subject matter of my research resembled that of an earlier Ph.D. student (Duane) who also researched under Dr. Dubeck. I demurred, as my research topic had been selected jointly with my advisor.

Dr. Dubeck strongly opposed such remarks and pointed out the many and significant differences between the research that I conducted versus Duane's. He enumerated them by counting on his fingers and fully pointed out the differences in minute detail. I felt that Dr. Dubeck took the oral examination more than I did, as the questions that I was pelted with in the beginning of the oral were easier to answer. With this heated exchange between the two professors and the strong defense that Dr. Dubeck launched as the future Chairman of the Physics Department, Dr. Havas quieted down and had no further questions for me.

With that exchange between the two members of the Committee, my oral examination essentially ended. I was asked to leave the room so the Committee members can deliberate the result.

I left the room and lingered outside awaiting their decision. I was serene and unafraid.

After about ten minutes I was called back to the room.

"I am speaking for the Committee," Dr. Dubeck began to say.

At that moment Dr. Havas stood up and eyed the door.

"You passed your thesis defense, Dr. Coca," Dr. Dubeck beamed. He then shook my hand and conveyed his heartfelt congratulations. So did Dr. Mihalisin. That was the first time I was addressed as Dr. Coca.

Defending my dissertation before a panel of experts who validated my contribution and acknowledged my ability to engage in research in physics felt so great!

Unfortunately, the timing of earning my Ph.D. did not coincide with the deadline for the graduation that academic year. As a result, I was forced to wait for the next Commencement Exercise schedule for January 1972 to officially receive my degree certificate. This was only a formality and it did not stop me from rushing out to use my credential to seek a job as physicist.

Earning my Ph.D. was a significant milestone in my life. It was the most important accomplishment so far in my lifetime. It took so much planning going back a decade or more, systematically working toward this milestone, spending essentially all of my time and energy to reach it. I felt extremely good about my success, but I did not gloat about it.

I sent a telegram to my parents conveying that I had earned my Ph.D.

However, the Ph.D. did not put me on the fast train to where I wanted to go.

JOB RESET

AS NOTED, FINISHING my schooling in 1971 and being officially awarded my Ph.D. in physics in January 1972 meant that I had achieved two major milestones. But I did not pursue the Ph.D. out of mere academic love of schooling and education was not an end in itself for me. I wanted to make use of this degree and earn money to financially aid my father. Accordingly, immediately after completing my Ph.D. dissertation in the summer of 1971, I set my sights on finding a job in the private sector which paid well. I craved working at IBM or Bell Labs of AT&T because both were attempting to find the high-temperature superconductor. However, the doors at IBM and AT&T were closed to me. I was in a conundrum. Yet I was not only looking for a purple squirrel, the exact right job fit for me, after I earned my Ph.D. I just wanted to be gainfully employed as a physicist.

The post-Sputnik era that drove the rapid growth in opportunities for Ph.D. physicists came to an abrupt end in the year I graduated. The Vietnam War was draining the science budgets. Concurrently, a political development caused an unexpected job shortage even for the brightest scientists.

In 1968, following the assassination of Robert Kennedy, Vice President Hubert Humphrey took on the mantle for the Democratic Party. He was roundly defeated by the Republican Party candidate Richard Nixon in that year's presidential election.

Nixon ran on a war platform promising to win against the Communist aggression in Vietnam. However, the war effort went badly, resulting in hundreds of thousands of more deaths of American soldiers. Nixon was now gearing up for reelection in 1972 and this time he promised to end the war. The war was costing the U.S. Government billions of dollars every year, and Congress was getting uneasy about continuing to spend on a war with no end in sight. Congress tightened such spending. Nixon was forced to cut back in U.S. defense spending, which meant a reduction of funds for weapons and other war machinery needed to fight the war. The ramifications of the reduction on defense spending spread across the military industrial complex, as well as the private sector which also depended on the federal money.

As a result, thousands of engineers and scientists in the public and private sectors were laid off from jobs in defense and related industries. In fact, when I graduated, such laid-off workers were reported to be driving cabs in cities in California, New York and Texas. A fresh graduate like me did not stand a chance to compete with this unexpected glut of talent.

I couldn't afford any time daydreaming about what my career might be. I needed to find a job, any job. I had no choice other than to redesign my life from innovator to instructor. I settled for teaching physics at the Abington High School in suburban Philadelphia to make a living.

Abington hired me to teach Harvard Project Physics, which was an innovative way of teaching physics. I enabled my students to discover the laws under which our physical universe operated.

One day, standing in front of my desk dressed in a blue shirt with a crimson necktie and a white lab coat, I watched bright-eyed teens as they slowly piled into my classroom. They occupied the lab tables where I had set up experiments for them to conduct. Giving minimal instructions, I asked them to play with the lab toys to discover the connection between light and waves.

The students were to electrically turn the tiny vibrating paddles immersed in a rectangular tray of water. The paddles generated waves in the water like in a pond. The students placed an obstacle that had two spaced-apart openings in the path of the waves. They were to observe the pattern that was produced on the other side of the obstacle and to didactically find the connection between light and waves.

After the experiment, I gathered the students in the classroom chairs and quizzed them about what they had learned from the experiment. Then I reinforced their conclusions with formal instruction about how light was composed of waves.

The geographic proximity of the job at Abington had an unexpected benefit. It enabled me to work with my Ph.D. thesis advisor to complete an unfinished task. I needed to write and publish papers in physics journals based on my thesis. Such papers were important credentials for a scientist's' resume. "Publish or perish" was the accepted norm for scientists then, as it has always been since. By collaborating with Dr. Dubeck, I was able to publish half a dozen papers in prestigious journals such as the *Physical Review*.

Teaching at the high school was not satisfying or rewarding. While the students in my classes were bright and eager to learn, I was saddled with chores by the school district. These included writing lesson plans for each class I taught, submitting to impromptu visits to my class by the principal who observed my teaching methods and how I managed any disruptive behavior in the classroom, participating in parent-teacher meetings, and dealing with emotional problems of kids who had trouble learning physics.

The teaching position required that I be certified as an Instructor by the State of Pennsylvania. This necessitated that I complete a set of prescribed courses in education. I took these courses at Temple on Saturdays. What bothered me was that I was forced to meet this requirement despite my lofty education and over five years of experience in teaching physics to undergraduate students at Temple.

Nevertheless, I dutifully fulfilled these requirements as I was a prisoner to the difficult job market. The investment I had made in my education, pushing myself to reach the pinnacle of study of physics, did not seem to readily offer the returns that I had expected. My degrees seemed like surplus schooling—more education than my teaching job needed. I was dissatisfied and kept my sights on something more productive, intellectually stimulating and lucrative. However, industrial jobs continued to be elusive. As it turned out, the 1970s started a period of financial stagnation with the weakest period for productivity growth since World War II. I graduated at the cusp of this period and unfortunately got caught up in this recession.

My inability to be more gainfully employed was an unexpected event which I did not foresee. Six years earlier, I had travelled the distance from India, and abandoned my family in search for a better life for me and my family, especially my unmarried sisters. My goal of earning wealth to help my father with funding for the dowries seemed to unravel. Although I was somewhat disillusioned by the dire situation I faced, I believed that America was founded on the importance of the work ethic. "If you work hard, study and learn, you'll rise in America because you have earned it" was the principle of success I staunchly believed in.

Rather than bemoaning the unfortunate situation I faced, I plowed forward seeking ways to supplement my earnings. I found opportunities in the evenings to teach more physics courses at the Montgomery County Community College in Lansdale, Pennsylvania and Weidner College in Chester, Pennsylvania.

On those evenings that I did not teach and on weekends, I worked as a front-desk clerk at the Sheraton Hotel in Fort Washington, Pennsylvania to keep myself occupied and earn money. It was an interesting part-time job where I learned methods of running a hospitality business. An enjoyable part was that I ate my dinners at the hotel and did not have to prepare my own meals at home. I also came in contact with well-known performers like singer Carly Simon when they checked into the hotel to stay for their performances at the nearby Ambler campus of Temple University Music School.

Now that I was employed and making some earnings, albeit not as much as I would have as a physicist, I continued to send money to my father to help out with family expenses. As before, I sent international bank drafts in U.S. dollars to my father who cashed them at the local Indian bank and received the equivalent money in Indian rupees. I did not send him too much money at a time as I was unsure that he would use it for the purpose I intended. I also saved money in my bank account for future transfer to him when he needed to pay the dowries.

In the summer of 1972, I went back to Bangalore to see my family. A lot had happened with my family since the dark episode of elopement by my sister Jaya. My mother told me that Raj and

Jaya had their child, a daughter. I was not sure when exactly she had been born—was it nine months after the two hurriedly got married or before? I never asked and no one in the family told me. I wondered whether Raj, who had converted to the Muslim religion in order to legally justify simultaneously having two wives, gave a Muslim name to his daughter. Not so. She had received the Hindu name of Jata. With the newly born daughter, who was the first grandchild for my parents, Raj and Jaya had seemed to somewhat patch up the family problems that their elopement had caused. My father, however, never embraced Raj and continued to be hostile to him.

In addition, my father had retired from his job as the Income Tax Officer. He started a part-time tax consultation business and met clients at home. When his clientele grew, he opened a leased office and hired a secretary to schedule appointments and assist him with his clients. However, his net income was nowhere near the income he earned before retirement.

My older brother Avi, who now had reached thirty years of age, started to show amorous tendencies towards marriageable girls. I was not sure whether my father or mother was then looking for a suitable girl for him to marry. However, unbeknownst to them, he was scouting on his own for a girl to marry. He had moved into a new house that my father purchased a couple of years earlier in Indiranagar on the outskirts of Bangalore. With the newfound freedom to live apart from our stern father and a Vespa scooter at his disposal, he apparently found leads through friends to meet girls.

One such lead was a female medical student, Wari, who was studying in Avi's birthplace of Kakinada. Apparently, she was the only child of her parents. I was told that Avi took a great liking to her. Without informing my parents, he brought Wari to Bangalore and showed her the sights of the city by driving while she was a passenger in the backseat of his Vespa.

Following a period of dating and then living together, Avi decided to marry her. I never found out whether my brother discussed his intention to marry Wari with my father and, if so, whether my father agreed to the arrangement. I could only speculate that they discussed it and my father demanded Avi to get a dowry from Wari's parents as a condition for the marriage. With him being his first son, I sympathized with my father's expectation of Avi to set an example for his younger brothers by collecting a dowry. This money could be used by my father to provide a dowry for one of his daughters. The next thing that happened was that Avi got married to Wari. After the wedding, she went back to Kakinada to finish up her studies.

I could only surmise that my older brother did not take a dowry from his in-laws. The family owned a house in Kakinada. My brother may have figured that Wari would eventually inherit that house whose value could more than compensate for the dowry that he did not take. Besides, she would be a practicing doctor and earn big money.

This was the second instance in my family's history when the children defied their parents and got married without the benefit of their consent or blessings. My parents did not have the benefit of being involved in Avi's wedding or celebrating it with relatives and friends. This incident caused more heartache for my father who was recovering from the elopement of Jaya with Raj. What Avi did by marrying Wari was tantamount to elopement since he rebelled against my father and defiantly married her.

When I visited my family in the summer of 1972, it was my second visit since I went to America seven years earlier. Avi's wife Wari had completed her medical degree, moved in with him, and started her medical practice. With the departure of the eldest daughter and son to their respective abodes as well as my own move to the U.S., my parents' house at 8 Miller Road looked less congested. My remaining siblings were getting older. My sister Mala had reached fourteen and attended secondary school along with Mini. My sister Swati was now employed as a technician at the Indian Institute of Science in the same department where Raj worked. Vitri continued to remain home uneducated. She had by now become the right hand to my mother for household chores. Vitri continued to worry me regarding what kind of life she would lead and who would marry her. My three younger brothers were employed in various jobs and continued to live with my parents. I got the impression that that my four siblings who were earning money were tight-fisted and were expecting me, the rich brother in America, to continue to foot a part of the increasing family expenses. Perhaps they also expected me to foot the dowries for my four unmarried sisters, although I gave no clues for such an expectation.

On this home visit, my sister Jaya, Raj and their infant daughter Jata appeared on the scene at my parents' home. Raj brought them on his scooter to meet me. This was the first time that I had seen Raj since our trip to Montreal—it had been exactly five years. It was longer than that since I last saw Jaya.

I met my niece Jata for the first time. She was cute and had the same facial features as her father. She would sit on the large red rock in my father's garden and try to utter words in English in a kind of baby talk. I did not see my father carry Jata in his arms as he generally did with other children, but my mother constantly embraced her. We never discussed the elopement and what lead to that desperate action. It was ancient history and none of us wanted to dig up that past painful incident. Raj and Jaya visited my parents' home more frequently than usual, because of my presence there.

A young student Kal, who was doing research in biochemistry for his Ph.D. thesis at the Indian Institute of Science in Bangalore under Raj, was beginning to make Sunday afternoon visits to my family at the invitation of my sister Swati. I assumed that she met him at the Institute. The body language and laughter that I observed in Swati when this young man visited gave me the impression that she was romantically drawn toward him. However, this emotion of attraction was somewhat tempered by the more friendly and mischievous behavior of my last sisters Mini and Mala who seem to joke with Kal and have a great time with him. Swati did not like the behavior of her younger sisters and felt jealous and threatened by their innocent friendship with her invitee. I noticed also that Mini and Mala, who were fourteen and fifteen, were beginning to show interest in boys. I wondered how my father would cope with these daughters who were beginning to show interest in the opposite sex.

I also wondered how my three younger brothers, Ohan, Enku and Kash, who were older than Mini and Mala, were behaving with the girls that they might be encountering in their lives. However, I received no clues from them about this.

My visit home was not joyous—not only because of the disappointment that my older brother and first sister caused my parents (whom I fully sympathized with)—there also was an unexpected health issue with my mother.

While in India, I generally did not visit the homes of my relatives in town, except there was one exception. My older cousin Mani and her husband, who admired me like a rock star because of my accomplishments, invited me to their home for afternoon tea. My mother accompanied me.

While we were in Mani's house, where my mother occupied a chair directly in front of me, I noticed an elongated and flattened mass under the skin on her neck.

After observing this, I queried her. "Mom, how long have you had that mass on you neck?"

She replied, "More than two years now."

I asked, "Is it causing you discomfort?"

She responded, "Yes, and the mass has been slowly enlarging. It is causing me discomfort when I swallow."

I decided to have her checked by a specialist. I was concerned that the growth in her neck might be cancerous.

The next morning, I took my mother to an endocrinologist. After examining my mother's neck, the specialist concluded it was goiter caused by enlargement of her thyroid. He speculated that it was caused by a diet deficient in iodine. I remembered that in India salt was generally not iodized and many people used untreated and pure rock salt in their food.

The endocrinologist added, "Another cause of her goiter could be an increase in thyroid stimulating hormone in response to a defect in normal hormone synthesis within the thyroid gland."

The specialist recommended that the mass in her neck be surgically removed. I lined up a small private hospital with a modern operating room and a reliable staff including nurses, an anesthesiologist and an experienced surgeon who specialized in treating thyroid cancer. I made arrangements for my mother's surgery.

On the morning of the scheduled surgery, a routine blood test was conducted by the hospital. The blood test revealed that my mother was diabetic. I was surprised that neither my father nor anyone in my family knew of this health condition.

The surgery was postponed. The doctors worked to bring her blood sugar to normal levels before undertaking the surgery. Making matters worse, on the later scheduled day of her surgery, the hospital did not carry the special type of blood that my mother needed for the surgery. Raj and I scrambled that morning on a scooter to find blood matching her blood type. We rushed to a remotely located blood bank and brought vials of blood in a refrigerated container for the surgeon to administer by transfusion.

The surgery went well, and the surgeon successfully excised the goiter and stitched up the skin on my mother's neck neatly. A biopsy of the tissue indicated that it was benign. I thanked God for this wonderful outcome. I thanked the surgeon for his outstanding surgery, too. Following the surgery, mother had to remain in the hospital for a few days.

The one person that I had not seen during this visit home was my brother Avi, who was now married and lived in my father's new house. He heard about our mother's surgery through Raj. I did not understand why Avi, who projected himself as a "know-it-all" type of person, or his doctor bride failed to notice the swollen goiter on my mother's neck earlier. If they did, why had they failed to take remedial action?

It was in the hospital that I saw Avi and met his bride Wari as well as her mother who paid a courtesy visit to my recuperating mother. I had seen the photos of Avi's bride but had not met her until then. We greeted each other in the waiting area of the hospital, after which I lead the trio up the stairs to my mother's bed. I explained the successful outcome of the surgery and the benign result from the biopsy. Their conversation with me was muted and focused on my mother's diabetes and the remedial treatments she needed to follow after the surgery.

The bitterness between my father and Raj continued. Raj never missed a chance to run my father down. He would draw me out of the earshot of my father and began a campaign of character assassination. He told me how humiliated he was when his colleagues read the postcards my father wrote to his office. He tried to woo me over by complaining about my father. Initially I tolerated it, but I resented this soon after it started when I realized that he was attempting to drive a wedge between me and my father.

I discussed Raj's divisive campaign with my mother on her hospital bed. She explained that Raj had been critical of my father ever since he married Jaya. She lamented that Raj had also been disparaging him in front of other relatives. The fact that Raj was a gossip came as a surprise to me. Gossip was normally a trait of women. His gossip was malicious. He tried to ostracize my father and gain personal satisfaction. This annoyed me and made me suspect the truth or veracity of his statements relating to people. By dishing the dirt on my father, he in effect began to alienate me.

My father probably suspected Raj's campaign against him and was concerned that Raj was poisoning his children with negative aspersions cast on him. He suspected that I was being corrupted by Raj's propaganda against him.

Before my mother's discharge from the hospital, the doctor instructed her to follow a prescribed regiment with medication to control her diabetes but also to manage her hormone levels through diet. For controlling diabetes, she needed a daily injecttion of insulin for which I made arrangements to have her taken to a medical clinic near our home.

After my mother returned and started her slow recuperation from the surgery, I decided to make a pilgrimage to the Hindu temple of Lord Venkateswara atop the seven hills in Tirupathi a couple of hundred miles from Bangalore. There, devotees kneeled and prayed in front of the God's formidable statue, which was adorned with new clothing, gold jewelry, diamonds and fresh flowers. Devotees considered a pilgrimage to this temple as sacred and believed the Lord would listen to their prayers and grant their wishes.

Many devotees climbed the seven hills by foot to show their devotion to the God. Men and women offered their hair by having their heads completely shaved by barbers in front of the temple. A shaved head was also a requirement for being ordained by the temple priests to wash away past sins or to show gratitude to God for having granted their past wishes.

I developed faith in praying before this God. I had made similar pilgrimages twice before: when I first embarked on my travel to the United States to thank Him for enabling my overseas adventure, and on my previous visit to India to convey my gratitude for the success in my Ph.D. preliminary examination. I decided to visit the temple now to thank Him for the successful surgery of my mother and for enabling me to earn my doctorate. I prayed for my success in finding a job as a physicist in America.

Raj and Jaya decided to accompany me. We rented a chauffeur-driven car and made a two-day trip. The weather cooperated, and the driver proceeded by negotiating steep roads and hair-pin curves across seven hills to the top of the seventh and highest hill station where the temple was located. We had good *darshnam* (auspicious sight of the statue of the deity). I felt great about this pilgrimage.

When we returned home, I discovered that my mother was not taken to receive her insulin shots for two days in a row. Before I left on my trip, I had a chat with my father and specifically told him to have someone take her to the clinic and make sure that she continued to receive daily doses of insulin injected into her body. I also discovered that my father went to his office. It was a Sunday afternoon and my sister Swati pointedly stated that he was probably with his office secretary.

I was infuriated to hear this. I immediately jumped into the car with my mother and Swati. I asked the chauffer to drop my mother and sister at the medical clinic so my mother could immediately receive the insulin shot. Then I went to confront my father in his office. Raj also jumped into the car to watch the unfolding of events.

I did not know what scene I would face at my father's office. However, when I barged into his office, he was chatting with his secretary. My father saw my unpleasant face and his disfavored son-in-law by my side and realized something was amiss. He ushered out his secretary and the three of us drove back home without saying a word in the car. The three of us were silent because we did not want the chauffer to listen in to our sensitive conversation.

After returning home, I said to my father, "Didn't you understand the importance of Mom receiving insulin shots on a timely basis? Didn't you understand the seriousness of her medical situation?"

My father remained silent.

I calmly explained to my father the serious repercussions on my mother's health if she failed to receive the insulin shots on a timely basis, which included the onset of blindness in her.

My father acknowledged what I explained, but he was furious at Raj. He stated that "someone set me up for this incident to have happened." He vowed that "someone," implying his son-in-law, "would pay for the consequences." I realized that my confrontation of my father in his office was a blow to him.

This was an ugly incident that I wished did not happen. I was ashamed and embarrassed at what I just did to my father. Passion born of youth and the prospect of my mother suffering from a diabetic condition, which when neglected might result in irreparable harm to her health, propelled me into this hasty action. I regretted my mistake of losing my cool and rushing to eject my father out of his office. I wished that Swati did not utter that my father was with his secretary as it implied something sinister was going on in my father's office. I also was disappointed that Raj did not stop me from rushing in.

That evening I reflected on my confrontation of my father. I sat on my bed in the garage and watched the lights to go out in our house as was normal before my siblings turned in for the night. My father silently sat in his wicker chair in the garden like he usually did before he retired to his bedroom. My brother Ohan in the other bed in the garage was already settled in with a mosquito net covering him. My mother was probably asleep in her own bed. A sense of remorse struck me. Perhaps I should have waited for my father's return from his office and quietly explained to him the repercussions of Mom not timely receiving the insulin. That would have been a better outcome than my hasty action.

Overall, this incident bothered me quite a bit immediately and for the rest of my life. That was one of the lowest points in my relationship with my father. I told myself that I would never again interfere with his personal life. My father's distrust of me began after this unfortunate incident.

I returned to the U.S. and resumed my teaching at Abington and continued to take the state-mandated courses for my certification as Instructor. Within a couple of years, I earned my Instructor certification from the State of Pennsylvania. I also became a fully tenured member of the faculty at Abington High, which meant that I earned a job for life as a Physics Instructor at Abington.

However, I was driven by goals beyond the comfortable life near the campus. My teaching job at Abington was not satisfying, both intellectually and monetarily. I faced difficulties accepting this career situation. It was stressful. I thought that after earning my Ph.D. I would make money through prize-winning scientific discoveries and develop inventions. Then at thirty-one, I came across a little ditty from the collection of poems written by Paul Dirac, a winner of the 1933 Nobel Prize in Physics. In it he gloomily warned that every physicist must fear "he is better dead than living when once he is past his thirtieth year" to make an important scientific contribution.

These lines scared me. I thought that my Ph.D. was getting stale. I feared a decline in my capabilities as a physicist. But tough times had a way of shining a light through the gloom. My gift of ambition and goal setting propelled me to overcome this stress and gloom. The gift of ambition was not for power but to make money and help my father from the potential bankruptcy he faced to meet the dowries.

Rather than lamenting my bad luck and being tormented by emotional distress, I decided to function in the face of it. I decided to redesign my life. I explored new careers. I wanted to elevate my career and my life to a higher level than what I originally planned and worked toward. I wanted to control my destiny. I plotted Plan B.

My Plan B was to engage in flexible thinking to analyze the circumstances I faced. I wanted a fresh approach to build on my strengths and overcome my obstacles. I needed to find new tools to help myself to become successful with a new, rewarding, sustainable and professional career.

I told myself, "I'm realistic about where I am but optimistic about where I could be. Failure for me is no longer an option. I may not have succeeded with what I really wanted the first time; I must just keep trying, trying and trying." I believed in Colin Powell's saying that "perpetual optimism is a force multiplier."

Plan B was to invest in myself for a radically new career which would not be subjected to the whims of the politicians in Washington, D.C. In effect, I wanted to have the freedom of control of my employment, my future and my destiny.

At first, I wanted to drop everything and go to medical school. I always wanted to be a physician but never received counselling from either my teachers in high school or my father to major in biological sciences which knowledge was imperative to become a doctor. Given my foundation in physics, I could get my M.D.

degree in record time and choose specialties like radiology, ophthalmology or nuclear medicine. However, not having a background in biology snagged me. To apply to medical school, I needed to earn sufficient knowledge in biology, organic chemistry, pharmacology, and human physiology to be able to pass the med school entrance examination. This would mean leaving my teaching job, going back to undergrad school during the day, applying for student loans to pay for tuition and taking chances for admission to the med school. Even if I was lucky enough to get into med school, for five or more years I would need to take more student loans to pay for the tuition to complete the M.D. program. These were hurdles which would set me back from my goal of earning money right away to help my father. My sisters were reaching marriageable age. Meeting the need for their dowries seemed imminent.

Another idea was to pursue a degree in business, like an MBA, which I could have done in the evening at Temple. However, I concluded that unless I earned my MBA from a top-ranking school like the Wharton School of Business at Penn or from the business schools at Harvard or Columbia, I might not get a lucrative job after earning the MBA degree. This also would mean attending the business school full-time during the daytime and leaving my full-time job as teacher.

The next idea under my Plan B was to consider pursuing the study of law. The idea to pursue law came from a brief excerpt that I read in the *Temple Alumni Quarterly* about a post-doctoral fellow Dr. Steven Brown who was studying for his J.D. at Temple's School of Law. I contacted Dr. Brown and met with him for lunch at Temple's cafeteria to pick his brain on what led him to pursue law after his Ph.D.

Steve was young, appeared to be in his mid-thirties. I was only thirty-one. He and I had remarkable similarities. He had earned his doctorate in Chemistry and ended up in a post-doctoral program as he could not find a job as a chemist. He did not love being a Chemist, but he wanted to become rich. I discussed the pros and cons of investing in the study of law. Steve told me, "I decided to take advantage of the free tuition that Temple offered me as a post-doc. I am single and have a lot of spare time. I opted to study law in my spare time." He explained, "I did not want to be stuck in the Chemistry lab. I figured, eventually, I would work in the petroleum or chemical industry as a compliance attorney." He thought that a law degree offered such an opportunity for him. Steve suggested that I talk with an Indian law professor at Temple by the name of K.G. Jon Pillai.

I'd never had any interest in law when I was in India. This was despite the fact that one of my closest friends, Shiv, who was my contemporary at St. Joseph's College, decided to pursue his bachelor's degree in Law at the Bangalore Law School when I veered toward my master's degree at Central College. Shiv had switched his career path from a technologist after earning his bachelor's degree in physics to become a lawyer. He switched because his father was a prominent judge in the state's High Court in Bangalore, and he was talked into following his father's career path as a lawyer and judge by his dad.

I disdained the legal profession in India because pursuing Law was a last resort for many students. Those who failed to get admission to professional schools which trained in medicine, dentistry, advanced sciences, or commerce migrated to the study of Law. In effect, the least desirable students went into Law. The legal profession and the court system in India were corrupt and hinged on extracting money from clients by procedural delays in litigation and the perennial backlog of court cases.

The law profession in the U.S. was much different. Lawyers occupied important roles in essentially every aspect of American life. This county was founded on a set of laws based on the U.S. Constitution. Almost all members of the U.S. House of Representatives and the U.S. Senate were lawyers. Most Presidents were lawyers. The rule of law was firmly entrenched. Strict adherence and enforcement of the laws by an elaborate court system was central to how everything in the U.S. operated.

I made an appointment to see Mr. Jon Pillai as recommended by Dr. Steven Brown. We met in Pillai's office at the Law School's new multi-story building. I knocked on the door to his office. A voice with a heavy accent growled, "Come in." I opened the door. Mr. Pillai was behind his desk and a young girl was sitting across from his desk. He looked at his watch and said to the girl, "The session is over," upon which she stood up and left the room. I introduced myself and shook his hand.

Mr. Pillai had a thick accent. He was from the state of Kerala in India. My prior research revealed that he had been employed as a full professor at Temple Law School for over five years. He impressed me as a down-to-earth sort of person, easy to converse with. He asked where in India I was from. I answered, "From Bangalore." I explored with him my intention to apply for admission to the law school. He was gracious. He was very helpful and reviewed Temple University's admission requirements.

Law schools in the U.S. were part of public or private

universities that granted the degree of Juris Doctor. The J.D. program took three years for full-time study and four years for part-time study to complete.

I gathered by talking with Mr. Pillai that getting into law school was not an easy task. First, the applicant should have earned good grades in undergraduate school. I easily met the GPA requirements. Next, the applicant should pass the Law School Admission Test, the LSAT. The LSAT score was on a scale of 120-180. To get into a top law school like Temple, the expected minimum score was 160.

Mr. Pillai also brought to my attention a special admission program being run by a committee known as SpACE that was underway at Temple for students like me. The acronym stood for Special Awards, Special Admissions and Curriculum Experiments. He advised that I might qualify as a candidate for the SpACE program and encouraged me to take advantage of it.

I mulled over the idea of applying to law school at Temple. I saw many positives in pursuing law. First, I was already educationally equipped and did not need supplemental coursework for applying to law school. I could study law full-time which took three years to complete or I could pursue it part-time in the evening which took one more year. The time investment of an extra year as a part-time student to earn my J.D. was not a major factor. The thought of continuing my teaching during the day and thereby still earning a living and also paying for my law school tuition appealed to me.

My new goal under Plan B was now more specific. It was to synergistically marry my background in physics with law to become an Intellectual Property attorney. Such a combination of law and physics was bound to fetch me lucrative employment.

While I previously had disdained the law profession, now I

was fascinated by how the Founding Fathers had written a fresh and thoughtful Constitution from which statutes, rules and regulations derived and enabled an orderly operation of the American society.

Applying for law school admission took months of preparation. I did not have the luxury of such time, as my idea to pursue law did not fully crystallize until the early spring of 1975. I hastily signed up to take the LSAT examination scheduled for mid-April at Beasley Hall of the Temple University Law School. Without any additional preparation I took the LSAT and received a score that surpassed the minimum required for admission to Temple Law School. With the LSAT scores under my belt, I filed a formal application for admission to Temple Law School.

I took up Mr. Pillai's suggestion and simultaneous with the application for admission I wrote to the SpACE Committee. The Chairman of this Committee was Handsel Minyard, who was also an Associate Professor of Law. I wrote a detailed letter to Mr. Minyard explaining my Indian heritage, the four degrees that I had earned including the M.A. and Ph.D. in physics from Temple, the GPA I had earned in each of the degree programs, the LSAT score that I just had received, and the fact that I was employed as a full-time teacher and sought admission as a part-time student in Temple's four-year program leading to the J.D. degree.

While I never received a response from Mr. Minyard, in mid-July 1975 Mr. Pillai called me to his office at Temple. I was curious why he wanted to meet with me.

He said, "I wanted to convey this news to you personally. The Temple Law School Admission Committee will be extending you admission to the J.D. program starting in the fall semester of 1975."

I was so thrilled at the news. I was pleased that I so quickly overcame all of the obstacles to get into law school. I expressed my sincere thanks to Mr. Pillai for being so helpful and paving my way to law school admission. I told him, "Mr. Pillai, but for your guidance and your informal recommendation to the members of the SpACE Committee, which I suspect you did, I would not have been admitted to law school in the record time I did."

The law school admission meant that I barely had two months to get ready for the new adventure. The thought of going back to school after four years of a comfortable life and as a beginner in a new area of study with new classmates scared me at first, but I was ready in every other way. I was determined to take this bull by the horn and subdue it to my full advantage and make my Plan B work.

A decade earlier I had arrived in the U.S. with great hope and many ideals. I arrived with the goal of establishing myself as a professional, earning a huge amount of wealth, and helping my father with the dowries. Certainly, I slaved for six years and reached the pinnacle in my field. However, that was not enough, and I did not find desired employment in a profession that I was trained for. My decision to switch to Law was to gain self-empowerment and I regarded it as entrepreneurship in my career. It was also a financial and intellectual investment. Here I was essentially starting all over again. But I knew this time around I would win and succeed. There was not an iota of doubt in my mind.

I signed up for the three basic courses—Contracts, Civil Procedure, and Torts—that most students in the first year of law school took. In addition, I signed up for an extra course in Lawyering Process, adding up to eleven credit hours. I was somewhat ambitious. I purchased the prescribed hard-bound books in their characteristic color of deep green from the law-school bookstore. I was ready for my law classes.

The law school enrollment was huge compared to the enrollment in my Ph.D. group. In the classes for the first-year law students, there were as many as two hundred students. The students spread across a huge galleried auditorium where they sat at flat oak desks and the professor stood at the central podium. All professors at Temple Law School used the Socratic Method of teaching. It involved the professor interrogating students on the assigned court cases and training them on how to identify the issues and analyze the cases. The Socratic Method was difficult for students like me to understand at first. When the professor randomly called upon students from the long roster that he had in front of him, some squirmed when they were questioned. However, when the professor asked a series of rhetorical questions in order to make a point, I found such teaching more beneficial than him directly stating his opinions or stating the textbook law. The Socratic Method forced me to think well, on the spot and under pressure.

I continued to live in my rented apartment in the suburb of Cheltenham north of Philadelphia close to the Abington High School. Teaching at Abington usually ended by 3:00 p.m., after which I stopped off at my apartment, grabbed an early meal and headed south to the law school. I spent an hour or more before the class commenced reading the cases that were assigned by sitting in the multi-storied law library. This became my routine for the first four weekdays when my four law classes were scheduled, every week. During the weekends, I trekked back to the law library to handle my assignments that were handed down by my law professors during the week and got prepared for the following week's classes.

While getting into law school was relatively easy for me, staying on top was a new obstacle. It became apparent that law school was not for the faint of heart. The study of law required a different approach. The logical and analytical thinking that I applied in physics needed to be thrown out of the window as law depended on subjective application to the facts at hand. Law required sifting facts from the numerous preceding case studies and drawing subjective legal conclusions as opposed to physics with its abstract problem-solving through applying the laws of physics in a logical, analytical and objective fashion.

The amount of reading I needed to do for each class was astounding. I was required to read cases, briefs and articles almost every evening and night in order to be prepared. I had to be ready to speak sensibly when called on in the class by the professor, and also receive value from the assignment when the professor engaged in the Socratic Method of teaching. The cases and court briefs were often complicated and required several readings to comprehend. The public speaking that I cultivated a decade earlier by participating in the Toastmaster's club came in handy when I was called on by the professor.

I joined small groups of five to six law students from my classes. All were white or Chinese males or females, except for one group in which we had a Japanese American, Yosh Miyazaki. Every student in my groups seemed to have a reason for going into law. For instance, Yosh as a child was incarcerated in a Japanese internment camp during World War II. He was employed by the Japanese American Citizens League and was determined to help JACL prevent a repeat of the racially-based internment. Wendy Chen, also U.S. born, was quick and tenacious and wanted to become a court judge.

We regularly met in one of the conference rooms in the Law School before the classes started or on the weekend to thrash out our reading material, brainstorm the legal issues and complete the assignments. Many in my study groups had a fine sense of humor and cracked lawyer jokes to ease the chore of reading voluminous material. Because of these study sessions, I gained more confidence in the classroom to rise up and speak sensibly when summoned by the professors.

The examinations in law school were often tough, but fortunately I had access to a lot of material that the law library amassed for our use. Some exams were open book, which came handy as I had full access to the library materials. After two semesters of taking law school courses, I began to develop a level of comfort in handling my coursework and received positive results.

There was something about the simple logic and rule of law, the sense of meeting out justice, and the respect for precedent and legal cannons that I was fascinated by. Upholding and respecting the law was the foundation of the American system of justice, which in turn was the bedrock of U. S. democracy. I was beginning to feel happy with my decision to become a lawyer.

MY ARRANGED MARRIAGE

IN THE SUMMER of 1976, I successfully completed my first year of law school. Many of my classmates and friends–like Frank, Tim and Mo–got married and started rising families even though they did not land in good jobs. I thought it was time to start looking for a wife who could share my sense of purpose and join in my adventure to earn credentials and start a new career.

I gave thought as to what type of individual I wanted to marry. I wanted someone who was beautiful but, equally important, a professional with zeal to succeed in the U.S. In particular, I wanted to marry a physician.

I wanted to marry a doctor as opposed to a person with an ordinary college degree for selfish reasons. A doctor might earn more money and compound my wealth to aid my father with the dowries but also uplift my future family into the upper levels of society. For the success of the continuing plan that I had laid out, finding a wife became my immediate goal.

I kept in touch with my former roommate Mo who now lived in Conshohocken, Pennsylvania with his wife. Two years earlier, Mo had wedded a Muslim girl from India. He now had an infant son. I visited him to find out how his married life had been. He expressed satisfaction and had no regrets.

After my talk with Mo, I settled for an arranged marriage as well. I wrote a detailed letter to my parents about my decision. I asked them to speak with their relatives and friends who might get involved in finding the right spouse for me by using their contacts. I wrote, *"I am relying on your judgement to identify compatible girls for me, but I reserve for myself the option to make the final selection."* I was frank and open in letting them know of my expectation to marry a doctor and stressed that they should focus on this requirement. I did not in any way want to rebel against them by marrying someone who they did not approve of.

I did not want to reveal to my father that I did not intend to take a dowry from my bride's father. This would have dissuaded him from looking for girls for me. I reaffirmed to myself that I would help my father with the dowry for my remaining unmarried sisters.

In the midst of my thinking about marriage, my father sent me a passport-sized photo of a possible match. She was a physician, graduated with a Bachelor of Medicine, Bachelor of Surgery (MBBS) degree from Osmania University in Hyderabad a couple of years earlier. She lived with her parents and siblings in Guntur, Andhra Pradesh where I had relatives. My father wrote that she was waiting to immigrate to Iran for work. In the photograph, she wore an Indian blouse and saree and had a facial makeup that was characteristic of Indian girls. This makeup included a round beauty mark on her forehead. She was adorned with jewelry around her neck and simple earrings. She looked somewhat angry in the photo as though someone forced her to pose for it against her will. I was amused by her angry look and set aside the photo.

In mid-July 1976, I travelled to India to see my parents. I planned to spend four to five weeks looking for a match and then return to start my second year of law school which resumed in late

August. My family had moved into the house in Indiranagar on the outskirts of Bangalore which my father had purchased years earlier. Avi and his wife who were living in that house moved into their own house. My family moved because the landlord of our house on 8 Miller Road decided to tear down our house and build a new one for his own occupancy.

The house in Indiranagar was small with only two bedrooms, a veranda, a dining room, kitchen and an attached bath. It had a one-car garage and a roof-top balcony, which was used to hang washed clothes to dry in the open air. Within days after I landed in Bangalore, we travelled to places in Andhra Pradesh where my parents had scheduled meetings with girls who were possible matches and their families. In addition, there was a match that was lined up by Jaya and Raj in Hyderabad for me. Jaya was eight months pregnant with her second child at the time and could not travel with me to check out the match. So the entourage that I assembled was my parents and Swati. I bought plane tickets for the four of us to fly to Hyderabad first and then to Vijayawada and then travel to Kakinada by car.

In Hyderabad, I decided that I should meet the girl and her parents without my family by my side. First, the referral was made by Raj and I knew my father outright disliked any of his recommendations. Second, she was a Muslim girl which I knew for sure that neither of my parents would favor. Third, she was not a doctor. Nevertheless, out of respect for Jaya and Raj, I decided to meet her.

I scheduled the meeting in the late afternoon and went to her parents' house. Once there, I waited for their employed daughter to return from work. I engaged in small talk with her parents and thought that my wait was going to be short. However, her parents apparently did not tell her about the arrangement to meet with me. As I was getting bored of waiting, she stepped into her house. I caught a glimpse of her face. She looked ragged and tired. After changing her attire, she made an entrance into the room where we were seated. Her father made a formal introduction for me to his daughter. She was tall and looked attractive but not beautiful enough to overcome the negative of not being a doctor. The encounter was brief with an exchange of pleasantries; I politely excused myself after thanking them for their hospitality. That was the end of the first match.

I met another girl in Secunderabad; she was a referral by my mother's younger sister Susheel, who lived in that city and hosted us during our visit. The entourage from my household accompanied by Susheel went with me to see the girl. The girl was a doctor who practiced family medicine in her private clinic. She appeared professional with an air of confidence, but her looks were not extraordinary. My quick observation of her physique did not make a positive impression that she would be compatible to me.

The next day we flew to Vijayawada, where we met another young female physician in her house while she was chaperoned by her parents. She spoke well but did not impress me one bit. She wore a white saree with a colorful border and a matching blouse, but her skin was jet black like that of her parents, reminiscent of a family from a lower economic class and lower caste. I did not have a requirement to marry a girl from the same caste in which I was born and she was probably from the same caste as mine, this young doctor's physical appearance did not attract me. My mother sensed from my body language that this was not the girl for me. So we marched on to the next arranged meeting.

Four more prospective girls, all doctors or medical students, were awaiting my visit over the next few days in Guntur and Kakinada. That evening we stayed in Guntur in a place known as the Medical Hall. The Medical Hall was actually a residence fronted with a medical facility and drug store. In the back was a large dwelling where relatives from my father's side resided. Our relatives owned the front office and its facilities. We stayed there with the expectation of meeting the girl with the angry look whose photo my father had forwarded to me earlier. My father told me that evening that the angry-looking match was identified by his younger sister Tripura, who lived near Guntur but could not join us.

The next morning, I showered and put on a colorful full-sleeved silky Hawaiian shirt and light-colored pants. The four of us from my family took a short drive in a car to meet the angry-looking girl in her house. A cool morning with a gentle breeze greeted us as we stepped toward the veranda which fronted the house where her family lived. In the front yard were tall coconut trees. The rest of the house abutted the veranda and was behind it.

Her father and his second daughter (who was the younger sister of the girl I came to meet) greeted me and my visiting family in the traditional style with both hands put together in a raised posture and saying *namaste*. I reciprocated. We all took seats in the veranda with the father. Her father hardly spoke English, but he spoke Telugu which was my mother's tongue as well. We exchanged pleasantries. The second daughter Arna, as she introduced herself, engaged in most of the conversation that took place between the families. Arna spoke perfect English without too much of an Indian accent. She was attractive herself, outgoing and joyous. She explained that her family included two younger brothers, besides herself and her older sister. I was impressed to hear that all four siblings were pursuing the medical profession. She herself was nearing completion of her medical degree and her brothers just had started their medical school. I admired her father's fortitude to educate all of his children to become doctors. Arna named each of her siblings and we greeted the two brothers with a hello as they were loitering in and out of their house. By now, I knew that the name of her older sister was Rama.

Rama happened to be also my mother's name. It was an old-fashioned name synonymous with the name Lakshmi, the Goddess of wealth, wisdom, fortune, fertility and generosity. This Goddess is portrayed as the embodiment of grace and charm.

The pleasant thought arose in me that if the younger sister was so outgoing, then the older sister Rama may also have a similar trait. Also, could I expect her older sister to be no less attractive than Arna? As such thoughts were crowding my mind, the girl that I came to see appeared in the veranda and greeted us with a beautiful smile, along with the gesture of *namaste*. She took the seat beside her father and directly in front of me. She wore a pure white cotton saree, which was starched and neatly pressed. Her facial makeup was minimal and displayed her natural beauty. She wore a red dime-sized powder dot (known as *kumkum*) as a decoration on her forehead between her eyebrows.

If there is anything like love at first sight, this was that moment for me. I was instantly attracted by her beauty and the slender body that she presented herself in. She was luminous. Rama had a beautiful smile. When she smiled, her pearly white teeth radiated. She was dainty and elegant, probably weighed no more than eighty to eighty-five pounds. She was graceful in her movements. She spoke in perfect English with me and in Telugu with my family members. We did not talk much as our parents and siblings were attentively watching us to glean our immediate reaction after our first visual encounter. Most of the time, we somewhat stared at each other on and off, while avoiding direct eye contact, as though our looks and physical appearance mattered the most at that moment.

After a while, sensing that I wanted to speak with Rama alone, the rest of the family members moved into the bedroom adjacent to the veranda where we were seated. This also provided an opportunity for my family members to meet Rama's mother who had not joined us in the veranda.

My conversation with Rama was somewhat limited, even though I wanted to ask many questions about her and tell her many things about me. I did not want to overwhelm her with questions lest she might think that I was interrogating her. I accentuated the positives in my life without boring her with the negatives of not landing employment as a physicist after earning my doctorate in America. I explained that I was in the teaching profession and laid open the fact that I was pursuing law in the evening to become a lawyer. Night school was an alien concept for most Indians, so I needed to explain it to her in some detail.

I asked, "Are you still thinking of going to Iran to practice medicine?"

To this she replied, "One of my classmates from the med school recently went to Tehran. I have been toying with the idea of going there as well."

I asked, "Then it looks like you are prepared to leave your parents and siblings and go to a foreign land?"

She acknowledged that she was.

I explained that doctors and lawyers made a good couple in the U.S. They tended to earn good salaries and were regarded as highly respected professionals. She did not respond one way or other to my statement.

The brief one-to-one conversation between the two of us ended when our family members rejoined us in the veranda. We were served some Indian snacks and sweets and cold soft drinks. The look-see and the associated pleasantries lasted for a couple of hours, after which the families bid good-bye to each other. Just before we left, Rama's father and sister asked about our plans and whether we were returning to Bangalore. When my father told them that we were proceeding to meet other girls in the next town of Kakinada, they simply listened and nodded their heads.

Soon after we had reached our relatives' home, my mother came to me in the privacy of the bedroom I occupied. She quietly asked, "Did you like the girl Rama we met?"—emphasizing the girl's name Rama.

As that was also my mother's name, I felt somewhat awkward repeating her name. I responded to my mother's question that I liked her immensely. I said: "She was beautiful. She appeared to have a graceful personality. Soft spoken. And she was already educated as a doctor."

With a sense of excitement and joy, I told my mother: "Mom, I liked her. I think I found my match."

She explained that Rama's mother, who I did not meet during our visit that morning, seemed to have some skin issues. This Mom explained as irregular-shaped white patches on her face and hands. No one else in her family had such skin pigmentation issues that we could notice, leading me think it is non-genetic.

Immediately I checked with our hosting relative Nath, who was a practicing physician and my elder cousin, whether the skin pigmentation was hereditary. He explained that "The skin issue is a condition known as vitiligo in which pigment cells are destroyed resulting in white patches on the skin." He said that "It is unknown whether vitiligo could be passed on by heredity to children or to grandchildren," adding his opinion that "It is unlikely." He then conveyed the bleak conclusion that "The cause and cure for vitiligo is unknown."

My initial impression and the conclusion that I had reached about Rama was not swayed one bit by the revelation of her mother's skin pigmentation problem. The fact that her father did not speak the English language did not bother me either. I stayed with my first reaction after I met Rama. The fact that all of the siblings in her family were studying to be doctors continued to impress me. I again silently lauded Rama's father for his wisdom. Even though the father was not highly educated, he had a keen sense of planning his family's size and had the foresight to invest in his children's education and drive them to be professionals.

I silently compared this with my own educated father's lackadaisical attitude to family planning and disinterest in grooming his children to earn the right type of education leading to professional careers. He essentially let them choose their own fate. I regretted that he did not guide me in my school years to become a doctor. Then I remembered his intention to send me off to the Army after I graduated from high school.

Perhaps, if I had studied to be a doctor, I could have avoided the long and arduous career path I pursued as a physicist. This unfortunately did not yield the monetary results that I had expected and that result now forced me to make a drastic change—seeking a new career path. I did not believe in karma. I believed that one could plan and shape one's destiny with determination and effort. However, the setbacks that I faced in my career made me sometimes rethink my belief.

The fact that I could converse with the siblings of Rama in

English more than compensated for the lack of English-speaking skills of her parents. I presumed that the parents would continue to live in India and my physical contact with them would be limited.

Having made up my mind, I decided that there was no reason to check out the other girls that we were scheduled to meet in Kakinada and the other towns. I wanted to immediately send word to them requesting cancellations of the scheduled meetings, but my mother wisely advised delaying such abrupt cancellations until Rama and her family reached their decision.

The question of dowry did not come up in the first meeting, as it was customary to use that meeting to primarily determine the mutual interest between the boy and the girl. However, I came to know from my mother that my father had a serious and protracted discussion through the night with Nath and other members of his paternal family who were hosting us. They had advised my father to ask for a huge dowry because of my special status abroad—namely that I possessed the potential to help not only Rama after marriage to immigrate to the United States but also possibly her entire extended family. This potential to immigrate would be especially significant to her three siblings, as it could considerably enhance their earning potential as doctors in America. My host relatives for some reason assumed that Rama's parents were wealthy; perhaps it was by the mere fact that all of their children were studying to be doctors. As expected, the relatives also encouraged my father that he must take the dowry from the newly met parents in order to help him defray the dowries for his four unmarried daughters.

I was not present in this internal discussion on dowry. In a way, that was a blessing as I did not want to reveal at that moment my grand plan to help my father with the dowries for my unmarried sisters. More importantly, I did not want to have a heated argument with my father because of my decision not to take the dowry from Rama's parents regardless of how wealthy they were.

While I had reached a quick decision about the girl that I just met, I was not sure as to where Rama stood in regard to me. I had received no clue from our encounter whether she liked my looks, speech and mannerisms. I was told that she had been somewhat choosy and turned down a few would-be matches in the past. I also had no clue from the short meeting earlier that morning whether her parents liked mine. In India, marriages were perceived as not only between the individuals who were going to wed but also between the families of these individuals. The compatibility of the families was important in Hindu families, albeit not to the same degree as the compatibility of the marrying couple.

That evening, we sent word to Rama's family that I and my family would like to have a second meeting with them the following morning, to which they readily agreed. Our request for the second meeting, particularly after we told them that we had plans to meet other girls, possibly gave them some hint of my interest in Rama.

On the second day of our stay at Medical Hall, I was getting ready for the second encounter with Rama when my cousin Nath came to the guest bedroom that I had occupied. He sat on the bed. In the past, I had found that he always had a smile and was easy to talk with.

He broached the topic of my dowry. He started with: "You should ask for a dowry from Rama's parents." He put forward the rationale that my father would need the money from my dowry to pay for my sisters' dowries, which I already knew.

I responded, "I've always believed that taking a dowry is immoral. It is also illegal, although almost every groom ignores the law against it. Ethically, I could not ask for dowry."

Nath did not balk at my rationale. He did not ridicule me for my altruistic comment.

I continued with my reasoning: "The money that her father invested in Rama to be a doctor must mean something. Rama's future potential to earn wealth by using her skills will more than compensate the dowry that I might expect to receive from him."

However, I did not share with Nath my grand plan to help my father with dowries for his daughters. I wanted it to remain hidden. Nevertheless, I told Nath that "Paying for dowries for my unmarried sisters is a collective responsibility of all sons in our family. I am prepared to help my father in any way I can with the dowries. I will not abandon him when it comes to paying for their dowries". Nath responded "It is laudable that you have such high ethical standards against taking dowry. Unfortunately most 'grooms in India do not generally feel the same way as you do. You are a good son to your father!" Our conversation ended after I implored "Please do not convey to my father what we just discussed. I do not want to set expectations for him". He nodded in agreement and left the bedroom.

Clean shaven and freshly bathed, I wore a dark green shirt with a contrasting pure white collar and belted a set of plaid trousers in green and brown colors for the second meeting with Rama. My parents and sister Swati accompanied me like the day before.

I was imbued with positive energy and a sense of purpose—to accomplish a major turning point in my life by taking on the responsibility of sharing it with another person.

The second meeting was friendly as though the two families had known each other for some time. Rama looked radiant, delicate and airy in her attire, which was a colorful silk saree. We got into a bit of a serious exchange where we revealed our respective ages, our religious practices—like visiting Hindu temples, dietary habits, and open vices—like smoking and drinking alcohol.

Satisfied that these matters were cleared up, I asked Rama, "What specialties in medicine are you interested in practicing?"

She became silent at first and with her sister's coaxing, I could faintly hear her utter the word "Dermatology." After that, I did not press anymore about her professional interest in medicine. Knowing that she had plans to go overseas to Iran, I asked whether she had a passport to travel abroad—for which she nodded her head and said, "Yes."

From our body language, it was apparent that Rama and I liked what we saw in each other's outward appearance during the brief exchanges we'd had that day and the day before. A similar sense of interest in moving forward was conveyed by my parents to Rama's parents and siblings. It was just a matter of coming out and saying that we should engage in a wedding. I took the initiative to express my satisfaction with everything I saw in Rama and my willingness to be engaged to her at that very moment. As engagements were uncommon in our families and I was in a hurry to return to the U.S., I proposed that if Rama was willing and her parents approved of my proposal, we should move forward with our matrimony. Rama appeared joyous at what I just had proposed. She flashed a smile.

There was no discussion of a dowry. This topic was not raised by my father or by Rama's father. Certainly, I did not bring it up as I already had made up my mind not to seek a dowry.

Rama's family then retreated to the back room of their house to discuss among themselves what I just had proposed. My family awaited their decision. After a long pause, Rama's father and her sister Arna returned to the veranda where we were seated. Her father approached my father, held his two palms in his, and indicated his family's acceptance of my proposal. This decision was smilingly reiterated by Rama's sister Arna to the rest of my family. With the approval of both parents, the match-making came to a successful conclusion.

I let Rama and her parents know the travel date for my return to the U.S. We then jumped to establish the date for the wedding in Guntur. My family also wanted to hold a wedding reception in Bangalore a few days after the wedding so we could celebrate with our friends and relatives back home.

Both families felt compelled to consult a Hindu astrologer to fix the auspicious date and time, known as the *muhurtam*, for the wedding. Using the bride's and groom's dates of birth, the astrologer calculated the position of the planets and stars to reflect the celestial union of the couple. It was determined that the wedding should take place on August 4, 1976 at 9:12 p.m. My family then decided to hold the wedding reception in Bangalore on August 8.

The names of the parents as well as the bride and groom were exchanged for printing the wedding invitations. We also gave a ball-park number of guests from our side of the family that could be expected to attend the wedding. Then it was time to we bid *adieu*.

I wanted to take another look at Rama before saying good-bye. We looked at each other. Something transcendent seemed to pass between us. Was it love at first sight, like I originally believed, or something more? Were we destined to marry, even though we were separated by thousands of miles and living in different continents across the world?

I and my family flew back to Bangalore after sending word to the prospective girls that I was scheduled to meet in Kakinada and elsewhere of our decision to cancel such meetings. In the plane while seated next to me, my mother relayed that "Your father is not happy with your decision to forsake the dowry, especially without consulting him." I nodded and expressed my understanding of his feelings. However, my father did not bring up my dowry at any time, nor did I. His silence on my dowry spoke volumes about his disappointment.

Upon returning to Bangalore, my father—who was now fully retired from his consulting business—set out to have my wedding invitations drafted in English. My siblings identified an auditorium with attached dining facilities at the Hotel Ajanta in Bangalore to hold the wedding reception, which I approved. After lining up the date, time and venue for the reception, we included the details about the reception in the invitation and had several hundred of them printed. My sisters Mini and Mala beautifully scribed the invitees' names and addresses on the wedding invitations and mailed them. The invitations were sent out to some of my former classmates and friends who I had left behind when I went to the U.S. I did not mail the wedding invitations to my friends in the U.S. I figured that given the short notice, no one from the U.S. would be able to make the long trip to India to participate in my wedding. In fact, none of my friends in the U.S.—including my host family—knew about my wedding.

I was advised to go to a gold merchant and have a ring made for myself, which I did. It was made from soft 22 carat gold with a diamond-shaped design on it. My father always wore a similar ring with a heart-shaped design on it. I chose the diamond shape, instead, not for any sentimental reason. This shape looked more symmetrical on my ring finger.

I went to my tailor and had a new suit made for the reception. I purchased a couple of white shirts, colorful silk ties and new slippers and shoes for wearing at the wedding ceremony and later at the reception. My siblings also purchased new clothes for themselves to wear at the wedding.

I was in a damned fine mood in July after I met Rama. I wanted to personally invite my brother Avi to my wedding. Avi's participation in my wedding—the happiest day in my life—was important to me. He was my older brother and the first born to my parents. We had quarreled with each other as children and competed for affection from our parents, but we were affectionate to each other, as well.

Avi was now living in his own house in another part of Bangalore with his wife, young son, infant daughter and his mother-in-law. I went to see Avi and his family and described with excitement the match-making trip that I just had returned from and my decision, with approval of our parents, to marry

Rama. I explained that Rama was also a doctor like his wife Wari. I extended a personal invitation and urged his family to attend my wedding celebration in Guntur, as well as the follow-up reception in Bangalore. Avi congratulated me, but his wife Wari showed no reaction. She did not smile or express joyous feelings after hearing the news of my decision to wed Rama. Likewise, Wari's mother was muted and did not react.

Avi came up with a work-related excuse that he was unable to travel to Guntur. However, he indicated that he would attend the reception. This meant that the other members of his family would not attend my wedding celebration either.

I was mystified by Avi's attitude and disregard for my feelings when declining my personal invitation. This incident took me back to my younger days. Although seventeen months older than I, Avi ended up in the same class-grade as I did. He generally received lower grades than I did. He could not get admission to the local Engineering College to pursue the bachelor's degree that he so badly wanted,

whereas I was admitted to the prestigious St. Joseph's College. While I earned my bachelor's and baster's degrees with top university rankings, my brother did not have the benefit of attending college but earned his A.M.I.E. diploma through correspondence school. While he succeeded in finding an excellent job locally, which I was happy about, I earned admission to Temple, travelled to America and accomplished a feat which was unheard of in our family—earning a Ph.D. from America. Now I was about to marry a beautiful girl, who was a doctor and with complete approval of my parents compared to his episode of eloping with his doctor girl. I could not help telling myself that perhaps jealousy was the reason for his unwillingness to attend my wedding. The fact of the matter was that I was not competing with Avi, even when we were in the same grade. I was competing with myself all through my life.

I already knew that my pregnant sister Jaya and Raj would not be able to travel for my wedding but would attend the reception. Their reason for not travelling to Guntur was understandable.

We barely had a week to return to Guntur for the wedding celebration. I asked my second brother Enku to make train reservations for all ten family members to travel together to Guntur. We travelled and arrived a day before the wedding date. My family entourage moved into the Medical Hall for that night at the insistence of our host there.

The wedding ceremony was scheduled by Rama's family to take place at the Collector's Bungalow of the Medical Club in Guntur. On the morning of the wedding, my family including me went to the Lord Ganesh temple. It had been a customary practice in my family before beginning a new project to offer a prayer to Ganesh, the God of good beginnings and good fortune and the remover of obstacles. We then moved into the Collector's Bungalow, which had many rooms that were reserved for the groom's party, while other rooms were already occupied by the bride's party and her relatives who travelled a distance.

In India, like in America, it was taboo for the groom to refrain from looking at or speaking with the bride in her wedding dress before the ceremony commenced. I respected this practice and remained in my room. There was a lot of curiosity from the guests on the bride's side to take a peek at the groom from America and meet him. While some sneaked glimpses of me, a few knocked on my door to greet me with a "hello".

The wedding day had dawned. The *muhurtum* (when the 'groom will tie the wedding knot) was set for 9:12 that evening, but other Hindu rituals that were part of the ceremony would precede it by a couple of hours. The *mehendi* ceremony, during which the bride's hands and feet were adorned with intricate designs with henna paint, had occurred a day earlier, as relayed by Rama's first bother Mali.

I got dressed in my new white shirt and new dark blue trousers. I did not wear the jacket as I wanted to be comfortable in my wedding attire. The rituals started. Rama's uncle (the older brother of her mother) accompanied by Mali came up to my room with a large silver plate and a jug of water. They laid the silver plate on the floor. It was a thick and solid platter with a raised rim, intricate carvings on its upper surface, and studs of solid gold in the center.

The uncle politely asked, "Son, would you please place your feet into the plate?"

I complied and rested both feet squarely on the silver plate with its rim. Mali poured water from the jug and my feet were washed, which was a ritual to wash away bad luck.

I joked with Mali that the real reason for washing was a practical one. "It is to make sure that my feet are clean before I sit at the wedding altar in front of the many guests who will be attentively watching me!" We all laughed.

I went downstairs to the wedding altar, known as *mandapam*, which is a structure constructed for the purpose of the wedding ceremony. Located on a slightly elevated platform, it was decorated with flowers, green mango leaves, colorful fabric and beads. There was a young-looking main Hindu priest with an assistant present to perform the rituals. In front of the *mandapam*, a fire was lit in a shallow pit. A Hindu marriage was not a contract but a sacrament. To signify the viability of the ceremony, fire was kept going as a witness.

I was asked by the priest to sit cross-legged on a low-leveled flat bench inside the *mandapam*. Our immediate families sat behind me and the empty seat next to me.

A veil was suddenly hoisted between me and the empty seat to my left signaling that the bride was about to enter the *mandapam*. The musicians played the traditional live music to signify her arrival. Her arrival was ritualistic. She carried in both hands a large fresh green coconut without any embellishments on it other than it glistened in the light. A procession of women from her side of the family escorted her to the *mandapam*. Rama gently placed the coconut in front for the priest to access and took the seat next to me.

Nothing had been rehearsed for the ceremony. The priests continuously made offerings to the kindled fire and the main priests directed the bride and groom to follow their motions.

Coconut takes a prominent place in Hindu weddings. The coconut, known as *sriphala,* is used as an object of worship. Coconut is used as a symbol of Lord *Shiva*, the destroyer in the Hindu trinity. The three eyes on the coconut, which appear after the outer fiber is peeled off, represent the three eyes of *Shiva*. The priest commenced the ceremony with a prayer to *Ganesha*, who was the son of *Shiva*

When the veil was removed, I noticed Rama in her beautiful wedding dress. She wore a deep purple saree with a wide gold border which graced down to her ankles, and the wide and gorgeous *pallu* which draped her shoulder over her matching blouse.

She had on long gold *jumka*-style hanging earrings studded with many tiny elegant pearls. The front of her jet-black hair was adorned with gold chains sliding from the center of her head to the back recesses of her ears. She wore a beautiful and highly intricate bridal tikka headpiece studded with pearls and precious stones embedded in gold, which was perfectly centered and elegantly stretched from the back of her hair and ended on her forehead. The head jewelry that she wore was very evocative. Colorful glass and solid gold bangles decorated her wrists. A black dot was affixed to her left cheek and a bright red dot of *kumkum* on her forehead. Centered between her neatly shaped eyebrows, the red dot added immense beauty to her already attractive face. Her long black hair was neatly woven with fresh and fragrant white jasmine flowers known as *pallipoolajada*. I was mesmerized by her beauty in her wedding attire.

After Rama sat, my mother offered her a silver plate on which were arranged a small stack of fresh green beetle leaves and a fresh yellow banana perched on the leaves together with a wedding gift which Rama graciously accepted.

Our wedding ceremony was attended by more than two hundred guests. Rama and I performed a series of rituals, some separately and some in unison, as directed by the priest. We sat for more than three hours in a continuous stretch. We bowed many times to heed the priest's instructions and to receive blessings from the guests. The priest uttered mantras in Sanskrit which I did not fully comprehend although I picked up bits and pieces from his hand gestures. Many of the rituals that he invoked were to worship the Hindu Gods of *Brahma, Vishnu and Shiva* and goddess *Lakshmi*.

After the junior priest peeled off the outer fiber on the coconut that Rama had presented, the main priest broke open the hard shell to complete the coconut ceremony while uttering mantras.

After the coconut ceremony, the bride's family escorted Rama from the altar to the back room. When Rama returned to her seat, she was in a different wedding dress. She was now in a pure white *Kanjeevaram* saree laced with a wide red and gold border and a lavish *pallu* that draped over her shoulder and a perfectly matching blouse. I noticed the round and colorful *bindi* on her forehead, which was known as the sixth *chakra* (or center of energy). The chakra was said to be the seat of concealed wisdom. The *bindi* was thought to retain energy, improve concentration and protect against misfortune, but most of all it immensely enhanced Rama's facial beauty.

We went through a ritual called *kanyadanam,* where Rama's father gently placed her hand into mine. Following this, he poured water through her hand into mine as a gesture of giving her away to me. After this ritual, under the Hindu principles, I was supposed to have claim to Rama.

Then, decorative and sacred cords dipped in turmeric were tied to our wrists and also separately around the forehead encircling our hair. These cords, called *raksha bandan,* were meant as protection from evil. Then followed the ritual of *jai mala* where Rama and I exchanged fresh floral garlands, which expressed the desire of the couple to marry each other. This was followed by the ring ceremony, where we exchanged rings; this signified establishing a firm bond between us.

Then we went through the ritual of *satpadi,* during which our outer garments were tied together with a knot and we took seven straight steps together side-by-side to signify our friendship. We then walked seven times around the fire while the priest uttered vows he asked us to repeat in each turn around the fire. Seven was a lucky number symbolic of the seven oceans, seven hills, and seven colors in the rainbow

Then the most important part of the ceremony called *mangala sutram* ritual took place at the *mahurtam*. Precisely at 9:12 p.m. I adorned Rama's graceful swan-like neck with a sacred yellow thread ornate with black and gold beads and tied three knots. I gently applied a dab of *kumkum* to her forehead. The live Indian classical music suddenly intensified to signify the arrival of the auspicious time and the occurrence of the *mahurtam*. The priest invoked the Hindu Goddess of wealth, fortune and prosperity in this ritual so the bride would receive these good blessings throughout her marriage.

Following this, we went through the ritual of pouring sacred rice tinged with turmeric from large bowls over each other's heads. We followed this with the ritual of retrieving a gold ring which was dropped in a narrow-necked brass container that was filled with gallons of water. Both Rama and I quickly and simultaneously inserted our hands into the narrow-necked vessel to retrieve the ring. This was a fun ritual. I ended up retrieving the ring to Rama's mild scorn.

The wedding ceremony was stretched out until ten o'clock that evening when all Hindu deities were invoked to bless us as a newlywed couple. Many guests already had moved from the *mandapam* to the dining area to feast on a sumptuous Indian meal.

During the dinner, Rama and I went around the tables and greeted her friends and relatives who she introduced by name and relationship. We posed for photographs with the colorful garlands still gracing our bodies. We posed for pictures with friends and relatives in different groups to commemorate the happy event.

As the long wedding ceremony came to a conclusion, I admired the tradition and vibrancy of the Hindu wedding which was absent in the wedding of my classmate Frank to Christine that I had attended in Seneca, New York eight years earlier. That had been a church wedding with a Catholic priest simply making the pronouncement of wife and husband after no one in the invited audience raised objection to their matrimony. Frank and Christine then exchanged rings and the priest pronounced them as man and wife and said the "You may now kiss" line. The wedding that Rama and I just had completed was not only highly ritualistic but also filled with special meaning for the performed rituals which invoked Hindu deities. It was also truly an occasion for joy—not just for the bride and groom but for all of the invited guests.

Rama and I sat at a designated table with the guests and shared pleasantries while enjoying our first meal as a married couple. It was past midnight by the time we were able to meet the many guests and personally thank them for their participation and blessings. The local guests started departing and the others who were staying at the bungalow stared to migrate to their rooms to sleep.

A guest house was arranged by my in-laws in a nearby bungalow for Rama and me to spend our first night together as married couple. Rama and I were driven in a car to the guest house where we were dropped off. No one else stayed with us at the guest house's main suite up the stairs; the servants were in the rooms below.

It was well past 1:00 a.m. and we both were exhausted. We both were ready to change from the wedding clothes that we were wearing. Rama carefully removed her head jewelry while leaving all other jewelry in place. She changed all by herself in an adjacent room into a delicate light saree. I slipped into my pajamas. While I waited for her, I munched on sweet grapes from the fruit bowl placed next to the bed.

The suite was nicely decorated. The large bed was adorned with garlands of fresh flowers. Single flowers and petals were strewn all over on the soft bed sheets and pillows. The fragrance of jasmine flowers imbued the air surrounding the bed with the whirring ceiling fan gently distributing the fragrance.

We both lay down on the bed side-by-side and talked, me clasping her soft hand. We talked about mundane subjects, like what our favorite music was and favorite foods were.

Rama asked, "Why are you studying law when you already have a Ph.D. under your belt?"

I was forthright and explained my predicament of not landing a good job as a physicist. Then I laid bare my goal to help my father with the dowries for his daughters. I expressed my hope and expectation that together we would have a happy life.

Communicating with Rama was easy for me, although she did not open up easily that night. Perhaps she had other thoughts in her head.

My heart was racing with excitement and joy. That was when intimate words popped out of Rama's mouth. "You know," she started, "I did not have interest in being a doctor. I never wanted to be a doctor." She paused for a moment and resumed. "My father forced me into medical school. He wanted me to be a doctor. I went along with his wish and pursued my MBBS in the Medical School in Warangal away from my parents, sister and brothers. I reluctantly completed my degree to satisfy his wish."

This revelation startled me. I could not believe what I just had heard from Rama. Here we were after having just completed an elegant and traditional Hindu wedding ceremony that was filled with rituals which we together meticulously satisfied and the many blessings which we together received from the hundreds of guests. After this entire happy celebration, Rama uttered a totally unexpected set of words which seemed to devastate me. I wondered in silence whether I would have continued with the marriage if she had told me about her experience of becoming a reluctant doctor a day earlier. One of my primary requirements in the girl I married had been to be a doctor who would practice her profession and enrich our new family. However, that requirement now appeared to lay shattered just moments after my marriage to Rama.

I did not respond to her statement and remained silent as various thoughts crowded my mind. Perhaps, I thought, her parents and sister Arna, who promoted Rama as a doctor during my first visit, would persuade her to live up to their expectations and mine. Perhaps, in due course after she arrived in the U.S. and spent time with her mates from the medical school who were now doing their residency in teaching hospitals there, Rama would change her mind. The uncertainty and doubt over marrying a doctor who was unenthusiastic about being a working doctor sapped me of my already drained energy. We just went to sleep lying side-by-side on the bed.

Neither of us realized that it was already morning until Rama's sister Arna gently knocked on our door. She softly addressed her sister by name and let us know that it was almost ten o'clock in the morning and that the family was waiting to have breakfast with us, the newly married couple.

We jumped out of bed, brushed our teeth, got dressed and joined my sister-in-law in a hurry. We had a nice Indian breakfast with my in-laws at their residence. I had a double serving of spicy *uppma* made out of cream of wheat. We then dashed off to meet with the Registrar in Guntur to officially list our marriage in the Hindu Marriage Register. I wanted an official certificate of our marriage in order to use it as evidence that Rama was now my spouse when I applied for sponsoring her for her Green Card.

When we arrived at the Registrar's office, my father and two relatives from the Medical Hall were waiting for us to serve as the required witnesses for our marriage certificate. The Registrar's office was desolate and dark with a couple of ceiling lights hanging from the ceiling and fans spinning. It was a hot and humid morning.

Rama and I presented ourselves before the Registrar at a desk inside the dark room. He was a heavy-set man in his forties. I explained that Rama and I celebrated our wedding last night with the customary rites.

The Registrar asked, "Are you both Hindus?" Before I could answer, he tutored us that "Under the Hindu Marriage Act, 1955, both parties to the marriage must be Hindus."

I answered, "Yes."

He followed up with a more specific question: "Did your wedding ceremony include *satpadi*?" He was apparently quizzing whether our marriage was performed with the customary Hindu rituals.

I replied, "Of course." My father, who was standing nearby, nodded in agreement to my reply.

We made a formal declaration attesting to each of our names, age to the day, residential address, father's name, and date and place of the marriage. The Registrar congratulated Rama and me on our marriage. He summoned a typist to his office to type up the certificate, including the names and addresses of the three witnesses. It was then examined and verified for accuracy of statements by two men. I whispered to my relatives: "The Indian bureaucratic system is fully at work to keep people employed!"

The document was then signed by Rama and me, the witnesses, the typist and the two people who examined it for its accuracy. After this, the Registrar affixed his signature and applied a large round rubber stamp of the Seal of the Hindu Marriage Registrar and solemnized. The certificate incorrectly stated that Rama and I were married on August 5, 1976. In truth, we were married the day before. I took the certificate, which was typed on an extra-large sized paper, folded it twice and left the Registrar's office with Rama, my father and relatives.

Rama and I went back to the guest house, where we had spent our first night, picked up our belongings, and vacated it. We then went back to my in-laws' house where my sisters joined me to spend time together. I spent the second night with Rama at her house.

My family had made arrangements for us to leave by train two days after the wedding celebration to return to Bangalore and get ready for the wedding reception scheduled for two days after that. Rama's siblings, father and her close relatives decided to travel to Bangalore the day after we left. The train journey took place at night with our arrival slated for the next morning. Rama and I shared a small private second-class compartment with an upper and lower berth wide enough for one person to sleep. I slept on the upper berth. Rama took the lower. The train chugged along piercing through the cool wind as we approached the hill station of Bangalore-Cantonment.

When we were away getting married, as anticipated, my sister

Jaya had given birth to her baby, another girl. We went to see her and the newborn in the hospital where she gave birth and wished their family good luck. With the addition of this newborn, my parents now had four grandchildren—a grandson and three granddaughters. I projected that if every one of my siblings had at least two children each, the total count of grandchildren for my parents would be at least twenty.

In India the wedding reception is primarily organized by the family of the groom. It was the first public appearance of Rama and I as the newlyweds after the wedding ceremony and a grand party to rejoice over the new alliance. Our reception also served as an opportunity for Rama to know and be acquainted with my friends and relatives.

The reception did not entail the Hindu rituals that Rama and I went through at the wedding ceremony, but it had a charm of its own. The auditorium where the reception was held was a large hall and it had nearly three hundred comfortable soft chairs, each with a white cloth covering. The ambience of the room with arched doorways and white pillars added to the ambience. Popular recorded music from Bollywood films played over the sound system. Rama and I sat in a set of elegant gold chairs on a 5-foot-high raised stage fitted with steps. The stage was decorated well with live potted plants and fresh flowers.

I had put on my dark-blue draper suit and a white shirt and pink silk necktie. Rama wore a wonderful new pink saree with an intricately made gold border and a matching blouse. She wore elegant gold jewelry and colorful bangles on her wrists and fresh flowers in her hair. She looked stunning. The bangles made a pleasant clinking sound when she moved her hands. The silver bells anklets which she wore made a pleasant jingling sound when she walked.

All of my siblings were also dressed in their best attire. The girls wore colorful sarees with matching blouses and the best jewelry they had. They all wore colorful glass bangles on their wrists. The guys wore suits or merely a pressed shirt and pair of trousers with a matching tie around their neck. My father wore a nice fitted suit and necktie. My mother wore a traditional red saree interspersed with a turquoise and white pattern and a wide gold border and a pure white blouse. Her pierced earlobes were filled with delicate floral diamond studs embedded in gold which brilliantly sparked.

My older brother Avi and his family, including his mother-in-law, came in somewhat ordinary clothes, which befitted attending a common and everyday event. I was taken aback by their attire. While Avi greeted the other relatives and my friends who he knew, his family seemed distant, aloof and disinterested in the celebration that was underway. This was the first wedding celebration in our family. I thought that Avi would share the joy in our family's celebration, but unfortunately I did not sense such warm feeling from him or his family at the reception.

The invitees trickled in as the evening progressed. Many guests came with their families; some came alone after work, as the reception took place on a weekday evening. The guests included many of our relatives who lived in Bangalore and its vicinity who could not take part in our wedding ceremony. Many of my friends and classmates from the middle and high school and college came. Many of my father's former colleagues and business clients were there. Likewise, the friends of my siblings—many of whom I had not meet before—also graced the reception.

Upon arrival, the guests were asked to take the seats that were neatly arranged in rows. From this vantage point, they looked at Rama and me as we sat on the stage in front of them. After viewing us, the wedding couple, they eventually climbed up the steps to the stage, greeted Rama and me in person and congratulated us. Rama and I bowed to them showing our respect and receiving their blessings. This way, I was able to introduce the guests to Rama and say a few kind words about my relationship or friendship with them. Some of my close friends openly complimented my selection of Rama as my wife. My close lawyer friend Shiv climbed up to our seats with his wife and openly stated, "Great selection." He supplemented this with "Perfect match." These comments coming from my best friend meant a great deal to me. When elderly relatives were unable to climb up the raised stage, I took Rama down to them and introduced her. An elderly friend of my father's after observing Rama commented, "You know, good things come in small packages"—referring to Rama's size and slender figure.

After greeting us and exchanging pleasantries, the guests were led by my siblings to an adjacent dining room where food and drinks were served. Before leaving the reception, all guests were handed a bag filled with goodies, mostly food, to take home.

While the reception was in progress, my brother Ohan, Raj and other photographers took photos of the guests—some with the bride and groom included.

The highlight of the reception was the cake cutting, when Rama and I jointly sliced a large decorated cake into pieces. As practice dictates in both India and America, the bride and groom stuff a piece of the cake in each other's mouths, followed by sharing the remainder of the cake with invitees.

I could not help noticing through all of these photoshoots the presence of my classmate Anda from middle school. Together we had fiercely played soccer during our lunch breaks. He attentively watched the happenings. His presence at my wedding reception surprised me as I was never close to him during my school years and completely had lost contact with him after high school. I wondered who in my family invited him to the reception. I was happy to see him and learn that he was working in a local bank.

After a dinner with our close relatives at the Ajanta Hotel, we returned home late that evening marking the conclusion of the celebrations. We rested in my parents' congested house occupying a bedroom for ourselves. In the privacy of our bedroom, I asked Rama to share with me her troubles and the problems she was facing. However, she did not open up, saying, "This is not the time."

Two days later, it was time for us to travel again. I took Rama by overnight train to the U.S. Consulate in Madras. During the quiet time of travel as the train sped on its tracks, we got to know each other a little bit better by simply talking about our lives and aspirations. Rama felt comfortable enough to tease me, even though we were abruptly married and did not know each other. I saw her willingness to tease as a good sign. Her charm was real and unrehearsed. I told myself that my alliance with Rama would be life-altering.

As a U.S. Green Card holder, I initiated the application process for Rama's own Green Card. I submitted a visa petition under the fourth preference of the U.S. Immigration & Nationality Act with the Consular Officer at the U.S. Consulate. I filed the visa petition with a copy of my marriage certificate furnished by the Registrar's Office in Guntur (which attested that Rama was my spouse), proof of my permanent residence in the United

States using my Alien Registration Card, and the payment of a fee.

That evening, Rama and I walked from the Sree Lekha Hotel where we were staying to the marina beach on the Bay of Bengal in Madras. The beach was not crowded. Couples and families came to the beach to spend time and relax. The moonlight leaked through the low clouds and fell across the gentle ocean waves washing up onto the sandy beach. As a cool breeze gently blew, we squatted on the warm sand and indulged in simple street food—something like freshly boiled peanuts and roasted hard peas spiced with masala. The quiet time at the soft sandy beach—where Rama kicked sand at my feet—such stillness, except for the roar of the ocean's waves—engendered a deep feeling of connection between us. That was a memorable period in my life.

We hadn't had the luxury of a honeymoon because of the pressure of time, with the reception taking place a few days after the wedding, our travel to the U.S. Consulate, and my imminent departure to the U.S. in a few days hence. The two nights that we stayed at the Sree Lekha Hotel in Madras was the first situation where we had privacy and time to spend with each other, get acquainted, and bond. It was amazing how close Rama and I got to grow over what was a short period of time after our wedding. We relied on each other for help, support and love, enjoying the simple things around us.

After we returned, Raj commented, "Madras was where you had your honeymoon. Isn't it?" Which was true and I agreed with him.

I had just a couple of days left to pack my bags before returning to the U.S. Rama's father travelled to Bangalore to bid farewell to me and take Rama back to Guntur to wait for her Green Card from the U.S. Consulate.

My departure at the Bangalore airport—for which my parents, all of my unmarried siblings, Rama and her father came—was emotional to my bride.

My father-in-law uttered with tremendous respect in Telugu, "Safe travel to America. Please write us as soon as you reach America."

With these farewell words spoken, Rama broke down in tears. Endless stream of tears rolled down her pretty cheeks.

Her father consoled her.

I assured Rama, "You'll join me in the U.S. in a short period." I uttered in her ear: "In just a couple of months, I promise." I whispered, "I love you forever, to infinity, through space and time." I wiped her tears, tenderly hugged her, and got on the airplane.

Rama's unencumbered emotion convinced me then that our marriage was founded on a strong footing and that we had bonded well. I felt like I was being deployed to a combat zone, leaving behind a dutiful and loving wife.

After I returned to Philadelphia, the fantasy of my wedding seemed to disappear. Yet by being with Rama for just a few wonderful days, it felt anticlimactic to unpack my bags and return to the humdrum of my life.

I called close friends including Ann and Len and told them of my marriage in India. They had no clue that I would jump into an unexpected marriage when I was on vacation to visit my family. They did not believe my story until I showed the album of my wedding photographs that I had carried with me to the U.S. Ann and Len were thrilled and could not wait to meet Rama. They were extremely inquisitive of the selection process of the bride that I had gone through, as well as the details of the wedding rituals. The entire marriage episode was just fascinating to them.

The second year of law school at Temple started in earnest during the last week of August. The deluge of study of court cases, briefs, etc. for the classes that I signed up for had resumed. Luckily, my teaching job did not resume till well after Labor Day and this gave me some breathing time to reflect upon my eventful summer.

My colleagues at Abington also were totally surprised by the sudden change in my marital status during my trip to India, which they merely thought of as a routine visit with my family. Again, I had to show my wedding album to convince them of my marriage to Rama. My friends were thrilled at my choice in a bride, like my friends back in Bangalore had been. When I bragged that Rama was a medical doctor, I could sense envy among my male friends. My colleague Sam Stewart commended: "You soon will be sweeping dough with a broom."

For me, my marriage was a dream. So was it for Rama, as she wrote in her letters to me. The match-making that we had participated in entailed commitment and the union of marriage followed by forging love.

Soon I was immersed in my teaching and studying. I neglected to communicate with Rama.

In the period of our separation immediately after our marriage, Rama showed her love and tender affection for me in her letters. She wrote incessantly. She wrote every other day or more often. She wrote letters filled with love, reminding me of the time we spent together. Some of letters were written in Hindi, which I struggled to read and comprehend. She was disappointed that I did not reciprocate and reply to her many letters. Yet on her own she recognized that I was busy with teaching and attending law school and apologized for expecting replies from me. Rama assured that she would not distract me from my job and studies when she joined me.

I saved those gems from Rama like this one:

My Very Own,

I have been waiting for your letters, but you do not seem to have time to write. Like you asked, I am having cassette tapes recorded with songs you like. Anyway, what difference does it make to you if I get them or not. I don't think you will have time either for the music or other simple pleasures. I know you will be extremely busy and will not be able to spend much time with me.

I also know I am a very plain girl and not to your expectations. But please give me a little time to get myself acclimatized to your way of life and also to the atmosphere over there in USA. Please do not rush me into things. Just now I feel shy and it is very difficult for me to mix with people. But if you are patient and gentle enough, I will try my best to come out of my shell.

When I join you, I will have left all near and dear behind. I will only have you and if you get mad or angry with me, I wouldn't know what to do. I will feel quite miserable. You know I am Dad's favorite and also all others spoil me. Anyway, what do all these trivial things matter as long as we love each other?

Yesterday, I was listening to beautiful songs played by Radio Sri Lanka. I was sitting in the moonlight, thinking of you and our first night together in the guest house. Also, I keep thinking of the very short time we were able to spend on the beach in Madras. I wish it were longer. You know, though I love you dearly, I also feel frightened of you sometimes and that was the first time I felt very free with you and enjoyed every second of it.

I am taking much of your valuable time. I will try to be brief in the future. I am always waiting for a word from you.

With tons and tons of love to you,

Rama

P.S. Please don't come into my dreams and spoil my beautiful sleep!

I reflected on her letters and told myself that I was lucky to have found such a wonderful person as my wife. In another epistle about dowries, Rama was very supportive of my plan to help my father by being willing to make personal sacrifices. She wrote this:

> *. . . I do not want you to spend money on me, for my luxuries and pleasures. I want to avoid this as much as I can. About your sisters, you are always welcome to pay for Swati and Vitri's dowries and also for your other sisters if you want to. You need not even mention it to me . . .*

From the letters that Rama wrote to me, I could see that Rama was definitely a romantic person whereas I was focused on intellectualism and driven by my goals. I always seemed to have a lot on my mind about chasing to the next milestone and accomplishing the next big thing. Rama wanted to enjoy the simple pleasures of nice music and song and treat others with love and affection. She wrote poetry in her letters.

I could tell that Rama was blessed with softer edges. I was sometimes abrupt and wanted to get where I wanted to in a big hurry. In law school, I may have started to develop the personality of an alpha male. Rama expressed to me in person when we were together that she wanted to be surrounded by family and friends. She told me that she wanted to marry into a large family anticipating close relationships with her in-laws, which came true.

Before I left India, I explained to Rama the process that I had initiated with the U.S. Consulate for her Green Card and the paperwork involved. I was required to furnish an affidavit of support for Rama to present to the Consulate. The affidavit was to assure the U.S. Department of State that Rama would not become a public charge after entering the U.S. In support of the affidavit, I was required to provide a statement of my income, my obligations for the support of Rama, and arrangements made for her reception and support. To substantiate my income, I was required to attach notarized copies of my income tax returns, a statement from my employer showing my salary and the length of employment, a statement from my bank regarding my account, showing the date the account was opened and the present balance to establish my financial ability to carry out my undertaking toward Rama.

I explained that Rama would be required to undergo a mandatory medical examination by a physician designated by the Consulate as a part of the process for receiving her Green Card.

As required, I obtained a statement of my employment and the salary I received and an account-balance statement from my bank. I filled out the official form titled the "Affidavit of Support."

Under the reasons for signing the affidavit, I stated that "Rama Coca is my wife and I have a moral and legal duty to live with her. I am delighted to carry out my duties as her husband." I executed the Affidavit before a Notary and mailed it to Rama.

Rama wrote me that she travelled to the Consulate in Madras with her uncle and all went well. The Consular Officer found my Affidavit as acceptable and instantly decided that she was eligible for her Green Card, subject to her passing the mandatory immigration medical examination. The Consular Officer then notified Rama to complete her medical examination and scheduled a date and time for the formal final immigration interview with him.

Her medical examination was conducted by Dr. Mahadevan in Bangalore who was among the list of immigration panel physicians. Dr. Mahadevan happened to be our family physician and it was a no brainer for Rama to have him conduct the examination. The exam included a blood test, verification of the record of vaccinations that she had received and an X-ray of her chest—all of which he quickly arranged at a local clinic. Dr. Mahadevan filled out an official form to document the results of her medical examination. He then gave her a sealed envelope containing the documentation of the medical results and the form he had filled out for delivering to the Consular Officer in Madras.

On the date scheduled by the Consular Officer, as advised, Rama travelled back to Madras and delivered the sealed envelope that Dr. Mahadevan gave her. Without any further questioning, the Consular Officer gave Rama a Visa Packet with clear writing on it of "Do not open this packet" and instructed that she should hand over the Visa Packet to the U.S. Immigration Officer at her port of entry into the United States. He also instructed that if the Officer after inspecting the documents admits her, then Rama would have lawful permanent resident status and be able to live and work in the United States permanently.

With the Visa Packet and Indian passport in her hand, Rama was now all set to travel to the United States to join me. After bidding good-bye to her parents and siblings in Guntur, Rama spent a couple of days with my parents in Bangalore. From there she travelled to Bombay to catch the international flight to New York. It was exactly three months since our wedding day when she left Bangalore. On that day, my father accompanied Rama to Bombay on a train journey. At the international airport in Bombay, as a parting or belated wedding gift, he presented her with a set of bangles made out of 22 carat pure gold.

MY WIFE'S ARRIVAL IN AMERICA

ON FRIDAY NOVEMBER 5, 1976, after a long flight, Rama landed in the newly christened John F. Kennedy Airport in New York City. I drove to JFK to greet Rama and bring her to our new abode as a permanent resident of the United States. I knew I'd be collecting a tired and fragile bride.

There was a dense mass of bodies and luggage moving around the immense Arrival Hall. Suddenly Rama emerged from the sliding glass doors of Immigration & Customs. She was wearing a lime-green saree with a matching blouse and looked radiant despite her long plane ride. A porter carried her baggage on a trolley and walked behind her. She anxiously looked to find me in the crowd.

An amusing thing happened. When she emerged into the arrivals area—although I recognized her from afar—she scanned for me and looked past me. When she came closer, I waved to her. She looked past me again until the porter spotted me and pointed me out to Rama.

Soon I embraced her. She hesitated until I uttered the gentle words: "Rama, I love you! Welcome to America."

The funny thing was that she was still unable to recognize me for sure. I had grown a mustache which seemed to have thrown her off.

She said, "I have missed you and am so happy to be with you."

We kissed.

She observantly looked at my face and commented, "You look folksy with your mustachioed face." She then added, "You look like your younger brother with your mustache."

That evening, I shaved off my mustache!

I asked her while we were still in the Arrival Hall, "How did the meeting with the Immigration Officer at the airport go? Did you receive your Green Card?"

She replied, "The meeting was a breeze" and pulled out her Green Card from her wallet to show me. It carried a different Alien Registration number than mine, the date of 11-5-1976, and identified the port of entry as New York JFK Airport.

Rama's preoccupation in watching me as I drove to Philadelphia and to be with me side-by-side seemed more important than entering a foreign country inhabited by a different kind of people. The highway was bizarrely free of traffic. The sky was crystal-clear blue. The scenery and the highways did not distract her one bit from her engaging looks at me and her incessant conversation with me. She had so much to tell me since our last time together.

Rama moved into my humble one-bedroom apartment at Temple University's graduate student's complex. Although the unit was small, it was ideal for a single person or a married couple. It had a small kitchen, a living room and a bath adjacent to the bedroom. I had the basic furniture. In the living room there was a small black and white TV and a music player and some leafy plants hanging from the ceiling.

Rama was terribly exhausted from her long journey from India. Nevertheless, she was determined to engage in continual conversation despite her shyness. I was glad that it was a weekend when she arrived. I could skip my preparation for the classes for the first time and spend quality time with her. Rama's jet lag did not get in the way as we reunited. For the first time I was so happy to share my simple life with someone that I adored, and I felt that I could count her as my best friend and co-equal partner.

After a blissful weekend, Monday arrived, and my daily routine restarted. I grabbed a meal of cold cereal, jumped into my car, and headed to teach at Abington. Since my commute to Abington was in a reverse direction to drivers who were coming into Philadelphia, my commute was a breeze.

When I returned to my apartment around 4:00 p.m., Rama greeted me with a warm embrace. I grabbed a quick TV dinner cooked in the oven and dashed off to prepare for my law class, leaving Rama all alone. When I returned around 10:00 p.m., we had some time to be together and then went to bed after I took a quick shower.

I wanted Rama to rest and get over her jet lag and exhaustion. She watched sitcoms on television. *The Mary Tyler Moore Show, I Love Lucy* and *Bewitched* quickly became her favorite shows. After she recovered from her trip, she bemoaned the fact that I did not spend sufficient time with her. She jovially threatened that she would tie me down so I could never leave her sight. "How wonderful that would be!" I said to myself.

No sooner than when Rama began to acclimate to our surroundings in Philadelphia, it became clear that her assimilation had a long way to go. When I was away at work, she decided to stroll around the neighborhood all by herself. When she told me about it, I admonished her not to do it again as we lived in a neighborhood with a high crime rate, even though her walk was confined to the Temple campus. We both laughed at Rama's adventure around the block and Rama risking her safety.

I taught her the rudiments of Indian cooking, starting with a few simple dishes for dinner, as she never had cooked before. Cooking potato and pea curry was easy to teach.

I briefly explained: "Boil quartered pieces of potatoes until cooked. In a pan, add oil, sauté thinly sliced onion until it turns brown; add the frozen peas. Spice the contents in the pan with turmeric, red pepper and salt. Then add the cooked potato pieces and turn for five minutes. Serve it with plain or Basmati rice."

Rama already knew how to cook rice by watching her mother.

Teaching her how to cook chicken curry took some showing. I showed how to skin chicken breasts, remove all fat, and slice the meat into thin strips.

I explained, "In a buttered pan, sauté the onion pieces until they are transparent. Add the chicken strips and cook for five minutes. Then add a pinch of turmeric, cayenne pepper, salt, crushed ginger and garlic, followed by adding a cup of plain yogurt. Cook for ten to fifteen minutes and add chicken masala powder."

Another dish I taught was sambar—a lentil and vegetable soup. I jokingly told Rama that "a simple trick to turn a good dish into a great dish is to add as much butter as you can."

Rama quickly came back with: "Sure, only if you wish your arteries to be clogged."

Rama was a good sport and soon started preparing delicious Indian meals. She had been a vegetarian in India, although her father desired occasional meat or chicken dishes which her mother made for him and for the other children. Because of my need to have non-vegetarian meals, inasmuch as Rama detested even looking at raw and blooded meat, she developed a tolerance for chopping raw meat and preparing non-vegetarian dishes. She did this out of love and respect for me. It was a sacrifice of being flexible and accommodating my needs, which I silently admired.

One afternoon after my teaching, I returned to my apartment complex and was walking in the corridor leading to our unit. A graduate student who also lived in the complex walked in front of me.

Abruptly he stopped and remarked: "I smell the aroma of delicious cooking. Someone seems be cooking Indian food."

As I approached our unit, I noticed that the main door to our apartment was ajar and the aroma was emanating from our kitchen. When I entered, Rama explained that she had left the main door ajar for ventilation. I told her that a passerby complimented her cooking for its aromatic flavor. Her response was "Yea, sure!" implying that I was teasing her cooking skills, which I was not.

Rama regularly received letters from her sister and brothers and importantly from her father. Her father encouraged her to do whatever I asked her, especially in building her career as a doctor. My father-in-law also wrote to me in Telugu pleading with me to be patient with his daughter that I had married. He reminded me that "Rama is a kind person and will not disappoint me." His letters provided me with a lot of comfort, particularly since he gave such strong moral support to his eldest daughter, which sometimes I neglected to do for my siblings in my preoccupation with my own studies. I had full faith that Rama would come through.

It was mid-Fall and the weather was turning chilly. We went shopping during the weekends to put together a warm and Western-style wardrobe for Rama. She started with long skirts and some pants and shirts but still needed more American clothes.

The first durable purchase that we made together was to replace my 1969 Chevy Nova, which was already seven years old and looked undependable, with a new car. We went to a couple of car dealerships and finally settled for a Chevy dealership in Cheltenham which I passed by on my way to and from work.

Rama was wearing a thin cotton sari and skimpy blouse without a jacket. She detested wearing anything heavy on her body, even hand gloves and shoes. The car salesman, a middle-aged male, showed us a number of swanky new cars, while all along sympathizing with Rama as she was shivering in the cold and blustery outdoor weather.

He abruptly interrupted the small talk he was engaged in and said, "I think your wife needs a coat more than car right now!"

We settled upon a high-end Nova, called Nova Concourse. The color, which Rama cared about, was white. It had a red top and two narrow red pinstripes along the doors and fenders. In the bright outdoor light, the car glistened. We picked up the new car the next day and sold off the old car to a young couple who lived in our neighborhood.

I wanted to execute my plan to preoccupy Rama with a career path rather than her getting bored. I figured that if she was doing what I was doing, namely studying for a new career, we might be able to receive moral support from each other and work toward the common goal of achieving good careers. With this in mind, I reopened the discussion of her career—which has been a topic that Rama wished that I would avoid. She once again explained that she went to medical school because of respect for her father who loved her dearly more than any of her siblings. She confessed that she hated the sight and smell of blood. Rama pleaded that she could pursue some other career. However, I was not persuaded. I rationalized with her that she already had earned her valuable medical degree and qualified as a doctor. I felt it was immoral to let her hard work go to waste and relayed my feeling to her.

A few of Rama's college mates from her medical school in India were senior to her and doing their U.S. residency in teaching hospitals around Union, New Jersey. We drove up to their house over a weekend not only to have Rama get reacquainted with them but also for me to meet them. My agenda was also to understand the requirements that Rama would need to satisfy to apply for the U.S. residency.

On another weekend, we met with my former roommate Mo whose wife was now doing her residency in pediatrics in a teaching hospital in New Jersey as well. When I introduced my wife to them, I felt proud because Rama was so graceful, gentle and beautiful.

On yet another weekend, we spent time with Rama's acquaintances from her medical school who were much senior to her and who came to the U.S. a decade earlier and were now living in Bethlehem, Pennsylvania. They were licensed in the United States as physicians and worked in hospitals and had two young daughters.

Equipped with the information that we gathered from these doctor friends, we together chalked out a plan of action for Rama's career.

The first step was to file an application for certification by the Educational Commission for Foreign Medical Graduates (ECFMG). Since Rama previously had filed such an application when she was in India, she only needed to update it with a new photograph and her present address, which she did, and this revived her ECFMG number.

The next step was to meet the written examination requirements for ECFMG Certification, which included passing two separately administered components: the English language and the Medical components. The former was a pass/fail test; the latter required a minimum passing scaled score of 75.

Even though Rama was not prepared, in mid-November 1976 she decided to take the ECFMG examination scheduled for January 26, 1977. This was intended to be a trial run to get a feel for the type of questions asked and to determine how current her knowledge of medicine was. She did not have the privilege of taking a review course for the Medical part of the ECFMG exam. I admired her courage to take the exam. When the results were communicated in early March 1977, as expected, she passed the English test but missed attaining the required score in the Medical component by a couple of points.

Rama then signed up for a ten-week Flex (Federation License Examination) Review Course from March to June 1977 sponsored by Hahnemann Medical College and the Hospital of Philadelphia. The FLEX course was designed for doctors who were preparing to qualify for the license to practice medicine, which followed after completion of the residency program. She signed up for this course to get an understanding of the latest state of medicine in the U.S.

While I headed to work, she headed in the opposite direction to downtown Philadelphia riding the Broad Street subway to attend the FLEX course. Over the weekends, she joined me in the cubicles of Temple's law library to study. She clutched books like *The Current Medical Diagnosis and Treatment*; I pored over law treaties on Uniform Commercial Code, Remedies, Torts, etc.

While Rama was focusing her time and energy on the ECFMG, I focused on my citizenship. Five years earlier in 1971 I notified the Immigration & Naturalization Service of my intention to become a U.S. citizen by submitting a Declaration of Intention. I completed the required five years of residency in the U.S. as a Green Card holder. It was the Bicentennial Year. I wanted to become a naturalized citizen in this moment of American history. The day before Thanksgiving in 1976, I petitioned by filling out Form N-400 and filing with the INS for naturalization.

I reflected on giving up my current Indian citizenship. I was grateful that I was a citizen of India by being born there and as a son of Indian parents. I was fortunate to have received a strong foundation in education, and to have been raised as a Hindu with Indian culture. My upbringing was the source of most of all the discipline and determination that was ingrained in me to succeed in essentially whatever I undertook in my life.

My decision to become a U.S. citizen was based on pragmatism. I didn't want my foreign citizenship to come in the way since I was still seeking a job as a physicist with the eventual goal of working as a lawyer after earning my J.D. As a foreigner, I could not have applied for a job as a physicist with the U.S. government or defense contractors who carried out secretive and sensitive defense work for the government. Defense contractors by far hired more physicists than the private sector did. The landing of a lucrative job continued to drive me as I remained committed to helping my father by raising the dowry money for my unmarried sisters back in India.

INS acted on my declaration and invited me to take tests in mid-December 1976 in the English language and civics, which I did and passed. INS then sent me a formal invitation to be sworn in on January 5, 1977 as a citizen of the United States in the U.S. District Court, Eastern District of Pennsylvania in downtown Philadelphia. I would have the privilege of being sworn in a short distance away from where the Declaration of Independence was signed two hundred years earlier.

I wore a dark blue suit and tie befitting the judicial ceremony of naturalization. Rama accompanied me to the Court to watch my swearing-in. I returned my Green Card to the INS officer who was present at the Court.

There were nearly two hundred other foreigners who were also invited to be sworn in. Minutes after the presiding judge ordered the Court to come to session, he asked whether an invitee was willing to say a few words to the audience about citizenship. I raised my hand and the judge thanked me and said that he would call on me at the appropriate time during the Court's session.

This gave me some time to collect my thoughts on what I should say. It was a moment for which I was prepared from the years of public speaking at the Toastmaster's Club in Bangalore a decade earlier. Also, the Socratic method of teaching that my law professors had drilled into me came handy for this occasion.

The highlight of the ceremony was taking the Oath of Allegiance where the Clerk of the Court read the Oath and I quietly repeated his uttered words verbatim. The Oath ended with the words of prayer of "so help me God?" which I also repeated.

After swearing in of all the invited candidates for naturalization, the judge nodded at me to speak. I rose to my feet. The court room around me seemed to disappear. It was as if adrenaline shut out all of my senses as I spoke with intense concentration on my words. I wasn't nervous but exhilarated by the great leap in citizenship that I just had taken.

I raised my voice for dramatic effect and said:

Your Honor,

Good morning. My name is T.R. Coca. I am deeply honored to have taken the Oath to become a United States citizen today. Over a decade ago, I came to the United States as a college graduate for educational advancement thanks to the student visa program of the Immigration & Naturalization Service and the generosity of Temple University which offered me admission and financial assistance without which I could not have come here. I came here to be a Ph.D. physicist, which I earned six years ago. I have been teaching physics since then.

This is a country which offers immense opportunities for individuals to realize. Anything under the sun is possible in the U.S. One only needs to dream big and apply himself to achieve that dream. After reaching the pinnacle of study of physics, I am now pursuing a radically new career to become a lawyer by attending law school in the evening. Such an opportunity to combine two diverse disciplines is possible only in the United States. I am hopeful that I will soon earn my J.D. degree and realize my new dream of synergistically combining my education in physics and law to serve the community as an Intellectual Property lawyer.

I must invoke the intellectual history of the American conclave of Founding Fathers, George Washington, Alexander Hamilton, James Madison, John Adams and Thomas Jefferson who enshrined this country on a set of legal, moral and ethical principles derived from our elastic Constitution. On this year of America's two hundredth birthday, the country continues to be the bastion of hope and decency for the entire world. Only a chosen few, like those of us assembled here, get this unique and wonderful opportunity to be a United States citizen, a citizen of a robust and enduring democracy, rooted in individual liberty and equal opportunity.

Our citizenship comes with the full range of moral, civic and intellectual virtues that together form the American character. As citizens we have certain duties and obligations through the privilege of voting, spirited participation on a jury when summoned, by running for public office, campaigning for political candidates that we support, speaking our mind on topics that are important whether at the local, state or federal level. Our patriotism is a duty and new attachment to the United States.

We the people are sovereign. The source of power of our government is us. I hope that we take the responsibility that comes with that power seriously and apply it righteously for the betterment of our society.

I have an immigrant's love for the United States. It is no less than a miracle to become a U.S. citizen. I am very proud of it and will cherish it for the rest of my life.

After the completion of the naturalization ceremony, I picked up my Certificate of Naturalization. I applied for my U.S. passport, filed for registration to vote, and updated my social security record with the Social Security Administration to reflect that I was now a U.S. citizen.

I further reflected on the long path that I took to reach the goal of becoming a U.S. Citizen. First, I earned admission for my Ph.D. and financial aid from Temple University based on my academic credentials from India, which took years of planning and accomplishment. Second, I obtained my student visa to enter the U.S. for my study. Next, after I demonstrated that my skills as a physicist were of value to the U.S., the immigration authorities allowed me to convert my student visa to a Green Card. Finally, after a five-year period of residency in the U.S. as a Green Card holder, I proved to be fit to become a U.S. citizen

I felt great and proud of my accomplishment of becoming a citizen of the U.S. I earned it!

TRANSITION: TEACHER TO PHYSICIST TO LAWYER

ALTHOUGH I WAS a tenured teacher, I wanted to succeed as a physicist like Niels Bohr, Ernest Rutherford or Enrico Fermi. However, my inability to find a job as a physicist after I earned my Ph.D. awakened me. I came to a realization that I was not in the same league as these physicists. I gravitated to law because I wanted the freedom to choose my destiny and not be subjected to the political whims of the U.S. President or Congress. I believed in making the right choices going forward, as the choices I'd make would determine my future life—success versus failure; extraordinary wealth versus an ordinary income; and supreme happiness versus discontent.

I believed in God, not necessarily in the Hindu Gods. Having attended a Jesuit school, I also believed in Jesus Christ. Regardless of the name of the God, I believed that there was a higher Universal Being who created life. This might seem antithetical to a physicist who could explain how the universe worked by the laws of physics discovered by man. I prayed for God to grant me the serenity to accept the things I could not change and the courage to change the things I could.

I wanted to make a difference in my family. That determination led me to break away from tradition and motivated me to new thinking before I reached fifteen. I was not about to give up that determination. My swearing in as U.S. citizen gave me impetus to try anew for a job as a physicist to earn more money while pursing my law degree. I was also getting concerned that my Ph. D. was getting stale and it may become more difficult to qualify for a job which required current knowledge. I continued to keep an eye on job advertisements in the local newspapers as I continued my law study.

Sure enough, I saw an advertisement in early January of 1977 for a materials scientist with the U.S. defense contractor General Dynamics Corporation based in San Diego, California. I sprang into action. With a freshly prepared resume and a personalized cover letter I answered the ad. Within days, I was invited for a personal interview with Melvin Campbell, who was the manager of the Mechanical & Physical Properties Laboratory in General Dynamics. I flew to San Diego at the end of January for the interview.

While Philadelphia was shrouded in dampness and had frigid temperatures in January, San Diego was basking in the sunshine with a pleasant dry climate typically in the mid-seventies. I said to myself, "San Diego, if I am to move here, it will be a God-send for Rama." Rama disliked the cold climate in the East. She hated wearing a heavy coat, gloves and even shoes. She suffered when it turned cold. Even short walks from our apartment to the law school library in winter or a trip on the subway train were tortuous for her. I felt sympathetic for her suffering in the frigid climate of Philadelphia having come from a tropical climate just a few months earlier. Her doctor friends advised that since Rama was so frail and fragile, we should consider moving to a warm climate like that in Florida, Arizona or California.

My interview with Mel Campbell and a number of other physicists and managers at General Dynamics went well.

Mel explained, "I am looking for a lead engineer in my lab. I would like him to handle materials and process engineering."

I promptly responded: "This is precisely what my Ph.D. research was all about. I pursued the elusive superconducting materials and processed them for zero resistance when chilled below a critical temperature near absolute zero."

Mel then stated, "I am looking for a trained scientist to run his lab. The lab now is comprised of four engineers, including a Ph.D. chemist, and three technicians."

I asked whether the seven people in the lab would report to the lead engineer.

He explained, "No. They will continue to report to me." He added, "We are running a flat organization. I am not looking for a manager but a person who can guide and lead the others on various projects in his lab."

He continued. "I would also like the new hire to collaborate with other scientists who are working on the electrical properties of materials under another manager to ensure that the materials are physically, mechanically, electrically, optically and chemically fit for use in certain classified space-based military projects."

I expressed my interest in the job and elaborated the details of my doctoral research on materials and produced the papers that I had published in scientific journals. I then added: "I also worked in optics for my master's thesis" and explained the optical occultation project I completed "to determine the diameter and distance of mutual separation of the double star Alpha Centauri."

Mel introduced me to another engineering manager, Dr. McKinney, who questioned me on my technical capabilities for possible collaboration on the projects he was working on.

I was impressed with the physical beauty of San Diego. Following the interview, I drove up to the University of San Diego Law School, which I previously had researched to have an evening J.D. program. I checked out the law classes that were in progress and picked up literature about the school. The physical location of USD was impressive. It was perched on top of a rolling hill overlooking the beautiful Mission Bay. It was a private Jesuit school not unlike St. Joseph's college in Bangalore—but more picturesque.

That evening I mailed Rama a postcard of the San Diego Bay with many sailboats and neatly lined up palm trees. I told her, "I hope we will be able to make San Diego our new home soon."

After returning to Philadelphia, I got immersed in my day job of teaching, in attending law courses in the evenings, and in preparing for my course assignments during the weekends. Rama, as had now become a routine, joined me in the law library with her medical books. We led a simple life, going occasionally to a movie, enjoying the New England style cheese pizza with no meat, and shopping for new clothes.

I continued writing letters frequently to my mother and at times to my siblings, particularly my younger brother Ohan and sister Swati. My mother wrote back loving letters wishing for my happiness with Rama. They were full of affection and blessings.

My father, on the other hand, became demanding for money. A letter I received from him shortly after Rama's arrival in the U.S. demanded that I pay for the set of gold bangles that he had presented to her on the eve of her departure to America. I was incensed by his demand. When Rama found out about it, she was unhappy. I decided to return the bangles to my father. When a friend was travelling to Guntur, I sent the bangles to my father-in-law for handing them over to my father. That turned out to be a huge mistake. When my father-in-law made a preplanned visit to Bangalore and delivered the bangles, my father became furious. He falsely blamed him for not teaching Rama respect for elders. My father deplored Rama for returning his wedding gift, while ignoring the money demands he had made to me which precipitated this incident.

I could not understand my father's anger. I could only think that he was angry with me for not asking for a dowry from my father-in-law for marrying Rama. I suspected his relatives chewed his ear even more with assertions such as that I was a groom with a Green Card (now an American citizen) living in America and worth more than an India-based groom in terms of a dowry, that I was earning tons of money in the U.S. from which Rama and her in-laws would benefit, and that my father needed my dowry to defray the dowries he would need to pay for his daughters. My father's angry response hurt me, but I decided not to further inflame his anger. I regretted my hasty decision to return the gift he gave to Rama. I had provoked a conflict with him on the matter of money. I hoped that someday he would thank me for the plan that I was working on to alleviate the strain of dowries on him.

Two weeks after my interview with General Dynamics, I received a phone call from Mel Campbell. We had a pleasant and cordial conversation. He stated that "General Dynamics would like to extend to you an employment offer as a Senior Research Engineer in the Mechanical and Physical Properties Laboratory. However, there is a condition: you should obtain your clearance."

Mel continued: "GD will apply for, process and obtain the clearance for you." He also mentioned that "your job title will be Senior Research Engineer, Material and Process Engineering."

I let him finish what he had to say. He laid out the salary and other benefits that I would receive.

I replied in excitement, "Mel, I am so thankful for your generous employment offer. I appreciate it so very much!"

The salary was about 30% more than my teaching job. Actually, considering that in my teaching job I worked only nine months per year whereas at General Dynamics I was required to work for twelve months, the average monthly salary was a wash.

Mel asked for a time frame that would work for me to start the job at General Dynamics. I could not commit to a time as I was in the early part of the second semester of teaching, which Mel was aware of. I thanked him again for the job offer and demurred on its acceptance. I told Mel: "I need time to discuss this with my wife and my employer. I will get back to you as soon as I can."

I was ecstatic to receive the job offer. This was the moment that I had waited for over six years. I thanked God for His blessing. I was convinced that Rama brought me good luck through our marriage. I immediately told Rama of the job offer. She was thrilled and was happy for me. She already had received the postcard from San Diego that I sent, and she was fixated on the warm weather and the beauty of the coastal city on the blue Pacific Ocean.

In as much as I wanted to drop everything I was doing then, dash to San Diego and build a career as an engineer/physicist, my precocious mind went to work. I already had invested three semesters of study and was in the fourth semester of the required eight semesters of study in my J.D. program. Summarily dropping my students at Abington from my teaching of the physics curricula will certainly disrupt them. Rama just had signed up for a three-month FLEX review course by paying a hefty fee. If she did not complete it, that would result in a loss of the course material review and coaching she needed for passing her ECFMG exam.

I conducted research on the requirements of Temple Law School versus the USD Law School if I were to seek a transfer to the latter and continue my J.D. there while working at General Dynamics. Temple had a requirement that I earn 83 credit hours of law study, 55 of which should be earned from Temple in order to earn my J.D. from Temple. On the other hand, USD would accept no more than 30 credits from Temple if I were to transfer my credits from Temple to USD and complete the remaining credits and earn my degree from USD. By that time I had earned 33 credits from Temple and was on path to earn 43 credits upon completion of courses I was then enrolled in my fourth semester.

I decided that I wanted to earn as many credits as I could from Temple and then transfer to USD with the expectation of receiving my J.D. from Temple University. Temple was ranked higher than USD by the American Bar Association. More than that, I thought my approach was a more expedient and seamless way of completing my J.D. What this meant, however, was that if I completed the fourth semester and additionally completed the summer semester of 1977 at Temple and earned another 5 credits, I would have earned a total of only 48 credits out of Temple's required 83 credits. However, it fell short of the 55 credits that Temple required.

Faced with this dilemma, as a law student who was learning

TRANSITION: TEACHER TO PHYSICIST TO LAWYER 179

the ropes of petitioning, on March 4, 1977, I formally filed a reasoned petition to the Student Transfer Administrative Committee at Temple. This is what I wrote:

> *I am an Asian American attending the Evening Division of Temple University School of Law. I came to the U.S. in 1965 to pursue graduate studies and earned a M.A. and Ph.D. degrees in 1868 and 1971, respectively, from Temple University. I started my legal studies in the fall of 1976 and will have earned 43 credits by the end of spring 1977. I plan to attend the summer session of 1977 and earn an additional 5 credits bringing the total credits earned from Temple Law School to 48 credits.*
>
> *Last semester I married a girl from India, and she entered the U.S. for the first time in November 1976. Ever since her arrival, she has not been keeping good health due to the cold winter weather in Philadelphia. Her family physician strongly recommended that we migrate to a warm part of the country to alleviate her suffering. In view of this serious personal problem, I decided to give up my tenured teaching position and move to a warm part of the U.S. I sought employment in cities in Florida, Texas, Arizona and California which have an Evening Law School and luckily found a position in my field in San Diego, California.*
>
> *I wish to move to San Diego and continue my legal studies at the University of San Diego. However, USD will accept a maximum of only 30 transfer credits, which means that if I were to matriculate from USD I will have to give up 18 of my hard-earned Temple law credits and spend essentially an extra academic year of study than I would have if I did not transfer.*
>
> *I am submitting this petition to request that I be allowed to matriculate from Temple University School of Law with a J.D.*

degree. I will have completed by the end of the summer of 1977 a total of 48 of the 83 credits needed to graduate from Temple. Normally, Temple requires that a student complete 55 credits and allows transfer of 28 credits from another accredited law school. In light of the personal problem that I am faced with, a problem over which I have no control, I request the Committee that I be permitted to transfer 35 credits of law courses from USD and be awarded a J.D. upon such transfer.

As I understand it, the intent of the 55-credit minimum requirement at Temple is to prevent rampant and unscrupulous student transfers in the middle of the J. D. program. Here is a situation where no such intent is present. This is a case where the physical well-being of the spouse of a student is being threatened by forces beyond her control. I urge that the Committee take this humanistic element into consideration and grant my request.

Exactly a month later, my petition was granted, which was communicated in writing by the Associate Dean of the Law School. With this issue resolved, I next sought admission as a Special Student to attend USD Law School by completing the application for admission, an official copy of my law school transcripts from Temple, a letter from Temple Law School Dean attesting that I was in good standing and that he approved my plan to attend USD as a Special Student. Since my final transcripts from Temple would not be ready until after I completed my planned coursework in the summer session of 1977, USD informed me that a decision on my admissibility as a Special Student would be made around August 1 after USD received my final transcript.

With the seamless continuation of my law study put in place, the next challenge was to convince Mel Campbell to hold the job offer he made open until August. I telephoned Mel in mid-April and opened with these words: "Mel, I am calling to thank you again for the job offer you extended to me. Much appreciated. As you know, the academic year where I am teaching does not end until June. I hate to leave abruptly now and disrupt my students. I feel morally obligated to finish up the academic year for the sake of my students."

Mel listened quietly. He then volunteered: "I understand. I was not expecting you to join GD until you finished the second semester at the school." He paused and asked, "Does this mean you will join us in June?"

I responded, "Thank you for your understanding. Your expectation for me to start my job in June is reasonable and I am grateful for it." I paused for a moment and resumed. "But I have another issue which I did not disclose. It might delay my start date beyond June."

Mel asked, "What is the other issue?"

I explained: "Mel, two years ago I started my J.D. study at Temple. I am now at the halfway point for completing it. I would like to complete the remaining portion of my J.D. at night at University of San Diego while working for you during the day. However, because of some peculiar credit transfer restrictions of the two law schools, in order to do so I must complete additional courses at Temple this summer."

Mel listened patiently as I nervously continued. "I need to take two law courses this summer at Temple, which I will complete at the end of July. I will start my job under you during the first week of August."

I supplemented all of that with this plea: "Mel, I know this is too much to ask. However, I assure you that I will definitely join as early in August as possible, if you could hold the position open for me until then."

I did not know how Mel would react to my unreasonable request. What he then said astounded me. He replied: "I applaud you for your ambition to become a lawyer. I applaud your stamina and determination to earn your J.D. on the side. I have nothing but respect for people who are ambitious. Yes, I am willing to wait for you until the first week of August to join GD."

I thanked Mel for his graciousness and accommodation in keeping the job open until then.

I followed up our conversation with a letter to Mel in which I expressed my sincere thanks and heartfelt appreciation and reassured that I would start my job in early August.

With my job as a physicist firmed up as well as the continuation of my law study without losing course credits, it was time to shift my attention to my family back home.

I reflected upon the naturalization status that I had earned a few months earlier and the new horizon it opened to make a major modification to my original plan to fund my father with dowry money. I discussed my modification with Rama, who was in many ways more intelligent when it came to family matters. The modified plan that I contemplated was practical and financially better. My rationale for a change in the plan was this.

My new job at General Dynamics did not promise a dramatically upward shift in my future earnings. The tuition at the privately held University of San Diego Law School was much higher than at the state-funded school of Temple. The cost of living in San Diego was higher as well. I could not count on a permanent career at GD as the defense contractors depended on U.S. government contracts from year-to-year for continued funding. Also, such contracts were known to get terminated by the government without notice due to changes in military spending and the ever-changing political environment that the President and Congress faced. The only path for a steady, successful and well-paid job that I could count on was to complete my J.D., earn admission to a State Bar, and be gainfully employed as a lawyer. Such dependable employment was at least two to three years away.

I could not count on Rama to supplement my earnings right away. She had many hurdles to cross in her career, which she was pursuing solely out of love and respect for me. The uncertainty over whether Rama would be able to overcome the hurdles and the long time it would take concerned me.

I came to the realization that I needed help from my siblings. I modified my Plan B to a new plan: I would enable my unmarried sisters and brothers in India to immigrate to the United States. My goal was to endow them with their Green Cards and have them establish themselves in the U.S. through additional education or straight employment based on the education and skills they already had earned from India. The crux of my new plan was to empower my unmarried sisters with a Green Card, which would enable them to attract grooms based in India to be their husbands by virtue of the prized possession of their Green Card. Importantly, the Green Card would entice the grooms to marry without demanding a dowry. Instead they would receive a legal pathway, as a spouse of a permanent resident, to immigrate to the U.S. The quid pro quo that I devised was that the potential value of the entitlement of a Green Card far exceeded the value of the dowry that the alien spouse could have received from marrying my sisters if they remained in India.

My new plan now took on a dual role: fulfill my duty to financially relieve my father of the dowry payment for my sisters; and be a benevolent brother to my siblings.

With this newer plan now permanently planted in my mind, I executed the process for immigration of my siblings to the U.S. Rather than pulling the immigration lever for all of my unmarried siblings, I wanted to test the process for the required paperwork and its speed of execution starting with two of them. I selected my first younger brother Ohan and my second sister Swati as the guinea pigs.

I selected Ohan since he already had earned his Bachelor of Engineering Degree from Bangalore University. He had been employed for five years with different employers based in India, was now posted in Bangalore, and lived with my parents. However, he had an inadequate job. I wanted to boost his earnings potential by him following my footsteps after he arrived in the U.S.

I selected Swati because she was next in line for marriage and I was sure that my father was beginning to worry about finding a groom for her. Like Ohan, my sister Swati was also educated and was now employed as a bio-technician in Bangalore. I knew that she would not accept any groom selected by my father as she distrusted my father and did not hold him in high esteem. She was emotionally close to her elder sister Jaya and brother-in-law Raj.

Having been away from India for more than a dozen years, I did not have the full knowledge as to the attitudes, feelings and aspirations of my unmarried siblings living in India. I could not attest to their morality, character, loyalty and dependability. Not everything that had happened back home in their lives during my absence was shared with me. Perhaps some dark issues with them were shielded from me. However, out of benevolence and brotherly love to my siblings and my duty to my parents to help their children to succeed, I lent a helping hand to enhance their individual lives in ways that I could.

I wrote home about my intention to sponsor the two eldest children now living with my parents for immigration to the United States. I guided my parents to prepare Relationship Affidavits attesting to the facts that I was related to my brother and sister and stating their respective dates and places of birth. Sometimes official birth certificates were unavailable and the Relationship Affidavit from the parents was accepted by the Immigration & Naturalization Service in lieu of the certificate of birth.

Armed with the Relationship Affidavits executed by my parents, I filled out two separate petitions—one for Ohan and the second for Swati. On March 4, 1977, I went to the Immigration & Naturalization Service office in Philadelphia and filed the petitions, under the Fourth Preference as brother and sister of a U.S. citizen, with the fee payment and supporting documents. This step initiated the process for Ohan and Swati to live permanently in the United States. I silently hoped that someday in the future Ohan and Swati would realize the value of my gift to immigrate to the United States and enjoy the benefits of their Green Card. I also hoped that my parents would see the wisdom in my plan to uplift their children, especially my sister who could likely later marry her spouse without payment of dowry.

On April 8, 1977, the INS office in Philadelphia approved my petition for my brother, assigned the fourth preference classification, and informed me that it had been forwarded to the U.S. Consulate at Madras, India for completing further action. The notification further stated that visas were issued only by the U.S. Consuls who were under the jurisdiction of the Department of State. Under the law, a limited number of visas were issued each year in the chronological order in which the petitions were filed for the same classification. When the beneficiary's turn was reached in the waiting list, the U.S. Consulate would inform him and consider issuance of the visa.

Without waiting for the visa number for Ohan, I filled out the Affidavit of Support to meet the public charge provision of the Immigration and Nationality Act and to indicate that I would assure my brother's support and notarized it. In support of this assurance I gathered a statement from my bank of the date my account was opened and the balance of funds in it, and a statement of employment from my employer. In the Affidavit, I stated that "I, as a citizen of the United States, am exercising my constitutional right to reunite my family in my new homeland. The beneficiary is part of my family—a blood relative." I sent the Affidavit and supporting documents to the U.S. Consulate at Madras, India. I was determined to fulfil my legal obligations under the Affidavit to financially support Ohan during the obligation period which could be for a long time until he became a U.S. citizen. This would be at least five years after he met the U.S. residency requirement as a Green Card holder or until he found financial means of his own to live. Morally, I wanted the sibling I sponsored to be reunited as a member of my extended family in my new homeland.

Strangely enough, even though I filed the petitions for Ohan and Swati simultaneously at the same INS office and under the same Preference category, my sister's date of approval of petition was three months later than my brother's. I was notified of her approval on July 9, 1977. As I was very busy finishing up my last set of summer courses in law at Temple and getting ready to have my household moved to San Diego, I held off sending the Affidavit of Support for Swati until after I settled down in San Diego.

At the completion of the academic year at Abington, I devised a plan to not tender my resignation from the tenured position that I had earned, even though I had accepted the position at General Dynamics starting in August. I wanted to hedge my bets against my successful continuation of law at the USD as well as my adaptability and capacity to lead in my new position at GD. I reasoned with myself that I would return to Temple to finish up my J.D. if things did not work out at USD, as I still had my tenured teaching job reserved for me at Abington. I also figured that if Rama were to pass her ECFMG examination, she most likely would have to return to the East for her Residency as California placed obstacles against foreign medical grads to do Residency in that state.

Accordingly, I notified Abington that "I taught at Abington High for more than five years. I am now a tenured member of your faculty. As I understand the policies of the Abington School District, I believe I now qualify for a year of sabbatical. I plan to take my sabbatical for a year beginning with the school year of 1977-'78." Abington agreed. I told my department head and colleagues that I decided to take my wife away from the cold winters of Philadelphia and continue my law study in San Diego.

In late July, the movers came to our apartment, wrapped up our meager possessions, and packed them in cardboard boxes for delivery to our new home in San Diego. That evening, we stayed with Ann and Len in King of Prussia. Their son and daughter were now off to college and they had become empty nesters. As always, they were happy to host us and continued to treat me as their eldest son. We decided to leave before dawn the next morning and drive cross country to the West Coast. Without awakening Ann and Len, we quietly left at 5:00 a.m. and drove on the Pennsylvania Turnpike heading west to Pittsburg.

I wanted to stop at the Hindu temple of Lord *Venkateshwara* that was under construction in Pittsburgh, Pennsylvania. Rama was not a devotee. She had visited many Hindu temples in India when she was a student. However, Rama told me she did not believe in God.

I asked Rama, "Would you like to stop at the Pittsburg temple?"

She responded, "Sure, if you like to. However, I am wearing jeans."

I asked, "Is there a rule against wearing jeans to a temple?" and laughed.

She did not reply but smiled.

I added, "I do not believe so."

Rama followed my faith out of respect for me. The temple was partially built and was open for worship. It was perched on the top of a mountain. Its positioning somewhat reminded me of the original temple for the same God that was built on the Seven Hills in Tirupathi, India. That was a temple where I had worshipped and developed immense faith.

Rama and I had stopped at the Pittsburg temple at midday. We purchased the traditional basket comprised of an unbroken coconut, bananas, beetle leaves and flowers for the temple priest to offer to the Lord. The priest broke open the coconut and offered it to the God while uttering sacred mantras in Sanskrit. After a vegetarian lunch at the temple, we jumped into our vehicle and headed through the flat lands of Ohio.

At one of the rest stops in Ohio, I took photos of Rama chewing on the tender meat of the fresh coconut on a shell that we had collected from the temple's priest.

I joked with her: "You are chewing the coconut like a monkey."

She quickly replied, "Then you are a monkey, too. You are my husband!"

Simple mischievous exchanges like this were an integral part of my life with Rama.

We hopped back into the car and drove to the outskirts of Chicago where we stayed overnight. Early next morning we re-started our 2,200-mile journey to San Diego not directly, but in a somewhat circuitous path. I wanted to see the Mount Rushmore National Park in South Dakota. It took another day of driving to get nearby where we stayed the second night. The next morning, we proceeded to Mt. Rushmore in the Black Hills in Keystone, South Dakota. The sculptures carved into the granite face of Mount Rushmore of 60-foot heads of four United States presidents—George Washington, Thomas Jefferson, Theodore Roosevelt and Abraham Lincoln—was awe-inspiring. Mount Rushmore had become an iconic symbol of the United States, and that was one of the reasons I wanted to see it. Another reason was that the memorial was famously used as the location of the climactic chase scene in Alfred Hitchcock's 1959 movie *North by Northwest* which I enjoyed seeing as an undergrad in Bangalore.

After spending the morning in the Black Hills, we drove

through Billings and Butte in Montana and headed south to Yellowstone National Park which spanned the states of Montana, Wyoming and Idaho. We went to this first national park in the U.S. to see its wildlife and its many geothermal features, especially the Old Faithful geyser which erupted every ninety minutes. We waited to see the Old Faithful in full action as it gushed out spewing warm mineral water out of the earth. We enjoyed driving through the South-Central Rockies' supine forests and headed down south to Salt Lake City in Utah.

Rama's best friend, who bore the same first name as hers, had been her high school classmate. She was now doing her medical residency in Salt Lake City. That city was going to be our rest stop for a few days. Having not seen her for years, Rama wanted to spend some time with her. It was on the third day of our long trip that we reached Salt Lake City. I previously had met her friend's husband Velu at our wedding. He happened to be in India at the time of our wedding and attended the ceremony in Guntur. He was a chemist working toward his Ph.D. at Brigham Young University in Salt Lake City.

It was a relaxing stay in Salt Lake City. In Utah, we saw sights like the famous Mormon Temple, the BYU campus, and some of the spectacular area mountains. Rama decided to stay with her friend in Salt Lake City for a week or so. I drove alone to San Diego on a route that took me through the Sin City of Las Vegas, Nevada. Finally reaching my destination, I checked into the Holiday Inn in the Mission Valley area in San Diego.

On the morning of Monday August 8, 1977, I reported to work at the Convair Division of General Dynamics Corporation in

Kearny Mesa, located in the central part of San Diego. I signed the required employment-related documents including the Invention Agreements and the Employees Savings and Stock Investment Plan Trust as requested by the General Dynamics HR representative.

Following this signing, I was led to Mel Campbell who I hadn't seen since the interview. Mel was a short gentleman with a crew cut and wore glasses. He had on a short-sleeved shirt and trousers. He seemed serious in his demeanor. I followed him to the Physical Properties Laboratory a block away in an adjacent building from his office.

There, he introduced me to all of the technicians and engineers in the lab who reported to him like I did, announcing, "Meet TR. He will be working with all of you." He added: "T.R. will be the lead engineer in the Lab."

The engineers had desks inside the lab amidst all sorts of measuring, testing and design hardware equipment. The technicians did not have desks. My desk was situated at a corner of the lab where the traffic was minimal, and I had privacy and the least noise to distract me.

Mel asked me to take care of my personal matters as the first order of business, like finding an apartment, bringing my better half to San Diego, getting my California Driver's license, registering with the voter's bureau, etc.

However, I immediately launched into my new job. I wanted to know the recent history of the Convair Division. A technician in my lab, Bob Wilson, who was active in the Hourly Employees Union at General Dynamics, took me on a tour of the sprawling campus. He led me to a large warehouse with a lofty ceiling where gigantic Atlas rockets that were in the design and development phase were stationed erect on the test pads. Some rockets were being tested by injecting liquid nitrogen and white gaseous vapors emanated from them.

Bob explained, "The Convair is an independent division under the umbrella of General Dynamics Corporation. This division made military jets for the U.S. Air Force until a few months ago. That plane business was moved to another division in Fort Worth, Texas. Convair now has shifted into space and missile development. The cruise missile program is now our main business here. We build the long-range all-weather and subsonic Tomahawk cruise missiles for the U.S. Navy and the Royal Navy. The cruise missiles carry conventional and nuclear warheads."

The projects that I was assigned to handle as the lead engineer involved establishing the physical, mechanical, hygroscopic and thermal properties of certain classified and unclassified materials intended for the building of Tomahawk cruise missiles and in certain classified space-based missions. One of the unclassified set of materials that I was asked to study were various carbon-fiber composite materials which were lightweight and yet as strong as steel. The classified materials posed a real challenge to me despite my well-rounded foundation in nuclear, optical and solid-state physics. I was essentially asked to discover a material with the following properties: zero thermal coefficient of expansion, zero hygroscopic variation, structurally stable in its shape, ultra-lightweight and strong as steel. These various material requirements were indeed daunting to meet. In the months following this assignment, I was consumed with research in theoretical and experimental aspects of the physics of materials.

One evening in mid-August, I stopped by the Dean's office at the University of San Diego Law School to find out about the status of my admission. Assistant Dean Doris Alspaugh informed me that the Law School granted me admission for the academic year 1977-78 as a Special Student and advised that I make arrangements to pay a flat fee for tuition for the upcoming semester and enroll in the courses that I wanted to select.

As advised by Mel, I took a few days off and drove back to Salt Lake City. Rama looked rested and relaxed after a week's stay with her classmate in Salt Lake City. Over the weekend, we drove to San Diego passing through the blistering heat in the desert area around Las Vegas, Nevada.

Rama instantly fell in love with San Diego. We stayed at a multi-storied hotel in Mission Valley. When I went to work, she would walk in the perfect weather of San Diego to the mall and plaza in the Valley.

We together looked at a number of apartments to rent. Since I was anticipating the arrival of my brother and sister from India, we decided to rent a unit with at least two bedrooms so that they could stay with us and share the second bedroom. We found an ideal apartment on Claremont Drive, which was convenient to General Dynamics and USD. It was located on the second floor with the bedroom windows facing west. The view from both bedrooms was spectacular—of the gorgeous Mission Bay. At sunset, the bay was mesmerizing with many sailboats floating by and the brilliant red and orange sun being swallowed by blue water.

We quickly settled into our apartment. This included purchasing extra beds, dressers and other furniture for the relatives I was sponsored for immigration to the U.S.

It was at this time that we came to know some news about Rama's sister Arna. Her sister was also a physician and I had helped her in April 1977 by paying the application fee for her to take her ECFMG examination in Manilla, Philippines. She suddenly had become married. We knew that Rama's parents were looking for a groom for their second daughter. Rama's mother previously requested that we be on the lookout for a groom for Arna who lived in the U.S. Her wedding had taken place when we were travelling from Philadelphia to San Diego and my in-laws had no means to contact us. We came to know that the man Arna married was also a physician who was presently working as an Anesthesiologist in a hospital in St. Louis, Missouri.

When Rama finally contacted her parents, we received details about this unexpected and quick marriage. The groom had gone to India on a visit to find a bride to marry. When he met Arna, they liked each other and abruptly decided to marry. The wedding itself was simple without the elaborate traditional wedding rituals that Rama and I went through. It was a simple exchange of fresh flower garlands and the tying of the *managala sutram* (the sacred thread). The groom, who was from India and had a U.S. Green Card, sponsored his new bride for her Green Card to the U.S. right after the wedding and returned to St. Louis.

This surprising news, although disappointing to Rama as she could not attend the wedding of her only sister, thrilled us both because her sister would soon be arriving to live in the U.S. That meant Rama could see Arna and meet her new husband and endlessly converse with her on the phone in real time. To me, it was a good sign that her close sibling made her way into the United States so soon after Rama's own arrival.

I signed up for courses at USD in Labor Law, Taxation, and Federal Government Contracts for the fall semester of 1977-78. These courses satisfied the minimum required credit hours that the Dean at Temple Law School stipulated. As the tuition at USD was steep compared to what I paid at Temple, I took a student loan for the required tuition by executing a promissory note with the University. As required, I formally notified the Dean at Temple of the courses that I was enrolled in at USD and received his approval.

The law classes at USD were quite different from those I was used to at Temple Law School. First, the doors to the classrooms were kept wide open to receive the cool air from the pleasant San Diego outdoors. The law school building did not require air-conditioning. The students, especially the males, were invariably unkempt and dressed in shorts, T-shirts and flip flops as though they just returned from a day at the beach. Not a single student was in a suit, which was common attire with the students that attended Temple Evening Law School. The professors were also lackadaisical in their approach to teaching. The Socratic Method was not practiced by many. They appeared to be courtroom lawyers or practicing professionals in a law firm or a corporate entity who taught part-time at the Law School. I was amused by the stark difference between the East Coast and West Coast law schools, but I chugged along with the legal education that I received.

Rama was very comfortable with the beautiful climate of San Diego. From our apartment, she walked to the supermarket situated just a couple of blocks away to do food shopping. The immense variety of vegetables and fresh fruit available in this California supermarket thrilled her. She stocked up our kitchen. A public library, which was also close by, kept her occupied. She loved to read mystery novels. She devoured a large novel in a matter of a couple of days. When she got bored at home, Rama sought a change of scenery and parked herself in the library where she read her medical books to prepare for her ECFMG examination.

Under pressure from me and persuasion from her father, who continued to regularly write to Rama, she signed up to take the next scheduled ECFMG examination on January 25, 1978 in Los Angeles, California.

During weekends I regularly went to the USD Law Library to prepare for the assignments for the next week's classes. Rama occasionally joined me in the Law Library with her medical books. During the weekends, we went to see some of the area's tourist sites, like Sea World, Wild Animal Park in Escondido, the shoreline of La Jolla, Old Town in San Diego's downtown area, and Tijuana, Mexico across the U.S.-Mexico border.

It was time that Rama learned to drive. The California Department of Motor Vehicles administered driver's licenses by requiring every driver to complete a three-part test: knowledge, vision and behind-the wheel. Rama easily passed the written test after studying *The California Driver Handbook* about road rules and regulations. After she passed that part, I attempted to teach the rudiments of driving our car in an empty and deserted parking lot. However, that was a bad idea. As she attempted to drive, we both got frustrated with each other.

I decided to enroll her in a driving course with an instructor. He trained her for ten hours by taking her on the road and instilling confidence that she was capable of driving in California. After he pronounced that she was ready, we went to have Rama take the behind-the-wheel driver's test.

First, the location of the test was in a remote place quite far away. Second, I made the mistake of scheduling the time for her test on a late weekday afternoon. I asked her to drive to get a warm-up before taking the driver's test. As Rama drove in the heavy rush-hour traffic, she got tense. From the tension, she had developed a splitting headache.

During the behind-the wheel test, the examiner, who was a police officer, sat in the front seat next to Rama and asked her to perform certain driving maneuvers. I watched them from a distance. The examiner asked her to parallel park, pull up on the right, reverse for two car lengths and rejoin the traffic, maneuver a turn in the road, etc. When the testing was all done, which lasted for forty minutes, the officer pronounced that she had passed. After that, Rama easily passed the vision test and qualified for her first-ever driver's license.

After returning home, over a glass of Chardonnay, we laughed at this experience of Rama earning her driver's license.

Now it was time to attend to my sister Swati in India who I sponsored for her Green Card. We had received her visa number from the State Department. It was time to fulfill my obligation to the U.S. Government by furnishing my Affidavit of Support for her benefit. I filled out the prescribed Form I-134 and gathered a letter of employment from GD and a statement from the bank where I newly had opened an account. I had the Affidavit notarized and mailed it in early September 1977 to the U.S. Consulate in Madras, India.

By signing the Affidavits of Support, I accepted my responsibility to financially support Swati, like I did a few months earlier for Ohan, until she found employment in the United States and was able to stand on her own feet.

In October, Ohan made his way into the United States by arriving on a flight from Bombay to Los Angeles. Rama and I greeted him at LAX airport with big smiles and my handshake which was a "welcome to America." I drove him to our simple abode on Claremont Drive in San Diego to share our life with him.

My brother Ohan was now a Green Card-holding permanent resident of the United States, a situation many foreigners only dream of. He was on the precipice of writing his own destiny.

However, my brother was somewhat timid and not driven. The new country to which he had immigrated intimidated him. He was unprepared for the foreign culture and fast pace of life. He probably never fathomed that he would land in the United States. He would have never come to this country if I had not opened the door for him to enter. He could not dream big and drive himself to achieve that dream, even if he had remained in India. As has often been said, you can only lead the horse to water, you cannot make him drink the water.

Nevertheless, I was very supportive of him. I wanted to lead by example by the manner in which I was conducting my life with a full-time job during the day and evening study toward my law degree. He also watched Rama clinging to her medical books and study for her examination.

I guided my brother as to how to look for jobs and apply for them. Finding a suitable job even for an accomplished engineer was a slow process. The fact that his degree was from a university in India did not help. Some employers were reluctant to lend credence to a degree earned from a foreign country. I suggested that he should go to school and earn a degree from a university based in San Diego, as that would improve his chances of finding a job. I explained that such a job based on an American degree could pay more than the job he might find solely based on his current degree.

Ohan expected me to find him a job at General Dynamics. I explained, "My employer hires only U.S. citizens. Over and above this, a security clearance to handle highly sensitive military projects at GD is mandatory, and you do not qualify." Ohan did not appreciate my reasoning and probably concluded that I was unwilling to help him find a job at GD. Being fresh off the plane from India, he thought that an employed person would help other people, especially his brother, to find a position with the same employer. I explained to Ohan that "such paternalism seldom has a place in the U.S., at least at the lower levels of society that we are in."

Ohan was an introvert and not very communicative. I could never understand what he was thinking. Nevertheless, he relentlessly pursued technical employment no matter how minor the job was.

It was in the later part of the year when Rama's sister called us from St. Louis about visiting. She had already immigrated to the U.S. She and her husband wanted to come over the Thanksgiving holidays. We wholeheartedly welcomed such a visit and were eager to meet her husband.

Their visit was a welcome relief from the day-to-day pressures that we faced. We spent quality time showing them the attractions and sites in San Diego. Rama's husband was friendly and spoke in Telugu for the most part. When he spoke in English, one couldn't help noticing that he had a heavy Indian accent. He attributed his accent to the village where he was born in India and the non-English speaking school he attended when he was a child. Although he earned his medical degree from a large city in India, his accent was already well-ingrained, and he was unable to get rid of it. In fact, one of the first compliments I received from him was "You speak excellent English with little Indian accent. I know of no one among my Indian colleagues who speak so well." I explained the years of effort I put into cultivating my English.

The highlight of their visit was an adventure that we unknowingly embarked on. We decided to rent a motorized raft with a flat tin roof on Mission Bay. The four of us ventured out into the bay of the Pacific Ocean. No driver from the boat rental accompanied us on the raft. None of us knew swimming in case of an emergency. In fact, Rama and Arna wore beautiful silk sarees in which it would have been impossible to swim. The rental company did not advise us on the use of the flotation devices, either. Despite taking this risk out of ignorance, we had a wonderful time for hours driving the rickety motorized raft in and out of the waters of the bay. The dark seals slipped in and out of the cool and calm waters and at places climbed on rocks to dry off their whiskered faces. We took a number of photos to capture the delightful moments of our adventure.

The beautiful sarees that the two sisters wore attracted many people in the places that we visited that day. The people could not help noticing how pretty they looked, particularly when we walked along the manicured lawns at the coves in La Jolla. Some admiringly asked me, "Are they were twin sisters?"

Now that Rama's sister also got married and made her way into the United States, I thought how lucky my father-in-law was. He was now completely unburdened from the shackle of dowry payments for his daughters. I admired his investment in his daughters to educate them as doctors. This investment served two purposes at the same time. He invested in their career, which made them self-dependent for life. Second, he made them lucrative enough to attract viable grooms, both permanently living in the U.S., and to wed without the demand of a dowry.

I could not again help comparing my father's undisciplined strategy, if he had a strategy at all. He was burdened with four unmarried daughters, whose dowry he needed to now manage as they reached marriageable age. In a way, he should have been thankful that his dowry payment for Jaya was taken care of by her plot to elope with Raj, no matter how despicable that plot seemed at first. He still had no idea that I would address his main concern of paying for the dowry for his remaining daughters, as I never told him of my plan. However, with my sponsorship of Swati to immigrate to the U.S., he must have been relieved that I was taking an active role to remove from his hair a daughter who developed independent thinking and defied listening to him.

Ohan continued to look for a job in San Diego. I gave many pointers to him on how to look for and apply for positions. The main way that was available to him for seeking jobs was to look for advertisements in the local newspaper to determine whether any of the advertised jobs matched his qualifications and experience and then apply. I gave him my typewriter to prepare his resume and customized cover letters to employers who advertised job openings. Months passed by, and he received no positive replies for the letters he wrote. It was frustrating for him and for me as well.

In December, I focused on studying for the finals of the courses I had enrolled in, while continuing to work full-time at GD and meet the demands of my boss. I did well in the finals and satisfied my residency point requirement laid down by the Associate Dean at Temple Law School.

Meanwhile Rama intensified her study for the ECFMG, which was only about a month away.

I did not get a long break from work at GD at Christmastime unlike when I was at Abington where I enjoyed nearly two weeks of holidays. Nevertheless, the spectacular weather in San Diego offered us a vacation almost every day to enjoy, while our relatives in St. Louis and friends in the East Coast were dealing with the snow and bitterly cold winter weather.

At the beginning of January 1978, Rama received her examination permit to take the ECFMG examination scheduled for January 26 that she previously signed up for. The designated examination center was at the Ambassador Hotel on Wilshire Boulevard in Los Angeles. This was the same hotel where five years earlier Robert F. Kennedy was assassinated right after he won the California primaries for the Democratic Party's nomination as the candidate for President. I narrated to Rama the tragedy of RFK's assassination, which gave her shivers. I drove Rama to the examination center the day before the exam and checked in to the hotel in the early afternoon and stayed with her. I pleaded with Rama to relax and get a good night's sleep so she would be refreshed to take the examination the next morning. However, she pulled an all-nighter to brush up on the clinical studies she might have missed.

The next morning after breakfast, she took the ECFMG examination with more than a hundred other foreign medical graduates. As before, the examination had two components: the English language skill test which she already passed and the test on the knowledge of medicine.

At the end of the day, Rama was not sure whether she had passed. However, she said that the postgraduate FLEX review course that she had completed earlier in Philadelphia was of some help. She had to wait for six to seven weeks to find out the results of her performance in the ECFMG. Yet completing the examination took a load off her.

I signed up for a new set of law courses for my second semester at USD, totaling 10 credit hours in Admiralty, Business Planning, Education and an Environmental Law Seminar. The tuition was again well over a thousand dollars which I paid in cash this time.

At work, I delved into the research of materials for optical applications, such as laser mirrors based in a low-gravity and low-temperature environment of the earth's outer space, and behavior of carbon composites at normal and cryogenic temperatures as a base of support for the optical coatings.

Swati, the sister that I previously sponsored for the Green Card, finally made her entry into the United States. On February 11, 1978 Swati landed at the Los Angeles International Airport, arriving from Bangalore. Rama, Ohan and I drove to LAX and picked her up with smiles and like with Ohan I extended a hand welcoming Swati to her new homeland.

I was not sure whether she appreciated the rare gift that I had bestowed on her in the form of the Green Card. I refrained from talking about the magnitude of this gift, lest she and Ohan might think that I was exaggerating what I did for them. I never expected gratitude because I never wanted to be disappointed when it was not expressed. I believed that gratitude cannot exist without deprivation.

Back then, it could be easy to forget at times that millions of people around the world were struggling to come to this country and become a part of the United States. Some never received an opportunity. Others would have to wait for many years for their turn to lawfully enter. Even after a long wait, they might be disqualified to enter this country. That is how the immigration process worked in the U.S.

I made it so easy for my siblings when I sponsored them as a U.S. citizen. However, my citizenship did not come easily. It required many trials, tribulations and much patience to earn it.

My sister Swati moved in with us and like my brother Ohan, she immediately started looking for a job. I advised that she should apply for a technician job at the Scripps Clinic in Torrey Pines in San Diego. I told Swati that "Scripps is a research institution and is now conducting research in biochemistry. Your previous experience as a bio-technician at the Indian Institute of

Science might help you find a similar job at the Clinic." She took my advice and applied without waiting for an advertisement by Scripps for such an opening.

In parallel, Raj, who had contacts at the University of California, Irvine, put her in contact with a biochemist who had unspent grant money from the National Institutes of Health. That avenue which she pursued immediately bore fruit. She went for an interview in mid-March and was hired soon thereafter by Dr. Eloy Rodriguez in the Department of Ecology & Evolutionary Biology at UC, Irvine as a Laboratory Assistant.

I wanted Ohan and Swati to integrate into the American economy and social fabric. I wanted them to buy into the American dream by finding a good job, earning a degree from a U.S. school, and advancing in their careers. I told them: "The opportunities for growth and personal enrichment that America offers to you are endless. Don't waste your time."

My brother went with Swati to Tustin in Orange County to see whether he would have better luck in finding employment there. Sure enough, after a couple of weeks of trying, Ohan also found employment. He was hired at the WEI Corporation in Santa Ana, California, beginning work on April 4, 1978. I called and congratulated both of them for finding their first Jobs in America. I told them that "landing your first job in the U.S. is so critical and important. It will serve as a steppingstone to climb higher for better jobs soon."

Another piece of even better news that we received in late March was that Rama passed her ECFMG examination. Rama and I were just ecstatic at her marvelous feat. Her success only reinforced my faith that she was well on the track to become a licensed physician in the U.S. She immediately called her sister Arna in St. Louis and conveyed the news, and Arna, in turn, notified their parents and siblings in India. I conveyed the news to Ohan and Swati now living in Irvine, California and notified my family back in Bangalore by a letter.

Passing of the ECFMG satisfied the prerequisite for appointment to accredited Medical Education Programs in the United States, including Internship and Residency. However, California Medical Programs had a catch-22 requirement that a foreign medical graduate must have completed Internship in another U.S. state to qualify for a Residency Program in California. This requirement essentially forced Rama to seek her Residency in the Eastern or Midwestern region of the United States.

Rama's sister had passed the ECFMG examination the previous year in Manila in the Philippines. She already had lined up her Residency in Internal Medicine in the St. Louis area. Her husband, with the physician contacts he had, was instrumental in lining up the Residency for his wife.

Medical education programs for new residents generally started in July. Most applicants for medical Residency in a specialty of their choosing use the National Resident Matching Program (NRMP), which matched the applicant with a hospital having an available vacancy. The deadline for filing the application with NRMP was generally at the end of September of the previous year. The Matching Program was usually completed by mid-March. However, Rama—who did not participate in the NRMP—could apply for any unfilled Residency positions after mid-March.

Through her sister, Rama came to know that the University of Missouri Teaching Hospital in Columbia had an unexpected vacancy in the specialty of Physical Medicine and Rehabilitation starting in early July. Columbia was only 120 miles from St. Louis, which was a plus for her as Rama could see her sister more often if she were to get into this Residency program. She net-worked with other residents who had completed their Residency in this specialty. They spoke positively about specializing in PMNR and convinced her that the Residency would be a breeze and she should apply. Rama applied for this vacancy and she was accepted.

I was so pleased that everything was falling in place so neatly and somewhat unexpectedly. I thanked God and renewed my faith in Lord *Venkateshwara* whose temple in Pittsburgh Rama and I had visited the previous August. However, the impending separation from Rama did not appeal to me one bit. Such separation was going to be hard for both of us, particularly for Rama who would be living alone in Columbia. However, I came to the conclusion that our separation would be only for a short period. I figured that as soon as I earned my J.D. degree, which would be in less than a year after she moved, I would find a position as a lawyer close to Columbia and we would be reunited.

Now that the two siblings that I had sponsored found jobs that paid for their living, I wanted to sponsor my last two sisters. They were both now pursuing their bachelor's degrees in Bangalore. This move was consistent with my master plan. I contacted my sisters Mini and Mala about my intention to file the petitions and asked them to send me copies of their birth certificates. Although Mala was exuberant, Mini was ambivalent about the idea of migrating to the U.S. I was puzzled by Mini's attitude. I knew all along that she was undisciplined and disorganized. Moreover, she was a dreamer. Neither my parents nor anyone else back home could explain Mini's reluctance to get sponsored for her Green Card.

I suspected that Mini and Mala were fun-loving and had their eyes wide open for young men. Perhaps Mini was presently involved romantically with a boy who my parents and other siblings living at home did not know about?

Certainly, Mini did not provide me with a valid reason for turning down my offer to sponsor her for the Green Card. However, her reluctance to immigrate threw a monkey wrench in my master plan. Nevertheless, I marched on and sponsored Mala by filling out and submitting the petition on April 18, 1978 at the Immigration & Naturalization Services office in downtown San Diego. I requested in my petition that the beneficiary be approved for permanent visa under the classification of 203(a) (5).

My petition was approved in my presence on the same day. Like I did before, I prepared, signed and had notarized my Affidavit of Support. I gathered the supporting documents of a letter of my employment from GD and a statement from my bank identifying my personal bank account balance. In addition, I made a declaration that "I will undertake to bear the cost of Mala's passage from India to the USA and provide for her during her stay in the U.S. and to repatriate her to India at any cost if necessary." I mailed these documents to the U.S. Consulate in Madras, India in June 1978.

It was mid-May when Rama went to see her sister in St Louis who was now expecting her first child. She went there also to meet with the Program Director of the Physical Medicine and

Rehabilitation Residency at the University of Missouri and to line up a rental apartment with a lease beginning in July.

It was also the time for taking the finals for my law courses. I decided to take a couple of days off and study at home for the finals. That's when my phone rang. A pleasant-sounding lady from the Human Resources Department at the Scripps Clinic identified herself and asked to speak to my sister. Swati had previously sent a letter to Scripps Clinic expressing interest in an unsolicited and unadvertised position at the Clinic. I introduced myself as her brother and said that my sister was unavailable at the moment. The lady conveyed that if my sister was still interested in working for Scripps, she should get in touch with her for an in-person interview. Immediately I called my sister in Irvine and suggested that she should line up the interview at Scripps and pursue this job. I advised that Scripps Clinic was a private and well-funded research facility as opposed to her project at UC Irvine which depended on annual NIH grant money.

The following week my sister attended the job interview at Scripps Clinic at Torrey Pines and soon thereafter she received a job offer as a Research Technician. The salary at Scripps was much higher than her current job as a Lab Assistant II at UC Irvine. She accepted the new job and moved back to San Diego and resumed living with Rama and me.

I thought that my presence at home on that weekday day in May when the phone rang was fortuitous for Swati to have landed her dream job at Scripps. Previously I had urged her to write to Scripps asking for a possible job opening for a person with her experience. It felt good that I helped my sister find this employment and she was now all set to have a dependable and successful career in the United States, particularly in beautiful San Diego.

I passed my finals and earned good grades as hoped. As a matter of routine, I notified the Dean at Temple Law School about the status of completion regarding my second batch of courses at USD.

The time was approaching to make a decision on renewing the lease for our apartment, and I decided to look for a house to own. I wanted to buy a brand-new house in the San Diego area, which was a sleepy town without much traffic and well-laid-out freeway and road systems. At first, Rama and I worked with a realtor to look at homes that were available for resale in Tierrasanta, Miramar, University Park, Rancho Bernardo, Del Mar, Carlsbad, Encinitas and other areas of San Diego, but we did not find anything that we could afford or fell in love with.

New housing developments were cropping up all over San Diego County. We looked at such developments. Rama and I liked one particular housing development in Rancho Peñasquitos north of downtown San Diego. This housing development in Penasquitos was convenient to Kearny Mesa where General Dynamics was located and was less than five miles away along the I-15 Freeway. We went to see the model homes that were already built in this development. We liked the terrain and the ability to pick the location of our house from the available home sites and the type, size and price of the house we could build on this site. I believed that the house should face east for good fortune. We made the decision to buy a house with four bedrooms, two and half baths, a two-car garage, a bonus room atop the garage with a nice picture window—all adding up to 3,200 square feet. The price was $75,000.

I wanted to own a house in San Diego for several reasons. First, San Diego was a highly desirable city. The weather was perfect, 365 days a year. The economy was booming with many businesses catering to the Defense Establishment as well as the private sector. A ballot decision, called Proposition 13, was in place by which the voters in the November elections could limit the maximum value of taxes on real estate to 1% of the purchase price of the property. If Proposition 13 passed, then it meant that the property taxes on this house will be limited to $750/year no matter how long I held on to this house.

I wanted to own a large house so the siblings I sponsored for Green Cards could live with me in the same household as a family unit. This would substantially minimize their rental expenses as I would continue to subsidize their housing expenses. Also, I wanted to own a house since I had ambitious plans to sponsor my other unmarried sisters in India. In my mind, I kept open the possibility of sponsoring my parents to immigrate to the U.S. at the appropriate time when all of their daughters got married and lived with their husbands in their own homes.

We decided to put down 20% of the house price as a down payment and apply for a mortgage. The mortgage officer examined my loan application. He hesitated to loan us $60,000 based on my salary alone. When Rama and I met with him at his bank's office, he said, "If you could increase your down payment to 30%, the bank would be able to give you a mortgage."

I replied, "No. For tax reasons, I do not want to increase my down payment."

He was pondering whether to reject my loan request.

Rama's mind went into problem-solving mode. She stepped into the discussion and said, "I am a doctor. I will be able to produce a letter from the University of Missouri, where I soon will be a Resident Physician. The letter will state my gross stipend. Would this help us qualify for the mortgage we applied for?"

The mortgage officer stood up and proclaimed, "Excellent! Why didn't you tell us you are a doctor in the first place? This changes everything."

Within days after I furnished the letter from UMMC that Rama had promised the officer, we qualified for the mortgage.

The house, which was not yet built, was scheduled for completion in late June. I pleaded with the developer to have the house built and made ready for our move in before June, as Rama was scheduled to start her Residency in Columbia in early June. Being the first house that we owned, I wanted Rama to be with me to make the *gruhapravesam pooja*—which is a ceremony done before moving into a new house to cleanse the place from evil forces. Such *pooja* is believed by Hindus to bring good fortune. However, by the time the house was ready to move into, Rama already had moved to Columbia and could not join in the *pooja*.

By this time, my brother, who had been working in Santa A na, managed to find a job in San Diego with Cubic Corporation. He once again moved back into our apartment on Claremont Drive. After Rama left for Columbia, my siblings and I vacated our apartment and moved into the new house on the last day of June 1978. We rented a U-Haul truck to move our furniture and other possessions.

After moving in, I asked my sister to light up the kitchen stove and then in a pot boil milk till it slightly overflowed. After this, I asked her to put some rice in the pot, cook it and make the sweet-rice preparation of *payasam* which we all shared. This was our simple *gruhapravesam* ceremony.

In the new house, each of us had a bedroom to sleep in. Compared to the apartment we just had left, this house was huge with two levels. Everything looked clean and smelled fresh, including the wood that was extensively utilized to build it. In addition to my bedroom, I utilized the den downstairs as my study. I quickly acquired a used washer and dryer set and I had it installed in the garage where the hook-up plugs, and accessories were placed.

The houses in the subdivision were tiered. There was just one house above the tier where the base of our house was located. In California, it was customary to have fences erected on three sides of the house except the front side. My neighbor on the upper tier, who already had moved in before us, had erected a wooden fence separating his lot from ours. What remained to be built were the fences on the back and on the side of our other neighbor the tier below. In the next few weeks, I ordered the wood planks and posts to build the fence and with help from Ohan, we fenced off the two sides.

There was no need for me to take law courses in the summer of 1978. I already had earned 67 credit hours from the law schools of Temple and USD combined. I needed to earn only 16 more credits from USD in the remaining two semesters of my fourth year of law in order to graduate. I already had planned out the courses that I would enroll in for the academic year 1978-79. I decided to sign up for 17 credits, one more than the 83 credits hours needed just to be doubly sure that the Dean(s) at either law school did not miscount or misstate the credits I needed to graduate. Not taking courses in the evening and slaving the weekends in the law library was a reprieve that summer.

I dedicated all energy to my work and observed various aspects of the defense contractor I worked for. The unionized technicians did not apply themselves with dedication to their jobs. They waited to put in their minimum required hours and promptly quit after logging in their hours. The junior engineers were also not devoted to their jobs. They frequently ran personal errands during the work hours and got away without being noticed by their superiors. There was a waste of resources as many of the contracted projects never materialized. People at my level were more dependable. However, in talking with them, I came to know that I was being significantly underpaid. This bothered me as I believed that Mel Campbell was a fair man and that he had paid me commensurate with my level of education.

While I was facing this frustration, General Dynamics announced a special intensive program to broaden careers of hardware engineers by acquiring on-the-job training in computer software sciences. The memo that was openly circulated proclaimed that General Dynamics had a special need for engineers all the way up to the doctoral level who were trained in two or more professions or intellectual disciplines. It further stated that the program would be fast track and would challenge the participants both mentally and physically. It was likely that not everyone would be able to do it, the memo warned. However, the memo also stated, "Those who succeed in mastering the software skills to combine with their engineering skills would be eligible for some of the most meaningful and important career assignments General Dynamics had to offer."

Being open for a challenge, I filled out the Candidate

Application and submitted it. I was immediately accepted into this training program, which started on July 1, 1978. I was one of ninety-six candidates that were selected out of seven hundred applicants.

It was an appropriate time to make this mid-career change within GD. Days before I was accepted to the software training program, Mel had made a formal appraisal of my job which was great, but the salary increase I received was essentially a cost of living increase. Following that miniscule raise I received, I felt no allegiance to Mel and was in fact glad to change my job assignments without changing my employer.

The Software Engineering Professional Development Program lasted for seventy-three days with an extensive curriculum. The curriculum was extensive. It covered digital computer concepts, fundamentals of computer language, structured design & documentation, Fortran and Basic programming languages, structured programming & testing, life cycle development, interactive terminal/control cards, PDF-11 assembly language, and microprocessors & microcomputer. I continued my law study at USD while receiving this professional training at GD.

I never had formal training in software engineering. This course was an excellent addition to my knowledge of how to write the code. It was like going back to school and learning a new discipline which complemented my knowledge of hardware techniques. All in all, I was pleased with taking it. I received a plaque in recognition of my successful completion of this development program.

During the Christmas Holidays, I visited Rama in Columbia. She could not take enough time off to visit her new home in San

Diego because of the tight schedule at the VA hospital. There she saw many injured veterans. Some of them were amputees and some others were severely injured on the battlefield requiring months or years of physical therapy in order to be rehabilitated to normal life. Rama narrated stories about the male patients, who were the majority at the VA hospital. Apparently, they looked forward to the young female doctor's visit to their wards and entreated her by calling her "Honey" and asking for favors.

I flew into St. Louis and Rama drove from Columbia to meet me at her sister's residence. I was so happy to be with Rama. During most of that Christmas and New Year's holiday season, it snowed incessantly in St Louis. We snugly remained in Arna's house with a number of other friends who also joined them to celebrate the holidays. After New Year's, Rama had to drive back over a hundred miles to Columbia on the frozen and slippery highway in her small car. I felt helpless that I could not drive her to Columbia but held tight until she reached her apartment and called me to inform of her safe arrival.

The software training took me well into the early spring of 1979. When I completed the training, my job title changed to Senior Software Engineer and I was assigned to the Global Positioning System project at General Dynamics. I was asked to redesign the code for the highly sophisticated GPS Kalman filtering algorithm—particularly, portions of the geopotential force model to improve the accuracy of satellite orbit predictions for Phase I of GPS. This was a lofty assignment and I made slow but steady strides to meet the challenges that were presented.

In my evening law-school studies, I successfully completed my seventh semester of coursework and finally entered into my last semester. Because of the financial commitment to my mortgage, I took a federally insured student loan to pay for the final two semesters of my law-school tuition. The set of electives that I enrolled in my last semester of law school did not demand too much of my time or attention. While regularly attending the classes and keeping up with the assignments, I was devoting time to look for a job as an attorney. I already had made up my mind that I would go into the specialty of Intellectual Property Law. So I contacted recruitment firms which specialized in placing patent lawyers, notably the Patent Placement Agency located in Carlsbad, California and headed by Bob Piehl. I did not want to work in a law firm but as an in-house counsel in an established U.S. corporation which was immersed in patent portfolio development. I also had decided that I would like to find a company based in the Midwest close to where Rama was employed so I could be with her on a regular basis.

In the meanwhile, in the spring of 1978, my youngest sister Mala was preparing to leave Bangalore to join me, Ohan and Swati. Although it was somewhat late, I rethought the idea of her entering the U.S. The truth was that she lacked work experience and she'd had less than a spectacular success in her undergraduate studies in India. I felt we should temporarily hold off her arrival because of an apprehension that I had developed about her finding suitable employment in the U.S. It took nearly six months for Ohan with a B.E. degree and years of work experience in India to find a job in the U.S.

When I notified Mala in India of my apprehension, my father got extremely angry. He demanded that I immediately send her the airline ticket and let her travel to the U.S. as originally planned. That demand only enhanced my apprehension. I thought perhaps my father was having trouble handling my rebellious youngest two sisters because of their by-then well-known romantic interest in boys. Certainly, if there was truth to the stories, I did not want to deal with this when my sister Mala arrived in the U.S. The peer pressure to socialize with and date boys was more pronounced here.

Once again, I thought that my father was not being reasonable. He did not want to listen to the point of view of others. My father never consumed alcohol. It was against Hindu practice. He was always sober but sometimes ill-tempered. He had gotten away with his dominance over my mother and with mistreating relatives from her side of the family and entreating relatives from his side of the family. Perhaps, he actually believed he was always right. I could not help recalling an incident that happened between my parents when I was seven. As my mother narrated the incident after it happened, one of my father's nephews (his sister's teenage son) visited our family in Kakinada. When my father was away at work, the nephew made some demands which my mother refused to meet. When my father arrived home, the nephew complained to him about my mother's refusal. Upon hearing this frivolous refusal, my father's temper flared, and he slapped her hard on her face in the presence of the visiting relative. She felt so humiliated by this incident that she was withdrawn for days. When she finally told me of this episode, I was unhappy. At that moment, I wished God magically could have made me big enough to jump between my parents and stop the slap.

I discussed my father's violent reaction to my intended temporary delay for Mala with my two siblings in the house and with Rama over the phone. It occurred to me that this might not go my way. I relented. I purchased an airline ticket and mailed it to Mala. She arrived in the fall of 1978 with a Green Card in her hand to join me, Ohan and Swati in this country. She shared a bedroom with Swati in my new house.

Since Ohan and Swati were working, they had to learn to drive which they did, and they also obtained their California driver's licenses. After initially depending on me for transportation to and from work, they purchased their own cars. Mala depended on her siblings for transportation since I left home early in the mornings for work and came back late after attending law school. Like I did with my brother Ohan and sister Swati, I encouraged Mala to find a job—any job—and acquire skills that she could use to find a better job.

Even though she was only twenty when she arrived in the U.S., Mala was intelligent and quick-witted. She was also slender and pretty. She spoke almost perfect English. All of these virtues helped her to land a job relatively quickly in the showroom of a company that sold pens. This was a good start for her to learn marketing and sales skills.

After Mala found employment, Swati used to drop her off in the morning at work on her way to her clinic. In the afternoon, since Mala finished work early, she took public transportation back. However, she needed to wait for the bus. Moreover, she had a long walk, albeit in the pleasant and warm San Diego climate, from where the bus dropped her off to go to our home. Occasionally, young Spanish-speaking boys offered to drive her home, which Mala took advantage of. During the weekend, these boys sometimes dropped by at our house to chat with Mala. Swati did not like these visits or the offers of rides from the boys. The two sisters used to have serious arguments over these incidents. This only reinforced my previous apprehension against bringing my youngest and still immature sister Mala into the U.S. I wanted her to be preoccupied with a tangible and meaningful pursuit.

I encouraged Mala and Ohan to enroll in a U.S. degree program in the evening school at San Diego State University or at another less-known local college. I advised that such a degree from a U.S. school would enable them to qualify for better paying jobs. They enrolled in some college-level courses but neither received a degree from a U.S. college.

Life is full of twists and turns. Nothing in life seems to be predictable no matter how carefully one plans events and works to attain them. I received a setback as I was looking for a job as a lawyer near Columbia to be close to Rama and give her support and encouragement to complete her three years of Residency in Physical Medicine. Rama indicated that she was not enjoying her Residency. She told me that the foul smells coming from the wounds of her VA patients repelled her and prevented her from functioning and carry out her duties. The foul smell upset her stomach. Despite advice from her colleagues who practiced in this specialty, she felt that it did not suit her. She mentioned again that she would rather do her Residency in a specialty like Dermatology.

This was a setback because in just a couple of months Rama would have completed her first of three years of Residency. A little bit of tolerance for the foul smells, which I expected would not last through the remaining years of her Residency program, was needed. I pointed out that the Rusk Rehabilitation Center of UMCM which hired her was bound to rotate her work to other hospitals rather than post her at the VA hospital permanently. She did not see the merit in my reasoning.

It looked as though she had made up her mind. I did not push Rama to stay and finish her Residency at UMCM. Rama's sister and her husband could not change her mind, either. I finally acquiesced and asked her to complete her first year of Residency at UMCM and at the end of June 1979 return home to San Diego.

I was beginning to receive overtures from NCR Corporation regarding hiring me as a Patent Attorney Trainee in the company's World Headquarter in Dayton, Ohio.

I wanted to graduate with my J.D. degree from Temple University as planned. I notified the Registrar at Temple of my intent to graduate in the spring of 1979. The Registrar said that before she could certify me for graduation, she would need an official copy of my transcript from USD. I arranged for this mailing.

Graduation was scheduled for May 24, 1979 in the Civic Center Convention Hall in Philadelphia. Earlier in March 1979, the Temple Law School's Associate Dean Diane Maleson urged me to attend the University Commencement as well as many festivities that were planned on the campus in conjunction with the graduation ceremony. My final semester of studies at USD was uneventful. I took my finals and passed them all, which fact was conveyed to Temple's Registrar who certified me for graduation.

Rama was unable to join me in Philadelphia as she already had notified UMCM of her intended resignation and was wrapping up to leave. I went alone to Philadelphia to participate in the Law School Commencement. It was an enjoyable reunion seeing many of my classmates from the first two years of my law study at Temple. I was happy to see Wendy and Yosh, who were in my study groups at Temple.

I asked Wendy, "Are you still on your course to be a Judge?"

She replied, "Yes, of course. I am clerking for a Judge in the Federal District Court in Philadelphia now."

I knew that the J.D. degree that I just had earned was going to be my last degree. I was completely satisfied and grateful that I had earned five degrees, three of them from Temple. I was fully satisfied that the personal career Plan B that I had orchestrated four or five years earlier was finally beginning to take shape. The change that I had initiated was to pursue a radically different career when I was a teacher. Then there was the subsequent maneuver to get on the career track of a Physicist and the marvelous opportunity to bend that track to a more desirable career as a Senior Software Engineer at General Dynamics. The law degree that I just had earned after four years of toil was bound to propel me into a new career orbit with glorious opportunities.

That evening after the Commencement Ceremony, I took Ann and Len Lovitz for a nice dinner to celebrate my graduation. I always associated my life in Philadelphia with the Lovitzes. They were a rock-solid moral force for me in my life ever since I first had arrived in the U.S. I could openly share with them my thoughts and feelings in all the years I was in Philadelphia and in my subsequent years as well. I cherished their counsel in the decisions that I made. Being physically near when I had lived in Philadelphia and available whenever I wanted to see them, they essentially became my parents by default. During our meal together, I thought about how the bonds that were established with them had become immutable. After dinner, I bid good-bye to Ann and Len and returned home to San Diego.

Rama returned to San Diego in early June. She left her car in St. Louis, and we made arrangement to have it shipped to San Diego. For the first time, Rama and the four of us from my side shared one house. Rama brought a lot of warmth and eased all of our lives at home. Her sense of humor and friendly and loving demeanor opened up the conversation among us. The completion of my law study alleviated the tenseness that I had suffered from for a long time. As a group, we took day trips to visit the movie studios in Hollywood, drove to Los Angeles to indulge in a good Indian meal at restaurants there and enjoyed other fun things. The summer of 1979 with my siblings and Rama was a happy time. I knew that we would never share those moments again, as I was looking for a job as a lawyer in another state and Rama and I would be leaving.

Normally, law graduates took the bar examination in the same state as the law school they graduated from. In my case, I went to two law schools. I received my law degree from a school in Pennsylvania, but I had no interest in being licensed in that state. Receiving my lawyer's license from California probably would have been wise. However, I was already thinking of moving back East or to the Midwest when Rama was engaged in her Residency in Missouri. As a result, I already had missed the application deadline to take the California bar examination in the summer of 1979.

Bob Piehl at the recruiting firm scheduled a personal interview with NCR Corporation, and he asked me to travel to Dayton, Ohio right after my graduation. I took a plane to NCR.

The Hiring Manager Philip Dalton, who invited me, had a

similar background as I did. He worked as an Engineer at AT&T, went to evening law school at night and became a Patent Attorney. He had been a Senior Patent Counsel at NCR for more than five years and was looking to fill two Junior Attorney openings under him. He was impressed with my education and experience. He drove me to Miamisburg on the south side of Dayton where NCR's center for design, development and manufacture of microelectronic chips was located. He said that if hired I would be working with the scientists, engineers and technicians at this center. I met a number of known inventors with advanced degrees in physics or electrical engineering as well as engineering managers who checked me out. After a nice lunch at NCR's wonderful cafeteria overlooking a beautiful golf course which included a put-put green, I met with other lawyers in the NCR Patent Department including the Chief Patent Counsel.

Phil laid out the requirements of the job: "You must be admitted to a state bar"—by which he meant the Ohio bar—and "you must obtain registration with the United States Patent and Trademark Office" (meaning, pass the Patent Bar).

Soon after I returned home, I received a formal letter from NCR containing an offer of employment as a Patent Attorney Trainee. The offered salary was nearly 150% of my then-current salary. Phil followed up his letter of offer with a phone call where he explained that "as soon as you are admitted to the Bars of Ohio and USPTO, the suffix in your title of Trainee will be dropped. You can expect a raise in salary." We discussed my start date at NCR and a timetable for taking the two bar examinations. I accepted the offer on the spot. My start date was going to be in mid-September 1979.

In the remaining months in San Diego, we attended to our house. Rama made new lacy curtains using her sewing machine and decorated our living room windows. We did some landscaping around the house by having a large silver-dollar Eucalyptus tree planted in our front yard along with dozens of rose bushes. Rama loved flowers, especially jasmine which we did not plant as this plant needed a lot of tender care. In the backyard, we planted strawberry guavas and colorful croton plants. We had paved the rest of the area in the backyard as well as a walkway on one side of the house linking the driveway to the paved backyard.

Our expectation was that my immigrant siblings would continue to live in our new house and take care of it. Although my monthly mortgage payment was large, I expected my brother and sisters, who would now each have their own bedroom, to chip in a nominal contribution—far less than if they rented an apartment. I wanted them to save their money and importantly live as a unified family in our home.

I told them, "Someday each of you will own your own house. And that day is not too far off." All three agreed to such an arrangement. I was happy to subsidize it and hoped that someday Rama and I might return to live in this house.

Rama and I drove for a short visit in San Francisco, as she never had visited this beautiful city—another gem in California. We enjoyed three nights of stay there and visited the tourist attractions, notably the famously steep and twisty-curvy block of Lombard Street in the heart of stylish Russian Hill. The brick-laid block with hairpin turns in the street, also known as the "crookedest street in the world," was exhilarating and fun to drive down.

On August 21, I notified my new manager, Les Niss, at General Dynamics of my resignation from the position I held as a Senior Software Engineer effective September 7, 1979. In my letter of resignation, I expressed my thanks for providing me an opportunity to work with him on the Global Positioning System.

In early September, the movers commissioned by NCR arrived at our house. They packed up our belongings and furniture for delivery to our new abode in the Dayton area in Ohio. Rama and I decided to drive cross-country in our Concours, leaving Rama's blazing red Chevette in our garage in Rancho Penasquitos for a later pickup or delivery.

DUTIFUL SON, BENEVOLENT BROTHER

WHETHER BY DESIGN or by coincidence, I wanted to lead my siblings by setting an example in my behavior. Ever since I was a teenager, they watched me bury myself in my books, regularly do my homework and wake up early in the morning—as early as 4:00 a.m.—before examinations to study in the cool and quiet early hours. I was told such day-break study enhanced concentration and enabled your mind to remember better the material you just had read. My sister Jaya woke up at this hour and made coffee to add sustenance to my study. She admired my dedication even though it was a chore for her to wake up at that ungodly hour.

My siblings were aware that I had obtained admission on my own to the prestigious St. Joseph's College in Bangalore, and of the distinctions of my being placed in the First Class and the top University Rankings in my Bachelor's and Master's degree programs. While my siblings were not aware of the planning and efforts I had exercised to land in America, they knew the end result—admission to Temple and the precious financial aid I received which made it happen.

Through my letters, where I detailed my life in America, and during the home visits in which I shared my experiences, my siblings knew that I had earned my Ph.D. While my siblings back home did not know what led me to study law, the ones that I sponsored for their Green Card and who now lived with me watched me in action as I juggled multiple balls in the air: I carried out a full-time job as a physicist; pursued law at night; spent the weekends in the library or at home studying for my class assignments; morally supported Rama with her nascent career; sponsored three of them for Green Cards; supported them to get on their own feet and succeed; and sacrificed mirth and merriment in marital life with my wife. I hoped and strived for a better tomorrow—a time when not only Rama and I could achieve our aspirations and enjoy happiness, but also my extended family located In San Diego and in India.

I wished I had such a benevolent brother when I was young. I could have observed and learned valuable life lessons from him. Also, the burden of rescuing a father usually fell on the firstborn son. However, my brother Avi did not seem to think of this responsibility placed on him. Instead, someone higher blessed me with an unconventional approach to become a catalyst for change which might result in fulfilling my duty to my father and in improving the lives of my siblings. The change that I contemplated was not merely rearranging the chairs on the *Titanic* but creating a future for them that did not yet exist.

Three of my marriageable siblings had now earned their Green Cards and were establishing their individual lives in the U.S. It felt good that it was only a matter of time before they would be in a commanding position to woo eligible bachelors or bachelorette, as the case may be. I began to think about the other remaining unmarried siblings in India, particularly my two sisters, and the financial contribution I would make for their dowries.

Although I was not religious, I believed in *dharma* or religious duty. This was a framework for the Hindu family to play the role of a welfare state. I believed that I had a responsibility toward the other members of my family who could not maintain themselves. I truly believed that charity begins at home.

I wanted my siblings who had joined me in the U.S. to achieve my values based on my moral standards, such as self-reliance, productiveness and integrity. I also wanted us to be reunited as a family and to rebuild strong family relationships. They needed to consciously realize the enduring value of staying together. This is what my mother expected of us, too.

My sister Mini, who did not jump at my offer to sponsor her for a Green Card, was being petulant. I concluded that in due course she was bound to change her mind when she found out from her sisters who now lived in America how good life was here. I was sure that I could use the Green Card for Mini as a trade for her dowry like I planned for Swati and Mala.

My paramount concern was with my third sister Vitri, who was neglected and remained uneducated. Bringing her to the U.S and gifting Vitri with the U.S. Green Card might not work toward her happiness. A potential husband in India might marry Vitri, if she held a Green Card, for the conferred benefit of the Green Card on him. After gaining entry to the U.S., he might divorce her. If such an atrocity were to happen to Vitri, I would encourage her to sue the estranged husband and force him out of the U.S. based on charges of fraud and violation of the letter and spirit of the Immigration & Nationality Act. However, such a situation would be extremely unpleasant and could embitter my family, particularly my then-divorced sister Vitri.

Instead, the only viable option that I could come up with for her was to establish a private endowment with sufficient cash. My thought was to have my parents find a suitable husband for Vitri by paying a dowry out of my endowment. I wanted Vitri and her husband to continue to live in India with no expectation of ever migrating to the U.S.

I discussed my thought with Rama. She embraced my thought without questioning who would contribute to the endowment. Even though I knew how sympathetic Rama had been whenever we discussed the neglected life of my sister Vitri, I presumed that she expected I alone would. I wholeheartedly agreed with her unexpressed expectation and was prepared to fully fund it. I put this thought aside for the time being as I wanted to discuss its execution with my sister Jaya in India.

I did not want to disclose to my father my grand plan of sponsoring his children in India, particularly my unmarried sisters, for their Green Card and using their Cards as a trade to entice husbands in India to marry them without a dowry payment. I never directly told him of my plan to rescue him from the strain of dowries. I did not want my father to put pressure on me to sponsor all four daughters at once for their Green Cards and have him ship them out to me once they received their Cards. I already had succumbed to such pressure from him when I attempted to delay the arrival of sister Mala to the U.S. My father would not have hesitated to transfer his parental responsibility to his daughters directly to me and then force me to deal with them. Such rapid chain migration would have disrupted my plan to complete law school and find a job as an attorney and Rama's own plan with her medical career.

I also did not want my father to know about my plan to establish the dowry endowment for Vitri because he might squander that money for other purposes, particularly if he had access to it. If he did not have access to that money, he would have pressured my mother to obtain access. This would have created much unhappiness to my mother and me.

In the past, I regularly had sent money to my parents to help them meet their everyday needs for raising our family back in India. During my last home visit, my father bemoaned that he had fallen behind in paying property taxes on his house.

I asked "Dad, for how long did you miss paying the back taxes on your house?"

He replied, "For over five years."

I went to the bank and exchanged my dollar bills and traveler's checks for rupees. I put stacks of cash in my parents' hands.

I pleaded with my father: "Please pay off the back-taxes you owe on your house. Otherwise, the city or the lender might put a lien on your house and force you to sell your house to satisfy the lien. That would make your life miserable."

I also told my mother, "Mom, here is cash for your household use. Please spend it the way you desire."

My father never let me know whether he heeded my plea.

My siblings who lived with me in San Diego discouraged me from giving my father control or even access to my planned dowry endowment, warning me that he would likely misuse the funds. Because of these reasons, I was reticent to disclose my dowry plan to my father. Instead, I made progress on my dowry plan methodically and at my own pace. I wanted to execute my plan my way. I expected my father to observe the execution of my plan and recognize it on his own.

Even though my father never asked me to sponsor his sons in India for their Green Cards, my thoughts shifted to such a possibility for my remaining brothers in India. I wanted to help them in the ways that I could to enrich their lives. Certainly, I had the power and means at my disposal to do it. Perhaps my father did not compel me to sponsor them for their Green Card because of the track record of dowry practice that I and possibly Avi already had established. In my case, I did not take a dowry, and in Avi's case, the dowry was not shared with my father. My father must have become resigned to the conclusion that none of his remaining sons would share their dowry with him.

My older brother Avi had a great job as an engineer with the India's Defense Ministry, which he had held for over fifteen years. His physician wife Wari had a thriving medical practice. His son and daughter were well entrenched in schools in Bangalore. Besides all this, my older brother never directly expressed to me his interest in migrating to the U.S.

My third unmarried brother Enku had some serious issues. He was unable to complete his undergraduate education. After some years of college, he decided to settle for a job. He was employed as a clerk in the state's High Court. He essentially was a paper pusher. More troubling, Enku suffered from a mild speech impairment which made his speech acutely nasal and unclear to comprehend by an untrained ear. I was not sure what caused this impairment. It was not genetic as none of the other siblings suffered from such impairment. Some in my family attributed this to a severe case of smallpox that he had contracted when he was nine or ten years old, but medically it did not seem to be the cause. I was sure that if he were to immigrate to the U.S., he was bound to have serious speech issues. His insufficient education was another negative. I recalled years earlier on my trips home imploring him to leave the court job and encouraging him to take courses in computer science or software coding to get a well-paid job. However, he never took my advice. If only he had earned such software skills, he might have been a candidate now for my sponsorship as jobs in software were aplenty in the U.S. and such jobs could be carried out silently without much oral interaction with his boss or other employees. In that scenario, his speech impairment would not have been a significant issue. My brother Enku needed to create his own future to some extent before my benevolence could have uplifted it.

My youngest unmarried brother Kash was well established as a banker in India. He was studious and had earned a bachelor's degree in commerce. He started out his career with a good job in a bank, which led to transfers across many branches. Then he voluntarily changed employers, which seemed to have resulted in rapid promotions. He was independent, cautious and risk averse. He never expressed interest in coming to America. I assumed that he was happy living in India and content with it.

Then there were my parents who were now aging into their late sixties or early seventies. Sponsoring them to join our family in the U.S. would have been a no-brainer. I already had a house that I owned in San Diego where they could live with my siblings or live with me in Dayton. However, I knew that they would not be open to it at least until all of their daughters were married and settled down and were leading their own independent lives with their husbands. I thought perhaps they would visit America when their first grandchild was born here.

9

BAR EXAMINATIONS

RAMA AND I MOVED to Dayton, Ohio with some reluctance and a degree of skepticism. After living in San Diego, which is a beautiful city perched along the U.S. Pacific Coast with year-round sunny and warm weather, Dayton did not appear glamorous. What led me to Dayton was the first job as a lawyer that I was offered—by NCR before I graduated from law school. Another reason for leaving was Rama's now suspended medical Residency. She could only complete her Residency in a state other than California (because of the rules there) and pursue her medical license.

I admired San Diego. Whenever I spoke about this marvelous place to Rama, which I incessantly did, I accentuated the positives of this city. At these times, she humorously would call me "Self-Dubba," which was a synonym that she coined for the acronyms of San Diego. *Dubba* is an India cookery term, and it stands for a round metal box used to transport hot food, either from home or from a restaurant, to a person's place of work. When the box is empty, one could make a lot of loud noise by hitting it with a utensil like a spoon.

I vowed that someday we would return to San Diego after Rama and I paid our "dues"—meaning Rama completing her Residency in another state and earning her medical license and me, earning my bar admission. Since I already owned a house in

San Diego in which my siblings were now living, I was confident that I would come back. Perhaps I should have taken the California bar after I graduated from law school. Had I secured my lawyer's license from California, then that would have guaranteed my return to San Diego. I may have made a mistake by rushing to Ohio and accepting my first job as a lawyer at NCR.

Months earlier, when I was completing my final year of law school, I had made up my mind that I would not work in a law firm. One reason: there were no law firms in San Diego which had national recognition in the specialty Intellectual Property Law that I was going to enter.

I toyed with the idea of going into Immigration Law as law firms in San Diego were doing thriving business in this area because of the illegal aliens flooding into the city from the border town of Tijuana, Mexico. However, because of the sunk cost of investing my time, energy and resources to earn my four degrees in physics and my professional experience in technology, such a leap to Immigration Law did not make sense. It was contrary to my goal of marrying my technology background with the law education I had acquired.

I had read tragic stories where young associates, fresh out of law school, were driven into the ground by the mounds of work that the partners at the firm hoisted on them. Such exploitation of rookie attorneys who were eager to earn the illustrious partnership at a future date was known to destroy the attorneys' family life. I wanted the work-life balance which in-house legal jobs in a corporation were known to provide. In a law firm, the attorneys were paid more because their remuneration was tied to their billable hours to clients, whereas an in-house attorney was paid a fixed salary which was lower. In other words, the choice that a starting attorney had was between earning a lot of wealth at the expense of a good family life versus earning less and enjoying a good family life. I chose the latter.

I chose the job at NCR first to settle down in Dayton, which took time. Second, I wanted to have the luxury of slow-paced work as a trainee and time to study for the two bar examinations: the Ohio bar and the patent bar. These were hurdles to overcome. NCR allowed me to achieve them at my own pace and did not pressure me, unlike a fast-paced law firm might have.

The drive from San Diego to Dayton was long, over 2200 miles without counting the detours we planned. We set out on a southern route as we wanted to see the Grand Canyon National Park in Arizona. We drove through Phoenix and up north through Flagstaff to reach the Grand Canyon, which took a day of travel from San Diego. We stopped for the night near Flagstaff and went to see the South Rim of the Grand Canyon early the next morning.

It was 6:00 a.m. when we drove up to the South Rim. The sky was blue and clear of clouds, and the sun was bright and beginning to rise above the vast horizon. The morning was still cool with gentle winds blowing from the west.

We parked our car and hiked a short distance to the scene. Rama was wearing a full-sleeved and full-length dress in pastel with purple dots, which perfectly fitted her slim body. Her outfit blended nicely with our surroundings, and we both found the scene of the Grand Canyon at sunrise to be just majestic. Rama could not believe the immense size of the Canyon.

I explained: "It is a mile deep, 18 miles wide and stretches for over 270 miles along the Colorado River."

I pointed to the river down below at the base of the canyon.

Rama said: "This is unimaginably spectacular. I have never seen anything like this before."

We admired the unique combination of layered bands of red rock revealing millions of years of geological history with hues that seemed to change with the direction of the sunlight. We drove around the Rim to catch glimpses of the canyon from different vantage points. The erosional form of the canyon, which was exposed over millions of years as the Colorado River and its tributaries cut their channels through layer after layer of rock, was a wonder to behold. I took pictures of Rama with the canyon as a backdrop.

At one of the scenic viewpoints, Rama was admiring the depth of the canyon by herself after I had stepped away to catch a glimpse of a different spectacular view. When I walked back to Rama, a photographer with a large camera on his shoulder was asking her, "Can I take your photo with the canyon in the background?"

He saw me approach Rama as he posed his question. Guessing that Rama was with me, he turned to me and repeated, "Could I take her photograph?"

I smiled and politely asked, "Who are you?"

He replied, "I am a photographer for the *National Geographic Magazine*." He added, "The bright purple dots on her dress match so perfectly with the purple, indigo and blue hues of the canyon rock. Her photo in that setting may find a place in our magazine."

I agreed with his assessment of the scene.

He politely asked Rama to be positioned between the red

bougainvillea bush on one side and the colorful canyon on the other. He quickly clicked a bunch of photos as I sipped from my water bottle.

After lunch at the Grand Canyon, we travelled to Albuquerque, New Mexico. Years ago, my classmate Tim Lambarski moved to Albuquerque and married a girl from New Mexico by the name of Gloria. Tim had been employed at the Sandia Weapons Lab there after completing his Master's in Physics at Temple. Rama and I met Gloria when I lived in Philadelphia, but we had lost touch with this couple after they moved to Albuquerque. I was unable to make contact with them as we drove past Albuquerque. It would have been a nice reunion if I had reconnected with Tim and Gloria after so many years.

We passed through Oklahoma City and went to St. Louis, where we stopped for a couple of nights with Rama's sister Arna. Arna's baby daughter was now eight months old. We both had seen the baby girl right after she was born by visiting St. Louis. Rama had made frequent trips from Columbia to see her newborn niece. It was a happy get-together with the new addition that brought a lot cheer to the family.

We arrived in Dayton on a grey afternoon with overcast skies. We checked into a bed-and-breakfast for our temporary stay. The B&B was a charming colonial house with four bedrooms for guests on the second floor. The owners were a middle-aged couple who lived on the first floor where all the house guests dined. The garden that surrounded the B&B was full of roses and begonias. The hosts were extremely friendly and gave us a history lesson about the Dayton area.

The Dayton region was essentially a flat land. The Wright

Patterson Air Force Base in the east part was one of the largest and most diverse, very organizationally complex and a fully operational base. Over 5,000 service members and 20,000 civilian and contract employees worked at the base.

Traffic in Dayton was nonexistent compared to the more densely populated San Diego.

The suburbs of Dayton—like Oakwood, Kettering, Centerville and Miamisburg—were very family-oriented with lots of outdoor parks. I was surprised to learn that most of the suburban school districts were ranked at the top of the state's school districts.

After I reported to work at NCR World Headquarters in Dayton, I quickly engaged a realtor to find a house to purchase. The realtor's name was Mr. Eisenhower and he resembled our past President. Once I accidentally addressed him as Dwight to which he responded, "That happens all the time to me!"

Home ownership was essential to wealth-building and a fundamental part of the American Dream for upward mobility. I was ready to invest in my second home—this one in the Dayton area. I was drawn to the suburbs of Oakwood and Kettering, which were only five miles from NCR. It wasn't only because of the convenience; they also were established communities with older houses with mature trees and manicured landscapes. I liked Kettering's character of the neighborhood, while Rama wanted to be in the southern suburb of Centerville where the houses were newer, larger and less expensive. However, with Centerville, my commute to work would have been nearly twenty miles each way.

Kettering was named after Charles F. Kettering, who invented the automatic transmission for motor vehicles. The town was self-contained with an excellent hospital and many conveniently located shopping plazas.

After looking at dozens of houses in Centerville, Kettering and Oakwood, we settled for a fifty-year-old three-bedroom house in Kettering. It had been meticulously remodeled by the previous owner. The home sat on a beautiful corner lot with established magnolia and Japanese maple trees and ever-green hedges around the house.

The drawback was that the house had only a single bathroom, and it was suited for a couple but would be somewhat inconvenient when overnight guests visited us. The house also was heated the old-fashioned way by conduction heating. Pipes arranged underneath the floors carried a hot fluid and heated the rooms by conduction up through the parquet floor.

I commented to Rama, "This is an inefficient way of heating the house, particularly pointing to the rooms in the house which were carpeted."

However, its location mattered to me. The purchase price was about $60,000 and I easily qualified under my NCR salary for a mortgage with 20% down payment

We closed on the house in record time after signing the contract. The movers delivered our household belongings, which were temporarily put in storage. I was eager to settle into our new home as I had promised my boss Phil that I would take the next scheduled Ohio bar examination in February of 1980. That was only about five months away. I needed time to study for it.

In early October, I initiated the application process for the Ohio bar by requesting the forms from the Admissions Clerk of the

Supreme Court of Ohio. The documentation that I was required to submit was intimidating. It contained an "Applicant's Questionnaire" (which was nine pages long) and an "Applicant's Questionnaire for Bar Examination" (five pages long), plus "An Application and Certificate," an "Application, Affidavit and Certificate of Law School" and a "Character Reference Questionnaire" (which together were seven pages long).

To complete this paperwork required meticulous coordination. I complied and submitted my application before the deadline. I signed up for a bar review course. As no live bar review course was offered in Dayton for the winter examination, I signed up for audio tapes of the bar review course.

As I was settling down in Kettering, my parents, Jaya and Raj in Bangalore started looking for a match for Swati. She was now twenty-seven years old and we felt it was time to get her married. She held a good-paying job at the Scripps Clinic and had saved up money.

Before Rama and I left San Diego, I took a number of photographs of Swati and sent them to India for the match-making process. Swati wanted to pose by the side of her new car, and I obliged.

Unbeknownst to me, Jaya and Raj already had lined up a match in Bangalore for Swati. I knew that she would settle for the match found by them, which she readily did. The person that she agreed to marry was a small-animal veterinarian who was five years older than her. He went by the name Subh. The date of the wedding of Swati and Subh was set for November 29, 1979 in Bangalore.

I felt great about how things were turning out. Swati had come to the U.S. based on my sponsorship and received her Green Card. She was able to marry a professional in India. The motivation for Subh was the Green Card that Swati promised him. A compelling attraction for Subh was also the nuclear family in the U.S. that I had reestablished. My stature as an American lawyer and that of Rama as a physician no doubt were additional key factors in Subh's decision to marry Swati.

I was not sure whether my father had agreed to this marriage arranged by Raj and Jaya, but it did not matter. My mother wrote to me that "your father is relieved that there was no dowry demand for Swati's marriage."

I dearly hoped that my father was beginning to realize the plan that I had orchestrated to precisely relieve him from paying the dowry for Swati. I knew that he was wise enough to understand that I had played her Green Card as currency for her dowry.

During the Thanksgiving holiday, I dashed off to San Diego to fetch Rama's car that we had left at our house there. I did not see Swati as she went to Bangalore to celebrate her wedding but had an evening to spend with Ohan and Mala.

The next morning, I jumped into the blazing red Chevette and drove from west to east along the southernmost interstate highway of I-8. I essentially drove continuously, except for short breaks to catch some sleep. I returned to Kettering by the end of the long weekend.

After I returned home, Rama's sister Arna came to visit without her toddler who she left back in St. Louis with her visiting mother. It was wonderful having her for the first time in our newly purchased house. It was a great family reunion. The two sisters were close and fond of each other's company.

Although they argued a lot, Rama and Arna easily made up and continued to be affectionate toward each other. We took her to the beautiful golf course at NCR and had a lot of fun playing many rounds of mini golf.

While I was preparing for my bar examination, my boss Phil and colleagues at NCR helped me expand my skills as a patent trainee. I started handling official responses from the USPTO by preparing amendments to patent claims and supplying associated arguments in support of them, which my boss was kind enough to critique.

Swati got married as planned and filed a petition with the U.S. Consulate in Madras requesting permanent U.S. resident visa for Subh. After returning to San Diego, she followed up the petition with her Affidavit of Support by adhering to the process I previously established.

Time quickly passed by and I assumed that sooner or later I would receive my ticket for admission to take the bar examination scheduled for the end of February. However, I received no communication from the Admission Clerk.

While I awaited my admission to the bar exam, Rama made inquiries to resume her Residency. Upon discussing this with her sister Arna and Arna's husband, she was beginning to lean toward pursuing a Residency in Anesthesiology. Both of her relatives talked up this specialty. In early December, Rama contacted the University of Cincinnati and obtained an application for a Residency in Anesthesiology. She promptly filled it out and put together a cover letter to Dr. Phillip Zaacks, the Director of

Anesthesiology Residency, expressing her desire to participate in the specialty training program he was managing. Dr. Zaacks responded that he would consider her application and let her know whether such a position would be available.

Rama would not give up and she contacted Dr. Zaacks again. This time she inquired about the twelve months of internship in Physical Medicine at the University of Missouri, Columbia that she had completed. Could it be counted toward her Residency in Anesthesiology if and when she was to start her Residency in this field at UC? Rama explained that during her Residency in Physical Medicine she spent 90% of her time in the clinical environment treating patients as well as taking night calls and a month in the Out-Patient Department at UMCM.

Dr. Zaacks was kind and took the trouble of writing to Dr. E.S. Siker, who was a member of the American Board of Anesthesiology. In his letter, he explained, "*I have an application from a resident who wishes to begin training in the Department of Anesthesiology at the University of Cincinnati Medical Center and would appreciate a ruling from you as to the validity of her Clinical Base Year.*"

Weeks later Dr. Siker replied stating in part "*. . . a year of training in the specialty area of Physical Medicine is not considered by the Credentials Committee as meeting the goals of a Clinical Base Year . . . Certainly, some credit would be considered if some minor portion (up to three months) of this years' training were submitted for consideration . . .*"

When Dr. Zaaks forwarded the letter he had received from Dr. Siker, Rama wrote back expressing her sincere thanks for making the case on her behalf to the Board. She reiterated her continued interest in the PGY-1 training program beginning July 1, 1981 at UC. The upshot of Rama's tenacious pursuit with Dr. Zaaks was that she was beginning to develop a sense of loyalty toward him.

In early January 1980, I called the Admission Clerk of the Ohio Supreme Court to find out the status of my application for the Ohio bar. To my consternation she informed me that she was unable to locate my application that I previously had mailed. I immediately duplicated a copy of the forms that I retained for my records and dashed them off to her. I emphasized an urgency to process them as the scheduled date of the bar exam was less than six weeks away.

When I followed up days later, the Clerk advised that I should talk to Professor Daniel Turack at the League of Ohio Law Schools regarding my application, which I did right away. Mr. Turack explained that my application was being held up since I did not furnish the required authenticated transcript evidencing my bachelor's degree.

I couldn't believe the reason for the holdup. I talked to Mr. Turack and went over the written statements I made in my application that I had completed my bachelor's degree at St. Josephs College, which was affiliated with the University of Mysore in India. I explained that universities in India were not equipped to send authenticated transcripts. Graduates from Indian universities used their original transcripts issued at graduation for proving their credentials. I also explained that I had earned three advanced degrees of M.A., Ph.D. and J.D. from an American school—Temple University, which granted admission by relying on my bachelor's degree received from India.

I followed up this conversation by sending him a copy of the transcript for my bachelor's degree that I had received from St Joseph's College at graduation. I pleaded that I had invested a lot of time and effort to prepare for the bar exam and requested a ruling that the bachelor's degree I earned in India was equivalent to that awarded by a U.S. university.

I received a handwritten note dated February 6, 1989 from Mr. Turack. He informed me that the Admission Committee completed its work and had made a recommendation to the Supreme Court of Ohio. The note further stated that I should be notified directly by the Court in the next few days. On February 13, I received a formal letter from the Admission Clerk informing me of the decision by the Court to permit me to take the bar examination scheduled for February 26-28. She also arranged to have me complete a personal interview with members of the Dayton Bar Association.

I successfully completed the interview the Clerk had scheduled. However, the episode of the Clerk missing my original application and the stress caused by dealing with Professor Turack took a toll on my ability to concentrate on my bar review material. My first reaction was to feel that it was unfair to lose my opportunity to take the bar exam over a paperwork glitz. Then I realized I was simply going through a blind following of the Rules by the Admission Committee than applying common sense. I discussed this with my boss and decided to postpone taking the bar exam until the summer.

Undaunted, I moved on to taking my Patent bar—the examination required to practice before the USPTO. On January 15, 1980, I applied for this examination which was scheduled for April 8, 1980 in Dayton. This examination was composed of two parts. I applied to take both parts on the same date. USPTO promptly approved my application.

My training at NCR and the work that I had put in to handle

the USPTO Actions came in handy for the afternoon part of the examination. The morning part, which tested for rules and regulations of the USPTO based on various U.S. Statutes and the Constitution, required a lot of reading and gaining knowledge of their applicability to various situations of patentability. *The Manual of Patent Examining Procedures*, which the Patent Office Examiner used during the prosecution of patent applications, was a required reading, which I read.

As scheduled, I took the exam in its entirety. Three other applicants also took this exam. Both parts of the test went without a hitch. On June 23, 1980, I received a notification from Ms. Lucille Parker, Chairman of the Committee on Enrollment at the USPTO, stating that I had attained a passing grade on both the morning and afternoon sections. I was bestowed a provisional registration number of P-29,784, and I was advised that this number must appear below my signature on every paper of correspondence I submit to the USPTO. Since I was not yet a licensed attorney, I could only call myself a Patent Agent.

Rama, more than me, was ecstatic when she heard about my passing the Patent Bar. She was an infinitely patient wife who supported me, and she regarded my happiness as her happiness.

My boss and colleagues at NCR were happy as well, and they congratulated me one after another by showing up at my cubicle when they found out about my success. For most of them, it was already a *fait accompli*. My boss reaffirmed that he was confident that I would pass and remarked with the classic statement: "I told you so!"

The next task for me would be to take and pass the once-postponed Ohio bar examination.

In the meanwhile, Rama had become pregnant with our first child. I was very happy with the news of her pregnancy. I wanted our child to be a son so he could carry my family name forward in my new homeland. Rama knew of my wish for a son, but she did not have the inkling to find out the sex of the baby in her womb. Neither did I. We waited until the birth to find out the gender of our child.

The timing of the delivery competed with the timing of the Ohio bar examination that I was scheduled to take. My bar exam was scheduled for late July and the baby was due during the first week of August. I did not like these competing interests. I tried to support Rama in her pregnancy as much as I could without getting distracted from my study for the bar.

Pregnancy was a life-changing event for Rama. She was filled with physical and emotional changes. She coped with these changes on her own, without moral support from her mother or elderly relatives. Her knowledge of medicine helped her understand the transformation that she was experiencing. Rama explained to me in medical terms what she was going through. She received assurances from her OB-GYN that the symptoms she was experiencing were normal and the pregnancy was on track.

Rama suffered from food aversion. She was repelled by the smell of food for months during her pregnancy, but nevertheless she cooked meals for me. Because of hormonal changes, Rama experienced mood swings. These she managed to control by taking naps, spending quality time with me, going for walks and getting involved in other physical activities on her own. She believed that walking was beneficial to her condition. She told me that: "Walking will strengthen my pelvic muscles and will make delivery easier. I just need to pace myself and try to stay on a soft surface like a lawn." Walking with Rama was a shared positive experience and was good for my health, too.

Rama continued to feel exhausted because of increased levels of progesterone which contributed to sleepiness. The fatigue became more acute during the late months of her pregnancy, starting in June, because she was carrying a lot more weight. Some of the discomforts of pregnancy made it difficult for her to get a good night's sleep. Rama's infinite patience and perseverance during her pregnancy amazed me and I felt blessed by her tolerant attitude.

Without receiving any guidance from anyone else, I studied the course material and listened to the endless audiotapes that the Bar Review Course Provider had sent me. Studying for the bar was much harder than any other examination that I ever took, including the Ph.D. preliminary examination a decade earlier. Its scope was daunting. This was an occasion when I was expected to be at the peak of my knowledge in law, equipped to answer any question that the examiners might ask. It was a confluence of all aspects of the law that I had ever studied.

The incessant reading and listening of the audio course material became somewhat monotonous and boring. I looked for a distraction—something different.

It had been over three years since Rama had become a permanent resident of the United States. As a spouse of a U.S. citizen, Rama's mandatory period of residency as a Green Card holder had been met. She was eligible to apply for her naturalization. While she could have remained as an Indian citizen and enjoyed the privilege of being a permanent resident of the U.S., she and I decided that converting her status to a U.S. citizen was in the best interest of our nuclear family. It was also in the best interest of Rama's career.

To us, America was not just a place on the map like Kettering or San Diego. It was an ideal and a profound concept. As a recently naturalized American, I had the foresight to understand this ideal and concept. I understood that America was about freedom, which I had earned by passing through many hurdles; and now Rama was about to earn it. Neither of us regarded America as about free stuff.

There was another good reason that motivated Rama to become a U.S. citizen. Her citizenship status would confer upon her an opportunity to reunify her side of the family who were living outside the United States. They could join our nuclear family in the U.S. Besides her parents, who have been citizens of India and were living in India, there were her two younger and unmarried brothers Mali and Rajen. They had both just completed their medical degree (MBBS) in India and expressed a desire to be closer to their two older sisters by migrating to the U.S.

In fact, we received the surprising news that both brothers had immigrated to Jamaica and were employed in Kingston as physicians. They wanted to be as close geographically as possible to the U.S. by being in the West Indies. Their physical presence in Jamaica helped Rama to call and talk to them frequently, and it increased our opportunities to meet with them.

Of the two brothers, the elder brother Mali was more attached to Rama and she looked to him for occasional counsel on family-related matters. Despite being younger than her, he was mature, and he had great affection toward her—just like her father did. Mali was family-oriented. He was easy-going, jovial and took life as it was handed to him.

The younger brother Rajen was more of a follower. He followed Mali. However, he tended to be somewhat timid and self-centered. He focused on his own profession as a doctor. The motivation for him to seek U.S. immigration may have been driven by money, as he could earn more in the U.S. than anywhere else.

We came to learn that a female classmate from his medical school, who had completed her MBBS degree with him, accompanied Rajen to Jamaica. This romantic relationship between Rajen and his girlfriend Sai was another surprise for me. Rama knew Sai from her days in Guntur. I noticed that Sai had a more intense desire to immigrate to the U.S. as I observed her during one of our visits to Jamaica. The motivation of clutching onto an eligible candidate for a U.S. Green Card did not escape my attention. Rajen and Sai appeared driven to become economic migrants to the U.S.

Having made our decision to seek U.S. citizenship for Rama, I started her naturalization process. Dealing with the Immigration & Naturalization Service was never easy, whether it was to convert from student visa to Green Card, to file a petition by a Green Card holder to sponsor his alien spouse for her Green Card, to apply for naturalization, or for a naturalized citizen to sponsor his alien brother or sister for their Green Card. The paperwork needed to be filled out carefully and a plethora of documentation supplied, personal interviews with INS officers satisfied, and health screening by immigration doctors completed.

Only when the applicant satisfied the requirements, which required patience and prolonged waiting, did one attain the end result.

I picked up and filled out, on Rama's behalf, the Application to File Petition for Naturalization. The form required Rama to provide personal data, the addresses where she resided since entering the U.S., the occupations she held, her relationship to me as a U.S. citizen and the continuous duration of three years to satisfy her marital union requirement. I had the prescribed Affidavit at the end of the Form sworn to by Rama before a public notary. On June 12, 1980 on behalf of Rama I prepared a letter, which she signed, explaining to the INS Examiner her request for naturalization. In the same package, I enclosed the completed Form, three photographs, a fingerprint chart and biographic information, and I mailed it to the INS in Cincinnati, Ohio.

On June 23, the INS acknowledged receipt of the Petition and indicated that processing had begun. A person from the U.S. District Court in Dayton would contact Rama. In anticipation of Rama's naturalization and the foregone conclusion that she would file petitions for Green Cards for her brothers, she set the ball rolling to have the necessary documents in India made ready for filing such petitions.

I took many timed practice tests in both the multiple choice and essay portions of the bar exam during the last weeks of preparation for the exam. The feedback I received for my essay tests was useful. The practice tests gave me some confidence in my readiness to take the exam. The review of my course material helped to kick my brain into high gear. It helped to fire up my neurons and flood back my memory of the principles of law. I was ready for the exam but felt ambivalent at the same time. I viewed it was an initiation rite of the legal profession.

Finally, the day for taking the examination arrived. The exam was scheduled for the last consecutive Tuesday, Wednesday and Thursday in July in Columbus, Ohio. I drove to Columbus the night before the examination and stayed at a hotel.

The exam had two components: an essay portion and the Multistate Bar Examination (MBE) portion, which consisted of multiple-choice questions. The MBE counted for one-third of the score; the essay counted for two-thirds. There was a total score possible of 360 points for the entire examination.

The MBE portion was held on Wednesday in two sessions of three hours each—in the morning and after lunch in the afternoon. I was required to answer the MBE questions in pencil by using my own pencils. There were 250 questions covering contracts, torts, constitutional law, criminal law, criminal procedure, evidence and real property.

The essay questions were timed to answer in twelve one-hour sessions—six on Tuesday and six on Thursday. The essay questions were given two questions at a time. I had one hour to complete both questions and thus was limited to thirty minutes per question.

For the essay portion, I was furnished answer books on the cover page of which I was asked to write my individual examination number (#238) as well as the name of the examiner giving that part of the exam. A separate book was to be used for each examiner. Two questions were submitted by each examiner, and I was required to answer both questions in the space provided in the answer book—making sure that my answer book corresponded with the questions.

Though the essay-questions were challenging, none seemed

tricky. I answered the questions in a precise way by writing legibly and by giving reasons for my answer. I wrote enough to show the examiner that I knew the principles of law applicable to the solution of the problem, and to demonstrate my ability to reason in a logical lawyer-like fashion. I ensured that I was concise, wrote grammatically, punctuated and spelled properly—again like a good lawyer. I read the questions at least twice to sort the wheat from the chaff and to discriminate between the legally relevant and the inconsequential facts. I formulated my answers in my mind before writing. For each question I stated the conclusion, and then gave the reasons.

The three days of the bar examination was terribly exhausting, and I was completely drained. I returned home on Thursday night after taking the bar and went to work at NCR the next day. I could not tell my boss for sure how well I did in the examination. Yet I needed to pass the Ohio bar now.

CHILDBIRTH

NOW THAT I had taken my Ohio bar examination, nothing else mattered more than looking after my wife's advanced state of pregnancy. She had reached the full extension of her baby-belly. Rama did sometimes wear the maternity slacks and light-weight shirts that she had purchased but seemed more comfortable in the sarees that she wore on a regular basis. I took many pictures of her clad in a saree and matching blouse in front of the flowering magnolia tree in our yard. Her colorful saree perfectly matched the pink and white magnolias. Rama looked more beautiful in her pregnancy with the cheeks on her face more rounded.

Rama gained fifteen pounds and possibly more. Much of her gained weight was attributed to the weight of the baby in her womb and an increase of blood and other fluids. It was the second week in August, probably the fortieth week in her pregnancy. The baby was due to be born any day now. We both waited. Rama waited to get relief from the delivery.

Probably nothing is more memorable to parents than the birth of their child. It is particularly more memorable and thrilling when the child about to be born is their first. I felt it would be even more memorable and cherished for me if our firstborn turned out to be a boy. In any case, the delivery and birth of our child was definitely an event. It was filled with drama, anxiety, suspense.

It started on the morning of Saturday, August 9, 1980. After carrying the baby for more than nine months and going from a few ounces to what appeared to be an immense weight, the somewhat diminutive, slender and delicate Rama was eager to bring the baby out from her womb into a beautiful world. She telephoned her obstetrician Dr. Ronald Loesch and informed him that it was game time for her delivery. She signaled to me that we should start executing our well laid-out labor plan.

I immediately drove her to the Emergency Room at Kettering Memorial Hospital a mile away from our house. A nurse helped Rama into a wheelchair and then rolled her down the hall. She was admitted to the hospital and I was summoned to the maternity ward. Rama was on a gurney undergoing various tests. Dr. Loesch arrived and after a brief examination of Rama's condition concluded that she should be monitored for commencement of contractions.

I took the time to call Rama's sister Arna in St. Louis. When she heard the news that Rama had gone to the hospital, she and her mother immediately headed by car to Kettering to join us.

At the hospital I wandered down the hallway into something the hospital called The Bullpen, where expectant fathers sat and stared into a small TV. Hours passed by. However, there was no action from Rama. It was evening. Still there was no action. My in-laws from St. Louis were scheduled to arrive at our house. I was beginning to wonder whether Rama had pulled a false alarm. Dusk set in. Rama had a light meal, and she was settling in for the night in the hospital, waiting for the event that she checked in to happen.

I went home to receive my in-laws and make them feel at home. Due to the lateness of the hour my in-laws decided not to go to the hospital to see Rama that night. I grabbed a quick bite and returned to The Bullpen at the hospital to be close to Rama. It was near midnight when Dr. Loesch was again summoned to the maternity ward because Rama had begun to show signs of serious labor. She was wheeled into the birthing room. A variety of electrodes were attached to her body to monitor the progress of the birth. The intensity of her labor contractions grew. With the encouragement from and the urging of the doctor and the nurses, Rama made gallant efforts to push, push and push the baby into this world by natural birth. Not much success, however. She was administered medication to induce labor and ease the delivery but to no avail.

It was already Sunday, August 10. I was biting my nails, sweating heavily, waiting and pacing alone in The Bullpen, wondering when I would hear from the doctor. It was 2:30 a.m. when Dr. Loesch came by. He was dressed in his hospital gown. He led me to a prayer room down the hallway and softly told me, "Rama has done her best to give birth the natural way, but her diminutive pelvic frame is proving to be not conducive for it." He paused and then added, "The labor has already taken too long and it is not safe to continue pursuing the natural course of birth. Any further delay may endanger the lives of both Mom and baby." He asked for my agreement to operate on Rama and facilitate delivery by the Cesarean technique. No sooner than I had given my authorization, he disappeared after assuring that he would keep me posted on the progress with the operation.

The lateness of the hour, the solemn words of the doctor about the impending danger, and the thought of surgical delivery for Rama created a sudden rush of anxiety in me. The prayer room appeared to be the most fitting place for my wait, given the dire uncertainty that I faced with Rama and our yet-to-be born child. Hours went by and there was no word from the OB-GYN doctor. I could do nothing but pray that everything would turn out all right. My hidden wish that my firstborn would be a son did not seem to matter much then. All I could wish for was the health of Rama and my long-awaited child.

Finally, Dr. Loesch appeared. It was close to five in the morning. As he approached, the doctor pulled off the OR cap covering the hair on his head.

He squeezed my arm and said with a smile, "It's a boy! Congratulations. Mother is doing well. Everything turned out well."

Those were the words that I was dying to hear. I could hardly contain my excitement and happiness. Tears rolled down my cheeks. I thanked the doctor for his marvelous feat.

Minutes later I was ushered in to see Rama. She was beaming with a smile despite her aestheticized state and the discomfort of just having come out of surgery. She showed off the prized extension of herself—her son! The baby's face glistened from amidst strands of silky black hair that completely covered his small head. He was a beautiful boy. He was serene and asleep with what appeared to be a smile radiating from his tiny lips.

The record showed that my son (named Coca Boy, by the hospital nurses) was born at 4:29 am. He weighed 6 pounds, 13 ounces and measured 20.5 inches. His birth ID# was 8039.

The miracle of birth! So much part preparation! So much part waiting! So much part anxiety! In the end, so much of joy and happiness for Rama and me. Our son's birth was such a memorable event, not just because of the drama that we witnessed and experienced. It turned out to be the only birth event in our personal lives, rendering it even more precious!

On that Sunday morning, when I reached home, my mother-in-law right away emerged from the bedroom where she was sleeping. She was so happy to hear the news of the birth of her first grandson and Rama's safe C-section operation.

Later that morning, I drove them to the Kettering hospital where they met the tiny baby in Rama's arms and were absolutely thrilled. I sent telegrams to my father-in-law in Guntur and my parents in Bangalore, conveying the short message of "Rama delivered boy 6 pounds 13 ounces by Cesarean. Both are fine." I telephoned my siblings in San Diego to tell them the good news. My last sister Mala wondered what name we had selected for our son.

She asked, "Would it be one of the names that we discussed a few weeks ago?"

I replied, "We have not settled on a name yet."

My second brother-in-law Subh, who had arrived in the U.S. a few months earlier as a Green Card holder, also congratulated me on the birth of my son.

While still in the hospital, Rama and I picked a name for our son, Dinesh. His name included both the Sun and the Moon in Hindu mythology. We simply called him Nesh. My son's birth certificate with his name on it and signed by Rama was recorded by the Ohio Department of Health under file 6379-80. A few days later we were delivered a Hospital Birth Record by the Kettering Medical Center certifying that our son by name was born to Rama and I specifying the date and time of birth. It was certified by Dr. Ronald Loesch and the President of the Center and carried a gold seal of the Medical Center. The back of the certificate carried the family's heirloom record of my son's left and right footprints and Rama's right and left thumbprint.

In Hinduism there is a strong belief that a son's birth is considered lucky and that if a couple is blessed with a male child they would definitely go to heaven. A son is considered to be the savior and one who will give *pinda daan*. That is, he will take his parents' ashes to the Ganges River in India and wash them so that they would go to heaven after death. A son was considered to spread the family tree into future generations.

More than these Hindu beliefs, I relied on studies showing that a firstborn is known to be 24% more likely to become a right-hand man to the father, a top manager or a leader such as a CEO.

I was satisfied now that my son had anointed me with the crown of fatherhood and gave me the exalted status of dad. My son was a precious part of my life. He was my sunshine, my pride, my hope.

My mother-in-law stayed with us for weeks to help Rama recover from the surgery and take care of our infant son. Rama regularly breast-fed him. Based on her medical knowledge, she believed that the mother's breast milk was by far the most superior nutritional food for her infant child.

During the weekends, we took our son and mother-in-law to the NCR golf course and enjoyed picnicking on the park. Rama and I played miniature gold. Simple pleasures like this satisfied our needs for entertainment.

The month of August had become a special month in our lives, with much to celebrate. I was born in August, and Rama and I were married in August. Now our son Nesh was born in August.

In addition to handling my clients at NCR's Miamisburg facility, I regularly travelled to Colorado Springs and Fort Collins near Denver where NCR had two other microelectronics design and development centers. I travelled to meet with my clients and explain the need to protect their inventions by patenting or by trade secret. I made presentations on Intellectual Property matters to engineers, scientists and engineering management to make them aware of the value of the intellectual property asset to the company. I continued to prepare patent applications on ideas that the inventors submitted and filed them in the USPTO under my name as their registered patent agent.

At the end of September, Rama finally received a letter of notification from INS in Cincinnati. With it came a Personal Description Form requesting, as the next step toward naturalization, that she appear for an 10:45 am interview at the Office of Clerk—U.S. District Court in Dayton on October 21, 1980. The notification required Rama to bring a number of documents, including her Alien Registration Receipt Card, passport, the filled-in Personal Description Form and names and addresses of two witnesses, our marriage certificate, my naturalization certificate and a filing fee of $25. The letter warned that the two witnesses that she named must be persons who can testify from personal knowledge and observation about Rama's qualifications for naturalization during the past three years.

The two witnesses that Rama named were my boss (we socialized with him and his family, and he knew her well) and our next-door neighbor Diane Fogle (she had been a friend of Rama's ever since we moved in to our house in Kettering).

On the requested day, I drove Rama for the interview at the U.S. District Court in Dayton. After examining the documents that Rama presented, a person at the Court appointed by INS then discovered that Rama's two identified witnesses were not in a position to testify about her qualifications for naturalization for the mandated full period of the past three years. Accordingly, he asked Rama to identify two witnesses—one in San Diego, California and another in Columbia, Missouri, places where she had resided during two different periods in the last three years.

A letter in a plain envelope, from the Board of Bar Examiners of the Supreme Court of Ohio dated October 29, 1980, was delivered to our home, and it made my day. Rama was not in the habit of opening letters addressed to me, and she didn't in this case either. When I arrived home that evening and opened the letter, it read: "Congratulations! The Board of Bar Examiners has awarded you a passing grade on the July 1980 examination. . . . You are now eligible to be sworn in as Attorney and Counselor at Law. The oath of office will be administered at a ceremony to be held in Columbus, Ohio on Friday, November 7, 1980."

I rushed into the bedroom and showed the letter to Rama, who was busy caring for our infant son. She read the letter and put the baby into the crib. She hugged me and planted a gentle kiss for accomplishing this major milestone in our lives.

Rama said, "I knew you'd pass."

I asked, "Rama, do you know what this means to us? The license to be a lawyer opens up a whole new world for us. I will never have to depend on anyone to support our lives. If needed, I can hang a shingle and get into the law business and make money."

Rama smiled in admiration and planted another kiss on my face.

While I was confident that I would pass the Ohio bar on my first attempt, the letter from the Board fortified my conviction. Obviously, my boss and the Chief Patent Counsel at NCR were satisfied that I had fulfilled my promise to earn my lawyer's license. I soon realized the impact of passing the bar. I took on a heavier load of legal work and become an advocate for my employer.

I took Rama with me to attend my swearing in on November 7, 1980 in Columbus, Ohio as an attorney and member of the Ohio bar. I was sworn in as a group with other attorneys who passed the bar examination with me. I received an official Certificate of Registration from the Supreme Court of Ohio, which proclaimed me as attorney and counselor of law in the state of Ohio. Along with the certification, I was assigned a registration number (0013600) which was expected to remain as my attorney number for so long as my name appeared on the attorney registry of the office of the Supreme Court of Ohio.

Now that I was a licensed attorney, I filed the paperwork with the Committee on Enrollment at the USPTO to convert my status of registration from patent agent to patent attorney and have the prefix of the letter "P" in my registration number dropped. On December 10, 1980, I was enrolled in the USPTO Roster of Patent Attorneys and Agents as an attorney with the registration number of 29,784.

With my accreditation as a licensed attorney and my accomplishment of specialization in Patent Law, I was now ready for the world to open new vistas based on my professional accomplishments. In order to reach my present career goals, I had to think big. I had to reinvent myself, which took creative thinking, risk-taking and innovation born out of necessity and a passion to succeed.

However, I could not rest on these laurels, as we still had unfinished business with Rama's career. Rama and I now needed to focus on her career advancement.

Rama and I wanted her to participate in the National Resident Matching Program for her Residency, which she missed in the previous cycle. This time she met the deadline of the end of September 1980 for participating in NRMP. The matching process required the applicant to check out and have an interview with the teaching hospital staffs in her desired specialty and furnish a rank order list to NRMP for matching her with the hospital that had like interest in taking her as a Resident. With the deadline for mailing the ranking order to NRMP looming, Rama had her work cut out to make contact with the Medical Directors or Department Heads of Resident Training at various hospitals that she targeted.

To identify her rank order for NRMP, Rama made contacts with a number of teaching hospitals to learn about their particular Residency program. These included: a flexible Residency program at Good Samaritan Hospital in Dayton, Ohio; Pediatrics Residency at Children's Medical Center in Dayton, Ohio; Residency Program in Pediatrics at the Cook County Hospital in Chicago, Illinois; Pediatric Residency Program at the University of Chicago, Illinois; Department of Radiology at the University of Michigan Medical School in Ann Arbor, Michigan; Department of Pediatrics at St. Louis City Hospital in St Louis, Missouri; Pediatrics Residency at St. Louis Children Hospital, St Louis, Missouri; Department of Anesthesiology at The Miami Valley

Hospital, Dayton, Ohio; Department of Anesthesiology at University of Cincinnati, Cincinnati, Ohio and more.

Rama was unsure what specialty she wanted to pursue. While radiology and dermatology were at the top of her interests, she could not apply to those because they were closed to foreign medical graduates due to the high demand for these specialties from American medical graduates. Rama initially thought of specializing in Pediatrics because she thought it would be manageable not only during her three years of Residency, but also when she went into private practice after receiving her medical license. Time to devote to her family was of paramount importance. Anesthesiology was still an attractive consideration

The process of filling out applications for each of the Residency programs, with a customized cover letter and identifying at least three references that each application asked for was a monumental task. As Rama was busy taking care of our toddler, I typed up her application blanks by filling in her data, prepared cover letters, kept track of which of her three selected references were identified in the applications and mailed them with her affixed signature. Many of her letters resulted in invitations for interviews at the respective hospitals. During the months of November and December 1980, I drove Rama to eight hospitals based in St Louis, Chicago, and Cincinnati and locally in Dayton. We dropped off our son with Rama's mother, who had returned to St. Louis to Arna's home while Rama attended her scheduled interviews.

The interview process was daunting but provided an opportunity to dismiss hospitals where she did not want to do her Residency. After she returned home with our son, on behalf of Rama I wrote personal thank you letters to the Directors and Department Heads who facilitated her interviews at their hospitals.

Rama then filled out the rank order listing of hospitals and mailed it to NRMP for the matching process to be completed.

Returning to Rama's naturalization, she identified to INS the mandated two witnesses (P.J. Lad in San Diego and Dr. Sreedevi Maddipati in St. Louis). INS scheduled a second interview with the Naturalization Examiner on December 9, 1980 at the U.S. District Court in Dayton. The purported reason for this interview was: "Examination of your knowledge of the American Government." Rama patiently attended the interview. She was asked questions on the workings of the U.S. Government, which she answered. Rama passed the test.

Three weeks later Rama received notification that her petition for naturalization had been approved. Along with it she received a "Notice of Naturalization Oath Ceremony" requesting that she participate in a ceremony scheduled for January 13, 1981 at the U.S. District Court of the Southern District Court of Ohio in Columbus.

I drove Rama to Columbus for her swearing in. At the naturalization ceremony, she took the Oath of Allegiance and became a United States citizen on January 13, 1981. She turned in her Alien Registration card and picked up her Certification of Naturalization.

Like I did four years earlier when I became a citizen of the U.S., she registered to vote in Montgomery County of Ohio where we lived, and she immediately applied for her American passport. Part of the reason for becoming a U.S. citizen was for Rama to assimilate fully into the community, taking local and national issues facing the country into consideration, and to become an instrument for change where needed. Rama now derived many additional benefits of U.S. citizenship, which she would exercise in the future when the occasion arose.

One such benefit, which had been pressing, was family reunification. In particular, the reunification of her younger brothers Mali and Rajen, who were now biding time in Jamaica.

Weeks after Rama was naturalized, on her behalf I filled out two separate petitions to classify the status of her brothers Mali and Rajen for issuance of an immigrant visa—the Form I-130. The supporting documents that Rama had requested from her brothers and parents months earlier were crucial in filing these petitions. I submitted her petitions with supporting documents to INS in Cincinnati.

The skills that I had learned as an attorney came in handy when filling out Rama's petitions and other legal documents. Without a question, INS found her submitted petitions acceptable. She received a Notice of Approval stating the petitions were sent to the U.S. Consulate in Kingston, Jamaica. The Notice further stated that "under the law only a limited number of visas are issued by the Department of State each year and they must be issued strictly in the chronological order in which petitions were filed for the same classification. When the beneficiary's turn is reached on the visa waiting list, the U.S. Consulate in Kingston, Jamaica will inform him and consider issuance of the visa."

We knew that the waiting period for the Green Card for Rama's brothers would be years away, and she was resigned to this long wait as were her brothers.

In mid-March 1981, NRMP matched Rama with St. Louis City Hospital in their Pediatrics program. The hospital followed up the match by sending Rama a congratulatory letter on April 19. It invited her to sign a contract as a PL-1 Intern in Pediatrics Service for a term extending from July 1, 1981 to June 30, 1982 for a specified gross stipend.

After reviewing the simple and yet binding contract, Rama discussed the offer with her family members in St. Louis. The separation of our family because of her relocation to St. Louis did not appeal to either of us. Also, it would be imprudent for me to quit NCR in less than two short years of employment. NCR was generous to train me and was patient with the months of time off I received to study for my Patent and Ohio bars. I felt it was not moral or ethical to abandon NCR at that time.

Nevertheless, to satisfy Rama, I explored patent attorney positions in St. Louis. There were a couple of major corporations located in that city, including the headquarters of General Dynamics, my previous employer in San Diego, and McDonnell Douglas, another defense contractor. In addition, a few law firms not particularly well-known for patent practice were operating their businesses in St. Louis. Since I did not want to work for a defense contractor again in my new capacity as a patent lawyer, it basically came down to working for a law firm. This meant that I needed to be licensed in the State of Missouri. The thought of taking the Missouri bar examination so soon after passing the Ohio bar repelled me.

Even though Rama had the support of her sister in St. Louis, she was ambivalent about the conditions, safety and security at St. Louis City Hospital since it was located in a high crime area. Her sister pointed out this fact which we did not know when Rama went for her interview at this hospital. She thought through the pros and cons of working at this hospital. The cons seemed to have outweighed. She made up her mind to not accept the position.

On April 7, 1981, I drafted a letter to the Director of House Staff Education at the St. Louis City Hospital expressing Rama's profound regret: "I am not in a position to accept the position of PL-1 Intern in Pediatrics Service at St. Louis Children's Hospital that was offered." In her letter Rama laid out the facts. "Recall our discussion at our interview last December in which I pointed out that my husband, who is a lawyer, may not find suitable employment in St. Louis? My husband has not found such employment in St. Louis, so far. If I were to sign the binding contract you sent, I may be forced to live in St. Louis apart from him for an uncertain period of time and thereby be subjected to considerable hardship." However, Rama left the door open by stating that "If my husband succeeds in his job search in the St. Louis area, I will be pleased to contact you to fill any unfilled PL-1 pediatric positions that you may have."

Rama signed the letter and mailed it. She followed the letter with a telephone call the next day to the Director to personally express her regrets. The Director listened. She had not yet received Rama's letter of April 7 so did not have the benefit of reading its content and being aware that Rama was open for working together in the future.

The Director wrote back a caustic letter on April 8, 1981, which referred to the previous day's telephone conversation with Rama. She quoted words from NRMP that "Students and Hospitals who are matched through the matching plan should consider themselves bound in the same fashion as they would be if the regular contract of the hospital has been signed by both parties."

This letter essentially turned off Rama and reinforced the misgivings she had in working at the St. Louis City Hospital.

Rama continued to focus on doing a Residency in Anesthesiology at the University of Cincinnati from which she had been receiving positive overtures of future acceptance. Finally, on March 24, 1981, she received a formal letter from Dr. Brian Robins, Director of Resident Education & Coordinator of the Residency Program at UC. It extended an offer for a PGY-1 position in the Anesthesiology Residency Training Program commencing July 1, 1981. Rama immediately accepted the offer.

Rama's accomplishment of lining up a Residency position was impressive, and she deserved to be applauded. This included: the time and effort she put into passing her ECGMG examination; the time and effort she invested in completing a year of her internship in Physical Medicine, while being separated from me soon after our wedding and living alone in a faraway place; the tenacious effort she made to visit nearly a dozen teaching hospitals and have personal interviews with the Directors of Residency programs; doing everything by the book to be matched by NRMP; and finally lining up her Residency in Anesthesiology outside the purview of NRMP, which by itself was a marvelous accomplishment. I felt that I was an integral part of Rama's accomplishment, albeit in a supporting role.

There was a purpose behind our joint accomplishment. That purpose was to invest time, effort and energy to accomplish something worthwhile in life, something within our reach, with the expectation of building a good and enjoyable life for our nuclear family.

When my father-in-law heard about Rama's acceptance in the

Residency position, he was thrilled and took pride in her. No doubt Rama's father was very proud because he always encouraged and supported her to be a successful doctor. He had made a huge investment in her medical education. Most important, he personally assured me that she would succeed as a doctor, despite my ambivalence immediately after I wedded her. Rama now demonstrated that she was on track to fulfill his assurance.

I was even more impressed by and admired Rama's immense desire to please me by securing her new Residency. Everything seemed to be falling neatly in place. I was pleased with Rama as my wife. She was also becoming strong and emotionally more capable and resilient to handle life's challenges.

While I focused on intellectualism, Rama had a great combination of intellectualism and romanticism. Speaking with her at a high level was easy. She readily understood what I was saying and grasped my thoughts and responded intelligently. Sometimes, Rama completed my unfinished sentences. That's how quick she was in grasping my thoughts. I joked with her that she read my mind and had a telepathic way to penetrate my mind.

Where did I stand with my plan? Well, there were the siblings who I had sponsored and facilitated for a Green Card.

For one, my sister Swati was now married without my father or me shelling out a dowry. She had managed to find an eligible and promising veterinarian who now joined her also as a Green Card holder. They were both living in my house in San Diego.

The other two siblings who I also had facilitated for Green Cards—my brother Ohan and sister Mala—were on the lookout to find suitable spouses who were based in India. I figured that it was now only a matter of time that they too would be wedded.

With four of his ten children now married, my father did not have to pay a dowry for marrying off his first two daughters. He did not have the benefit of receiving a dowry for marrying off his first two sons, either. So far, the dowry score seemed to be even, unless my older brother received a dowry from his parents-in-law in some other material way than cash, which I did not know. He never shared the quid-pro-quo of his marriage. For all outward appearances, the dowry score for my father was even and it was a zero-sum game.

MEDICAL RESIDENCY

THE UNITED STATES was attracting scholars from abroad at the time that Rama accepted her second Residency program. This was particularly true of medical scholars, as there was a shortage of physicians in many parts of the USA. Many of the foreign medical graduates held a medical degree from an accredited medical school. They successfully had completed an Internship and Residency and were trained to practice medicine in their native countries, like my wife Rama before her arrival in the U.S. Yet barriers had been erected in this country against their continued practice of medicine. These barriers involved duplicative training to make sure that the foreign medical graduates met this country's educational and quality standards which the American medical industry groups believed were unmatched elsewhere in the world. Also, specialization in fields like Dermatology, Ophthalmology and Radiology was out of the question for foreign medical graduates. Rama's passion was to specialize in Dermatology, but she stood no chance to gain admission for such training.

The offer that Rama had received in March 1981 from the University of Cincinnati for the Anesthesia Residency training was less desirable and less attractive from her interest perspective. Nevertheless, Rama was grateful and accepted her Residency at UC. Anesthesiology was one of the top-paying specialties and generally attracted far more applicants than available Residency slots.

She rationalized her acceptance this way: The Residency training would be completed in three years or possibly sooner; the American Board of Anesthesiology already had indicated that the previous full-year Residency training in Physical Medicine that she completed might receive consideration toward her Anesthesiology Residency. More than this, the practice in Anesthesiology did not demand being "on call" around the clock so she should be less stressed during the Residency. It also appeared to offer good work-life balance. This specialty, while being intellectually demanding, was yet likely amenable to family life, with high-pressure workdays offset by possibly ample personal time.

Although Rama accepted the offer of Residency at UC, travel from Kettering to Cincinnati was not within the normal commuting distance. Cincinnati was accessible by car via the interstate highway but was located nearly 60 miles away. Selling our house in Kettering in less than two years and moving to Cincinnati did not make sense as we would face a financial loss from this. We needed to find a solution to the housing problem for Rama so that her daily commute to UC would be manageable.

The University House Staff noted that Rama was eligible to rent rooms or an apartment at the University through the Housing Office. However, we decided to remain as a family unit and live together in our own dwelling. Accordingly, we scouted for a rental dwelling in the northern part of Cincinnati, closer to Dayton, so my daily commute from the rented unit in Cincinnati to NCR in Dayton would be somewhat less than 60 miles. We decided to rent a two-bedroom single family row-house in the nice and modern Williamsburg Apartment complex in the Wyoming section of Cincinnati beginning on June 1, 1981.

Almost everyone in Cincinnati believed that their "Queen City," as it was called, was one of the most livable cities located in the "Tri-state" area of Ohio, Kentucky and Indiana. Northern Kentucky where the airport that served Cincinnati was located was quite accessible to Cincinnati's central city area. Fountain Square was the city's heart with lots of entertainment and restaurants. A few blocks south was the riverfront park for fishing or just viewing the Ohio River. In short, Cincinnati offered a good way to life, far superior than Dayton.

No sooner than when Rama accepted the offer of her PGY-1 position, paperwork started flowing to her in the mail. This included membership applications for the Ohio Society of Anesthesiologists, Academy of Medicine of Cincinnati, and American Society of Anesthesiologists. The membership to these societies was mandatory. A temporary license was required to work as a Resident at the Medical Center and was issued by the Ohio State Medical Board. I meticulously filled out these forms with Rama's assistance and sent them back to UC with notarized copies of her MBBS degree and ECFMG certificates, her photograph and a money order toward the application fee for the temporary license.

While we were awaiting the temporary license, Dr. Brian Robbins, the Director of Resident Education at the Medical Center, sent Rama a detailed timetable of her three-year residency program. Dr. Robbins stated that Rama would spend the first six months in Anesthesia. She would receive a total of four months in Clinical Sciences rotation a year in her first year as well as in each of her succeeding two years. The Clinical rotation was usually in Internal Medicine, Pulmonary Medicine,

Cardiovascular and Neurosurgery.

Rama responded fully to all requirements of the Department of Anesthesiology and she was appointed to the House Staff of the U.C. Medical Center. She knew how hectic and demanding her training was going to be for the next three years. On the top of this demanding training, she wanted to earn her permanent license to practice medicine as soon as possible as the University made subtle hints to get this license under her belt during her first year of three-year Residency. This entailed studying for, taking and passing the Federation Licensing Examination (FLEX) which is now renamed as the United States Medical Licensing Examination (USMLE).

The FLEX was an objective multiple-choice examination with testing in the areas of Basic and Clinical Science as well as in Clinical Competence. Rama felt comfortable and was prepared to handle the testing in Basic and Clinical Sciences. However, she needed more knowledge in Clinical Competence, which she would gain after completing her first year of Residency. Accordingly, she made plans to take the FLEX examination, which was offered only twice a year, in June of 1982.

Despite our preoccupation with lining up Rama's Residency and my own professional advancement as a patent attorney at NCR, our newborn—who was now less than ten months old—had been receiving well-deserved attention, albeit less than 100%. He had been growing in a normal fashion and was now beginning to take gentle steps and utter simple words. Neither Rama nor I believed in stimulating his mental abilities to increase his IQ by playing Mozart while he was in the womb or soon after birth or playing Baby Einstein videos in his crib. We were convinced that by being the offspring of two highly intelligent parents, he naturally would have inherited smartness. We regularly played with him and stimu-lated him with love, affection, music and song. My wife was more adept at childrearing and had more time to devote to these important needs of our son than I could.

As the summer approached when Rama would commence her Residency, we made the heart-wrenching decision to send our infant son to India to be taken care of by Rama's parents. We arrived at this conclusion for many reasons. Keeping our son with us would create a huge distraction for Rama's Residency training. It would also create undue hardship for her. Moreover, my mother in-law—who had spent some time with our son Nesh—developed a strong bond and wanted to take him to India and care for him. Both of my parents-in-law were lonely living in India without any of their four children. They pleaded to take care of our son for their own joy in raising their first grandson and to help out Rama during her Residency.

With the decision made to send our son to India, I had applied for his U.S. passport four months before Nesh reached his first birthday. I also applied for and obtained a visitor's visa for him to facilitate his stay in India. With his American passport and Indian visa in hand, in late May of 1981 Rama and I drove our infant son to St. Louis to deliver him to my mother-in-law to take him to India. We expected our son's stay with his grandparents to be temporary, just long enough for Rama to gain her footing in the Residency training at UC and pass her FLEX.

What remained to be done was to rent out our house in Kettering. Luckily, through our neighbor realtor Diane Fogle, we were fortunate to find a dentist to lease our house. The tenant turned out to be a single man with a fiancée and a large German shepherd. He was also the son of the current Mayor of Kettering.

I drafted a lease agreement for a one-year term for him to sign, and then we vacated our house and moved into our rented unit in Cincinnati.

Back to the story of my siblings who were living in my house in San Diego. My sister Swati was now married to Subh, who had joined her in Southern California. With this development, the other two siblings in the house received an impetus to seek their respective spouses in India.

Although my motivation to sponsor my sisters was to alleviate the strain placed on my father by the dowries for his daughters, I had opted to sponsor my brother Ohan as he was inadequately employed in India. I wanted him to improve his career by gaining additional education in America, like I did, and end up in a well-paid job. After arrival in the U.S., Ohan had signed up for technical courses but he never applied himself to earning an American degree.

Ohan had been a follower. I thought he would follow in my footsteps but not so when it came to earning a higher education. He also never had shown a passion to come to America. But for the fact that I sponsored him and enabled Ohan to earn his Green Card, he would have never set foot in the U.S., certainly not as a permanent resident.

In my conversations with Ohan before he set out to find a bride in India, I advised that he should look for a compatible girl who had similar credentials as he did. Particularly after the hardship that my wife Rama had been experiencing as a doctor working on requalifying herself in the U.S., I conveyed my practical view that he would be better off staying away from marrying a doctor.

I was also concerned that Ohan's low-paying job and poor prospect of advancement as an engineer might stifle his status as the head of his family if he married a doctor. I was concerned that he may feel inadequate in his family household if his wife earned more than him.

Nevertheless, I found out that Ohan had asked my father to find a doctor bride for him. Likewise, my parents also set out to find a doctor groom to match up with my sister Mala. It was understandable that my parents bypassed alliances for Vitri and Mini who were living with them, and instead focused on matching my last sister. Vitri had an issue with a lack of formal education to readily find a suitable groom for her. Mini, although attractive, educated and smart, was known to be flaky. She refused to be considered for marriage. In 1977 she had declined my generous offer to sponsor her for a Green Card.

While my father had little influence in matching my sister Swati with a groom, he now understood the value of the Green Card held by Ohan and Mala. He emulated the example set by me and my older brother Avi. He sought doctor spouses for Ohan and Mala.

It turned out that during the same week that Rama commenced her Anesthesiology Residency at UC, Ohan made a visit to India to check out the girl that was selected for him to view. Her name was Shree. She was a doctor holding an MBBS degree. I came to know that Ohan decided to marry Shree. Their wedding was hurriedly set up and performed in mid-June of 1981 in India.

I never asked and no one shared information of a dowry that my father may have received from the parents of Shree. The prospect of my younger brother Ohan sponsoring his new bride for the U.S. Green Card was a lucrative factor for Shree and her family. The mere prospect of qualifying for a Green Card by virtue of simply marrying Ohan and Shree's subsequent potential to become a U.S. citizen opened up priceless opportunities for chain migration to the United States for her siblings and parents. Despite the fact that Ohan did not have a well-paid job in the U.S., his Green Card enabled Shree to permanently immigrate to the United States. This was indicative of the immense value Shree placed on her Green Card.

Soon after my younger brother married Shree, he followed the process of sponsoring his bride for her Green Card that I had paved way in 1976 for sponsoring Rama and that Swati emulated in 1980 for sponsoring Subh.

A parallel development in the matchmaking department surfaced in the spring of 1981 involving Mala. Apparently, through the connections of family and friends in India, my parents had identified a prospective groom for Mala. The prospective groom (Shank) and his family lived in Bangalore. Shank's father was a lawyer, and he knew about me through my classmate Shiv who was also a lawyer practicing in the State High Court in Bangalore. Shank was a medical graduate who lived with his parents.

Unbeknownst to me, the discussion of this match advanced to such a high level that Shank and his family attended the wedding reception for Ohan and Shree. Shank and his family figured prominently in photographs that were taken at this reception and later sent to me.

Even before attending the reception, the father (MR) of Shank took the unusual step of writing me a personal letter. The letter (relevant parts) reads as follows:

Dear Dr. TR Coca,

You must have come to know by now through your kind father that we have almost finalized the alliance of your beloved sister Mala with my son Shank. I have taken the permission of your father and liberty of addressing this letter to you to clarify the following as you were responsible for sponsoring your sister Mala in California, namely: Whether you sponsored her as a citizen of America with all privileges as an immigrant? Whether Mala is a Green Card holder? Whether Mala's present employment is sufficient to take her spouse without any legal hindrance?

As my son is a doctor, I thought it necessary to clarify with you as lots of restrictions were imposed upon the situation before granting of a visa in the Madras Consulate General's Office of America. Recently one of my relations who also immigrated to California had to undergo rigorous stress and strain to complete the formalities in getting the visa which took nearly one year.

As you are now an attorney, I am sure that you will not hesitate to give your considered opinion in the interest of your sister and my son as my son intends to take the necessary entrance examination in America itself at the earliest point of time either this year or in the beginning of the next year instead of wasting precious time.

My wife joins me in conveying her personal regards to you . . .

Yours sincerely,

MR

On May 25, 1981 I replied to MR as below:

Dear Mr. MR:

I am glad to receive your letter mailed May 11, 1981 informing of the settlement of marriage of my kid sister Mala to your son

Shank. As you know by direct conversation recently with my father, Mala is planning to be in India about July 1 to celebrate her wedding on July 10.

With reference to your questions, as a U.S. citizen I sponsored Mala under the Fifth Preference using Section 203(a)(5) of the U.S. Immigration and Nationality Act. Mala is a lawful permanent resident of the U.S. and has the right to sponsor her alien spouse under Section 203(a) (2) of the Act. Mala's present employment is not a hindrance to sponsor. The requirement by INS of submission of an affidavit of support by Mala—in support of which adequate employment and bank savings are needed—is to assure the U.S. government that Shank will not become public charge upon entering the U.S. What is important is the marital relationship, as evidenced by a valid certificate of marriage to my sister.

Please advise Shank to make arrangements with ECFMG to take his examination in Los Angeles. He should study for this exam after the wedding and avoid wasting his time. . . .

Finally, my sister should file the Petition at the American Consulate office in Madras. I do not have hard evidence that Petitions filed at another U.S. Consulate will be processed faster than that filed at Madras.

I hope that I answered your questions to your satisfaction...

Sincerely yours,

TRC

This was the first time a parent of a prospective suiter contacted me to inquire about my sibling and to double-check what my father and other relatives conveyed to him for truthfulness of information. Perhaps, being a lawyer, he was being extra cautious to verify facts before he committed his son to marry my sister. Or there might have been some undisclosed trepidation of the authenticity of the qualification of Shank as a medical doctor or questions about the character of his son that made him launch this inquiry to safeguard him?

In retrospect, the parents of Subh did not make similar inquiries about Swati before they settled for their matrimony. Perhaps, they were convinced enough of my U.S. entrenchment as a professional to doubt the veracity of what they had been told. Perhaps they were too enamored by the unexpected and imminent prospect of their son moving to the USA as a Green Card holder and decided not to question anything?

With the wedding date set for July 10, my sister Mala in San Diego begun to make preparations to travel to Bangalore. Then, an unexpected quirk developed. It involved a taped narrative by my sister Mini about Shank, which she sent to San Diego. After meeting Shank, Mini made cryptic comments about her observations of him which she recorded on the tape. The comments, while not critical about the character of Shank, were directed to his behavior and mannerisms. These comments threw Mala off-balance, and she had been somewhat reluctant to an arranged marriage to begin with.

I and my siblings decided to delay Mala's travel to Bangalore until we got to the bottom of these cryptic comments. While waiting to talk with Mini, we made the decision to postpone the wedding date. An unexpected issue with the health of my sister was conveyed to my parents as the reason for the change of travel and wedding plans. The wedding was now postponed.

Days later when Mala finally spoke with Mini, it turned out that her comments on the tape were a false alarm. They were merely personal observations of Mini about Shank and not intended to be in any way critical of him.

We wondered if perhaps Mini herself wanted to marry Shank and conjured up her vague and cryptic comments to throw her younger sister off-balance. However, Shank's reason for marrying Mala was to immigrate to the U.S. Any alliance between Mini and Shank was highly unlikely, and it was immediately ruled out. I thought that Mini, who rejected my offer to sponsor her for her Green Card in 1977, was probably now regretting her decision. If she was in the U.S. and held a Green Card, she might have been a candidate to marry Shank, instead of Mala. I said to myself that God acts in strange ways to determine the destiny of us mortals.

With the clarification that the taped comments of Mini were benign, it was collectively decided by me and my siblings in San Diego to move forward with Mala's wedding. However, it took considerable effort on the part of my parents and older brother Avi to sooth the nerves of the groom and his family. They seemed to have gone wild and conjured up all sorts of nefarious issues that might relate to Mala and be responsible for the abrupt postponement of the scheduled wedding date.

Nevertheless, when Mala finally travelled to Bangalore in the summer of 1981 and met with Shank and his family, all of the suspicions about her imagined nefarious issues melted away. Instead they were impressed with the charm, beauty and sense of confidence and humor that my sister displayed. They were all ecstatic to have settled for the alliance which exceeded their wildest expectations. Over and beyond this, she was going to sponsor Shank for a Green Card so he could immigrate to the United States.

With the priceless gift of a Green Card that was offered to Shank in return for marrying Mala, there was absolutely no discussion of any dowry payment by my father. The realization by the groom's family that the Green Card would in due course dramatically enhance Shank's potential wealth as a successful American doctor rendered the discussion on dowry mute.

Mala's wedding with Shank took place as planned. As expected, the wedding was conducted in the ceremonial style of a Hindu wedding and was attended by relatives and friends from both families. After the wedding, Mala took her newly married husband to the U.S. Consulate's office in Madras and filed the petitioned for his U.S. Green Card.

By the fall of 1981, Ohan—who had sponsored his bride Shree for a Green Card in June—received her permanent visa, and she soon arrived to live with her husband in our house in San Diego. The number of relatives living in my San Diego house had now grown to five. It was only a matter of time before this rose to six with the anticipated arrival of Shank to join Mala.

I felt very good that I had fulfilled part of my objective of bringing my siblings into the U.S. and facilitated them with their Green Cards to live permanently in the U.S. This in turn made each of them a very valuable draw to attract professional spouses. All of this happened without my father paying a single dollar of dowry. Could I declare this as mission accomplished? Not yet. There remained the unfinished business of my sisters Vitri and Mini in India, who were still unmarried and continued to live with my parents. Their marriages needed to be completed before I could make such a declaration.

I never expected or received a word of thanks or an expression of gratitude from my father for enabling the weddings of my sisters Swati and Mala without him paying a dowry. Over and beyond this, his two daughters were fortunate to have wedded educated and attractive sons-in-law who were destined to build successful professional careers in the U.S. This would directly benefit these married daughters with life of greater good. I consoled myself that my father was sometimes too quick to criticize and too slow to compliment. But then again, an overt display of affection or affirmation of gratitude by hugging, embracing, kissing or expressing in words was taboo in the Hindu culture, and my father certainly never practiced them. It seemed that there was nothing I could do to improve his ingrained attitude of financial expectation toward me. Nevertheless, I continued to faithfully move forward to fulfill my duty and self-avowed goal to financially help him with the dowries for his remaining unmarried daughters.

In January 1982 I received a letter from my sister Mini in Bangalore, who in 1977 turned down my offer to sponsor her for a Green Card. She expressed interest in being sponsored. Perhaps she realized how her other sisters with a Green Card in their possession were able to garner good husbands from India. Perhaps she got tired of my father's control over her social freedom and wanted to get away from him.

No matter what the reason was for her change of mind, in February 1982, as a benevolent brother I filled out a formal petition, as I did before for Swati and Mala, to sponsor Mini for an immigrant visa under the appropriate preference of the Immigration & Nationality Act. I had the petition notarized by my legal secretary at NCR and mailed it with associated documents and fee to INS in Cincinnati.

As I anticipated, three months later the INS approved my petition and forwarded it to the U.S. Consulate in Madras, India. As before, the Letter of Approval reminded us that only a limited number of visas may be issued each year and Mini was placed on a waiting list. I knew that the waiting period for Mini was going to be five to six years.

Rama's Residency as an Anesthesiologist began to take hold soon after she started her training at the UC Medical Center. She realized that the requirements and demands placed on her in the Anesthesiology Residency were strict. She needed to be observant, think and act fast. She had to be detail-oriented should something go awry with her patient's life hanging in the balance. She needed to be in the operating room during most of her time. She was able to handle occasional emergencies with help from her team of nurses and technicians.

As part of her training, Rama regularly had pre-operative and post-operative duties with the patients slated for surgery. She assessed them pre-operatively and developed an anesthetic plan. She took care of them in the operating room. And she took care of them during the post-operative period and wrote orders for that patient's case.

Rama realized early in her Residency that she needed to accept or at least tolerate the company of the surgeons who she was working with in the operating room. She told me that "Some surgeons were arrogant and sometimes thought that they were the captain of the OR." She needed to adapt and deal with the surgeons with a sense of humor and grace.

In the weeks and months that passed as she got used to the Anesthesiology Residency, Rama came to grips with the idea that she was not the person the patients regarded as their doctor, and that they looked to the surgeon for that esteemed role. Rama's interaction with her patients was intense but short-lived. Rama used her interpersonal skills to make her patients feel comfortable with putting their life in her hands after just a few minutes of acquaintance. Often the patients seldom remembered much about Rama's interaction with them as an anesthesiology trainee.

In the Operating Room, Rama's duties as the Anesthesiology Resident had become quite technical. After administering a medication through the patient's IV, it took effect quickly and the patient lost consciousness. After induction, Rama needed to manage maintenance and emergence. Though she depended initially on her assigned staff anesthesiologist, in time she became self-dependent for her part while also depending on the surgeons, nurses and technicians for a successful outcome with each and every patient.

Rama was on-call two days a week while she was doing her rotation in Pediatric Anesthesia. She learned a great deal while on-call about pediatric respiratory care. During this rotation, she was instructed in techniques of blood gas analysis and the logistics of maintaining an inhalation therapy service, including sterilization techniques and maintenance of equipment.

When Rama was on-call, the staff's anesthesia library located near the OR and the neonatal respiratory care unit came in handy. She was able to use her free time to study for the FLEX examination that she was planning to take during the second year of Residency.

While my wife was busy with her Residency, I continued my job at NCR by commuting with two other co-workers who lived in Cincinnati near our house and also worked at NCR in Dayton. Taking turns driving made the commute of nearly an hour each morning and evening more tolerable. We drove to work typically at 7:00 a.m. and returned home by 6:00 p.m.

In contrast to my leisurely schedule, Rama was forced to leave as early as 5:30 a.m. to be in the operating room where surgery was scheduled invariably at 6:00 a.m. In the winter mornings, when it was still dark and at times of morning precipitation, I used to worry for her safety while driving. Cincinnati was situated at latitude which was prone to form black ice on the road's surface, which could be treacherous even with proper snow tires and other safety equipment fitted to her car. As an added safety measure, I regularly loaded up her car's trunk with sandbags to increase traction while driving in slippery road conditions.

Rama put in long days of ten to twelve hours at the Medical Center. Sometimes Rama came home in an intoxicated stupor having inhaled the anesthetic gases that she had administered to her patients and so she hit the sack immediately after arriving home. On other days, especially after being on-call, she arrived home early, showered and awaited my return from work. This was a very pleasing experience to me. We occasionally went out to our favorite Chinese restaurant in the city and enjoyed spicy Sichuan food.

We regularly made phone calls to Rama's parents in India to listen to our son who had now picked up the Telugu language from his grandparents and the other children that he played with in India. I felt guilty for sending my son away during the critical formative years when interaction with parents was so important for his mental and cognitive development. I believe that the environment interacts with the genetic predisposition, particularly in the first few years when the brain is most malleable. Although the environment that my parents-in-law provided to my infant son was good, I still felt it was not the same as what Rama and I could offer him.

I told myself that it was only a matter of a short separation from our son that we needed to endure. As soon as Rama had a solid footing in her Residency training and passed her FLEX examination, I vowed we would bring him back to live with us.

At the end of spring of 1982, Rama successfully completed her PGY-1 to the complete satisfaction of the evaluators of her Residency training. Based on this successful evaluation, the Medical Center extended her Residency for the PGY-II level for the next year beginning on June 1, 1982.

From observing Rama and regularly discussing her hospital experience, I thought that Rama cultivated a warrior spirit in her early part of her Residency at UC. There was no doubt in my mind that she was also a dedicated and caring member of her healthcare team. Her professional experience in the Operating Room of inducing, maintaining and terminating anesthesia in patients and her dedication to conduct and record pre-operative and post-operative evaluations with no occurrence of death or permanent disability among patients she evaluated gave me immense confidence that in time she would be an outstanding anesthesiologist.

Rama was feeling confident about the rapid progress she was making toward a successful completion of her Anesthesiology Residency and excited about the knowledge that she had been gaining, particularly in Clinical Competence. So, in the spring of 1982, she decided to take the Federation Licensing Examination the next time it was offered. She decided to take the FLEX conducted by the Kentucky Board of Medical Licensure rather than by the Ohio Board since the application process for the Ohio FLEX was strewn with many requirements about her MBBS degree that she had earned from her Medical College in India. These requirements reminded me of the hurdles that I had faced when I applied for my Ohio bar examination for my license to practice law. Compared to the ominous requirements by the Ohio Board, the application process at the Kentucky State Board was straight forward.

Rama filled out the application for the Kentucky FLEX scheduled in Louisville for June 15, 16 and 17, 1982 and sent it together with the required documents that were already in her possession before the deadline of April 1. The only document that she could not furnish was the Certificate of Medical Education which needed to be completed by the Dean of her Medical College in India. The Certificate had some requirements imposed on the Dean. In addition to identifying Rama by her name and dates of attendance and date of graduation, it needed to be notarized to affix the appropriate seal of the college. Rama promptly forwarded the blank Certificate to the Dean of her Medical College in India to fill out and satisfy the formalities requested.

Despite this missing Certificate, her application was tentatively accepted by the Kentucky State Board, and Rama received her Federation Identification Number (FIN) card #470531004. This FIN number was to be used to identify her answer papers for scoring in the examination; she was to record it on the back cover of each of her test books. On May 11, 1982, she received her admission card to gain admission to take the FLEX examination given at the location of Executive West, Freedom at the Fairgrounds in Louisville.

The Kentucky FLEX was an objective, multiple-choice examination involving testing in the areas of Basic Science (Day 1), Clinical Science (Day 2) and Clinical Competence (Day 3). The examination resulted in a weighted distribution so that the Basic Science counted as one-sixth of the total score, Clinical Science as one-third and Clinical Competence as one-half. A FLEX weighted average of 75% was required for passing.

Rama diligently studied for the FLEX whenever she had free time during her long days of Residency. She paid more attention to gaining knowledge in Clinical Competence which carried a higher weight in the overall scoring.

Rama always had loved reading. She took refuge in books. In fact, reading has been a life-long passion for her. She had devoured thousands of books of fiction, particularly mysteries, while in India and continued incessantly to read novels after she came to the U.S. She probably has read every book that Agatha Christie ever wrote. Reading was the last thing Rama did before she went to bed. It seemed to calm her nerves, transported her into a different, imaginative and fantasy environment, and lulled her to sleep.

Rama's avid reading habits were a god-send for preparing for her FLEX. She read innumerable textbooks in preparation for the examination, including multiple volumes on Anesthesia, Medical Pharmacology, Medical Neurology, multiple volumes of *Principles of Internal Medicine, Midwifery, and Clinical Methods* as well her bible, *Current Medical Diagnosis & Treatment*.

When the time rolled around to take the FLEX, Rama was as ready as she could be to give it her best shot. I drove her to Louisville, where a block of hotel rooms was reserved by the Kentucky State Board. This made it convenient for her to stay and take the examination, which was given on the hotel premises.

Even though the Certificate of Medical Education from the Dean of Rama's medical school had not arrived, the Board was gracious enough to allow her to take the examination.

As expected, there were three days of rigorous testing that Rama and her fellow Residents participated in. Rama was so relieved when I went to pick her up at the completion of the test. She felt that she had put her best effort into this endeavor to earn her license to practice medicine.

After taking the FLEX, Rama resumed her regular Residency training of all-night on-call duties twice weekly, intensive clinical training including a rotation in the pain clinic of 100 hours per week, attending to the patients under her supervision for pre- and post-operative evaluation, etc.

I waited with baited-breath for the results of Rama's recently completed exam. Sure enough, on August 10, 1982, which happened to be our son's birthday, a letter addressed to Rama arrived from the Kentucky Board of Medical Licensure. It read in part: *"It is our pleasure to inform you that you passed the recent Flex examination for medical licensure in the State of Kentucky. Attached are the results of this examination . . ."* Her weighted average well exceeded the required minimum score.

I was euphoric at this news. It called for a celebration. I rushed to the local wine store and picked up a chilled bottle of sweet prosecco spumante and put it in our refrigerator along with two flutes to frost. I waited for my wife's return home.

Rama shuffled into our home at around 7:00 p.m. and went straight up the stairs to take a hot shower. Cleaning up after she returned from the hospital was a habit Rama had cultivated. The shower relaxed her tense muscles and refreshed her.

She walked down as *Mozart's Overture to the Marriage of Figaro* was softly playing on the radio. Rama saw me with the frosty flutes and the chilled prosecco on the cocktail table in the room.

"What is the occasion?" she asked, as I popped the bottle and poured the bubbly into the flutes.

I pulled the letter received from the Board and gently thrust it into her hands. Rama took a glance at it and knew instantly that she had passed FLEX. I hugged and kissed her. After a clink of the flutes, we sipped the bubbly.

I said with a beaming smile, "Rama, congratulations! This is a marvelous accomplishment. I am so proud of you!"

Rama acknowledged that this was superb news. She was so pleased and felt satisfied with her success. She realized that she had crossed a significant milestone in her personal and professional life. On the personal side, she had revalidated her medical knowledge by successfully crossing the hurdles that were placed in her path by the American medical industry groups. On the professional side, she was now essentially licensed to practice medicine in the United States.

We retraced Rama's journey to where she had arrived now. It took Rama six long years after entering the U.S. to achieve the milestone of earning her license to practice medicine in this country. She passed the ECFMG examination, was forced to move away from San Diego to Columbia to complete a year of Residency in Physical Medicine, crossed the restricted gates of NRMP to be matched for a Residency in Pediatrics, settled for a less desirable Anesthesiology Residency at UC, and finally passed the FLEX examination—all to demonstrate that Rama was perfectly qualified to practice medicine in this country. What an extraordinary journey this had been for a physician who was already established by the Indian Medical Establishment as a licensed doctor only to reestablish this in the United States!

Later that evening after a nice dinner, the first thought that occurred to us when the news of her passing FLEX had sunk in was to bring our son Nesh back from India.

There also remained the unfinished business of fetching the Certificate of Medical Education from the Dean of her Medical College in India, which was required by the Kentucky Board of Medical Licensure to complete the final step in granting her license. Rama notified the Kentucky Board that she would travel to India and hand-carry the Certificate signed by her former College Dean.

We decided to take advantage of the 1982 Labor Day holiday weekend, in order to minimize Rama's absence from her responsibilities as a PGY-II Resident. These duties would be shouldered during her absence by other Residents on her team. Soon Rama and I dashed off to India for a two-week trip.

The reunion with our son was somewhat unexpected. At first,

Nesh refused to be embraced and clung to his grandmother. He could only speak Telugu, which both of us spoke. Actually, it was our speaking with him in Telugu that helped him to open up. His appearance, hairstyle and attire were quite different from the time, fifteen months earlier, when we had handed him over to my mother-in-law.

Nevertheless, in a matter of a day or so, he began to accept our warm embraces and kisses and started to slowly and shyly speak with us. From our gentle touches to his hands, cheeks and face, he instinctively realized that we were fond of him and loved him. The bond between the son and mother was quickly reestablished.

Nesh soon became playful and started showing off his friends and what and how they played together. I realized that he made friends easily and felt good about him developing such an affinity. We heard from our parents-in-law about all the mischievous things that my son did over the course of the fifteen months he was with them.

Rama sent an emissary on a mission to fetch the Certificate of Medical Education from the Dean of her Medical School in Warangal. The Dean filled out the prescribed form and executed it in accordance with the formalities of the Kentucky Board. Such a personal mission turned out to bear fruit.

As my parents had not met my son yet, we travelled to Bangalore where they continued to live. It was a wonderful reunion with my mother and sisters Vitri and Mini. They took a fond liking to our son. My father was somewhat reserved initially but soon enjoyed carrying Nesh in his arms.

I sensed that something heavy was hanging over my father. Even though my two sisters in the U.S. who had received Green Cards were now married, it seemed that the remaining dowry problem associated with the two sisters still living with my parents was bothering him. My father did not know that I already had set up a private endowment of cash to pay for Vitri's dowry. However, I continued to believe that getting Vitri married was going to be a challenge—no matter how large a dowry was offered.

On my visits with my parents, I always inquired about their financial situation. Then I generously showered with them with the needed cash. On this visit, my father finally opened up about his financial picture. He said that he had continued to neglect the payment of the property taxes on his house. He added that he was unable to meet these payments out of his pension and savings. I asked whether his children in San Diego were financially helping him. While wryly acknowledging that Ohan sent small amounts of money on a sporadic basis, he said Swati so far did not share her fortune with them. His statement referring to Swati disappointed me. I did not expect Mala to chip in as she held a small job and was not earning much.

I decided not to question my father about the stacks of cash I put in his hand on my previous visit when I pleaded with him to pay off the back taxes he owed then. Instead I asked how long he had been neglecting to pay taxes.

He said: "A decade."

I quickly estimated the net property taxes due, plus the cumulative interest that the City might add to his overdue bill. I immediately exchanged U.S. dollars for rupees in the amount due for his tax bill and urged him to pay it off to remove any encumbrances on his house.

My father was aware that earlier in the year I had filed paperwork for my sister Mini to immigrate to the U.S. However, the time for processing a Green Card was now taking many years, as compared to the time when I had applied for similar petitions for my other three siblings. They had received their Green Cards almost instantly. It would take longer for Mini to receive her Green Card, but it was inevitable that she would enter the United States, find suitable employment, and establish herself. After that, it was only a matter of my father finding the perfect husband based in India who would be willing to marry Mini without paying a dowry as a quid-pro-quo for gaining his foothold in the U.S. as a Green Card holder. This modus operandi had worked well with the three siblings that I had sponsored previously. I remained confident that there was no reason to doubt that it would work with Mini too.

Rama and I returned with our son to Cincinnati in mid-September. Rama mailed the original Certificate of Medical Education that she had fetched from her Medical School to the Kentucky Board of Medical Licensure. The Board notified Rama that she was now licensed in Kentucky to practice medicine and surgery and her license number was 22335 effective immediately. After receiving this letter which constituted Rama's authority to begin practicing, and as advised by the Kentucky Board, she applied to the Drug Enforcement Administration in Chicago for her DEA permit. The DEA permit allows a practitioner to write prescriptions for her patients.

The Director of Resident Education at the Cincinnati Medical Center and all members of the House Staff were extremely pleased with Rama's accomplishment of having earned her permanent medical license so early in her Residency. The American Society of Anesthesiologists, which had elected Rama for Resident membership for the years 1981 and 1982, assigned her the permanent membership number of 30881.

With the medical license neatly buttoned up, our attention shifted to the care and well-being of our precious child Nesh. Before leaving for India to bring Nesh back, I researched all available and reputable daycare centers and nursery schools in our neighborhood. Terry's Nursery School, in the city of Wyoming where we lived, held a license after meeting the rules and regulations set forth by the state of Ohio governing child-care centers. Terry's School was licensed for children from eighteen months through six years of age, with a teacher-pupil ratio of 1 to 6.

I checked out this daycare center in person and spoke with the Principal Terry Delgado. I was satisfied by the stated operations for food inspection, emergency procedures, fire safety and their enrichment program. The convenience of the location of the Terry School near my home and on my way to work was perfect. They opened as early as 7:00 a.m. and stayed open late till 6:00 p.m., which particularly suited my needs.

I made arrangements with Terry Delgado to accept our son in her daycare beginning about mid-September, soon after we brought him back from India.

My morning ritual commenced with the baby in tow, dropping Nesh off at the daycare before making my detour to pick up my carpool mates and driving to NCR. This became the structure of my mornings, and there was something comforting about knowing exactly how my day was going to start out.

However, dropping off my beloved son early each morning to the company of other unknown toddlers seemed so cruel. I felt so guilty for abandoning him for hours each weekday at the daycare. Nesh was struggling to learn the English language from his caregivers and other toddlers who he interacted with at the school. He looked forward to my arrival late in the day and beamed a big smile my way and hugged me when I got there.

Meanwhile, my wife was extremely busy with her intensifying Residency and the more than usual number of hours she had to put in to make up for the time she took off to study for and take the FLEX, plus the two weeks of vacation she used up to bring back our son from India. It appeared that she hardly spent any time at home. In her absence, I played with Nesh and attempted to keep him physically occupied and intellectually stimulated.

The long hours that Rama was asked to work and her inability to spend quality time with our son began to take a toll on her emotional stability and physical ability. She used up her entitled vacation when she travelled to India to bring back Nesh and earlier in the year when she took time off to study for and take her FLEX. She desperately wanted to get away from this dredge. Faced with an intolerable situation, she wanted her brothers, especially Mali, stationed in Jamaica, to visit with us in Cincinnati during the Christmas holidays of 1982. She wanted Mali's support during the tough times she was going through. However, the Interviewing Officer in the U.S. Consulate in Kingston, Jamaica apparently did not feel that there were compelling enough ties to Jamaica which would draw her brothers back after entering the U.S. on a visitor's visa.

I then took the extraordinary step of writing on behalf of Rama to Ohio's two United States Senators John Glenn and Howard Metzenbaum. The letters were dated November 15 and 20, 1982 to Mr. Metzenbaum, who was just reelected to the Senate, and Mr. Glenn, respectively. The letter that I crafted for both was identical except for a congratulatory opening line in Mr. Metzenbaum's letter and in part read as follows:

> Dear Senator Glenn / Metzenbaum:
>
> I am a naturalized citizen of the United States. I am writing this letter with the hope and expectation that you will assist me in my efforts to obtain visitor visas for my two brothers, who are citizens of India and living outside the U.S., so that my family can enjoy a long-awaited reunion during the upcoming year-end holidays.
>
> Two years ago, I filed petitions with the U.S. Immigration & Naturalization Service for issuance of immigrant visas for my brothers. However, to this date they have not been granted this visa. Attempts by my brothers to obtain a temporary visitor's visa in order to visit me have not been successful.
>
> I have not seen my brothers in years and am eager to have them in my house during the upcoming Christmas holidays for a family get-together. This will be possible only if the Immigration Officials in Kingston are convinced that my visiting brothers will not remain in the U.S. beyond their temporary visa expiration period. I (a physician) and my husband (a practicing attorney) are responsible citizens of this country and give assurances that my brothers will depart from the U.S. prior to expiration of their visitor's visa.
>
> I request that you, through your good office, convey these assurances to the U.S. Consulate in Kingston, Jamaica and urge them to grant temporary U.S. visitor's visa to my brothers . . .
>
> I fully appreciate your promptness and kindness in this matter.

Yours sincerely,

Rama Coca

Both Senators Glenn and Metzenbaum acknowledged the receipt of Rama's letter and promptly forwarded it to the U.S. Embassy in Jamaica. To Rama's disappointment the hoped-for reunion did not take place in our home. After the holidays, both Senators received an identical telegraphic report from the U.S. Consulate in Jamaica which they forwarded to Rama. It was a denial of the visitor's visa. There was nothing in the report that I was not previously aware of.

I voluntarily took this extraordinary step of contacting our state's senior politicians for two reasons. First, to facilitate the family reunion that Rama has been craving for to preserve her sanity. Second, to have the U.S. Immigration authorities accelerate the processing of the Green Card for my brothers-in-law.

Ever since this wasted effort, I never again sought the help of any influential politician or anyone else on immigration matters. I went back to my belief that self-help was my best help. I reminded myself that the laws, rules and regulations in the U.S. were followed to the letter by the responsible government authorities. Influence peddling did not work when it came to legal immigration, at least at the low level of the U.S. society we were in.

Beginning with the New Year of 1983, serious health issues with my wife and our son Nesh began to surface. Rama suffered from exhaustion with over one hundred hours per week of demanding duties as a Resident. Due to the press of time, she neglected her diet to meet her incessant and heavy responsibilities at the

Medical Center. She became weak and lost weight, which was already low to start with. Compounding this agony, she needed an unexpected invasive surgery which strained her more. Rama felt guilty that her surgery and recuperation placed more burdens on her fellow Residents at the hospital.

Even though the Consular Officer in Jamaica refused to grant visitor visas for Rama's brothers, it turned out that the doctor girlfriend Sai of her younger brother who lived with him in Kingston managed to receive such a visa. She flew to Cincinnati to spend time with us and also to meet other acquaintances from her alma mater who were now living in the U.S. Although Sai was not related to us, I sensed that she had a hidden agenda to her visit. Still, she was tight-lipped and did not share her reason for visiting. It soon became obvious from the phone conversations she had with her former classmates, that Sai had visited to assess opportunities for her medical Residency in the U.S.

We were delighted to host Sai during her trip. However, with the health issues that my family was facing with Rama's hospitalization which just had preceded her visit, Sai's stay was not an enjoyable experience for our visitor. She witnessed firsthand the hardship we were going through.

With the onset of a chilly winter in Cincinnati, our son Nesh hated to wake up in the cold, dark and early morning hours and then be summarily dropped off at daycare. He used to complain, "Dad, it is so cold!" Even though he had been generally healthy, his mingling and close interaction with other children at the daycare center, some of which suffered from serious ill health, left him vulnerable to respiratory illnesses. Soon he started contracting colds and seemed to have a constant running nose.

One persistent cold turned into pneumonia. He needed to be quarantined from the other children.

Our son's pneumonia compelled Rama to take more time off to attend to his health by staying home with him. This annoyed her fellow Residents and the attending Staff who were no longer sympathetic as her absence overburdened the other Residents and upset the schedule that the House Staff depended on for the smooth operation of the training program. They could not understand Rama's dire predicament. They unrealistically expected her to perform at the same level as the other Residents and no special provisions were made by the Staff to accommodate her difficult situation at home.

After nearly a week of taking time off to enable Nesh to recover from pneumonia, Rama resumed her duties. Our son was back at the Terry Daycare Center. However, within a matter of two weeks, his nose started running again. When I came to pick him up at the end of a day, his upper lip was crusted dry from his nose running for a length of time. I was unhappy that Terry or her staff did not have the decency of washing off his nasal drippings. Their neglect of my son's health bothered me to the extent that I wanted to report it to the local health authorities.

Sure enough, this neglect led to a relapse of Nesh's pneumonia. Rama had to take time off for additional days to stay home with my son until he recovered again.

When Rama returned to the Medical Center, she could feel a mild disdain from the Residents she knew and worked with. This was the beginning of a subtle rejection of Rama's Residency despite her extraordinary accomplishment of passing the FLEX in just about a year after commencing her three-year Residency program and receiving a good evaluation of her performance after the first year. Rama could sense some hidden hostility from the

Staff as well. One or two attending Staff members hinted that Rama should take time off for an extended period and attend full-time to her son.

The cumulative effect of these happenings began to take a toll on Rama's psyche. She began to lose her vibrancy in everything she did. I could feel a sense of despair in her as she was unable to meet her own personal expectations. Rama was disappointed that she might not be able to complete her Residency and become a full-fledged Anesthesiologist, which was what I had pushed her for. The disappointment she faced became overwhelming. She felt helpless and became despondent. Rama expressed to me her struggle with a low sense of personal control over her life. I provided moral support to the extent that I could, but her inevitable resignation from the Residency position at the UC Medical Center seemed imminent.

Rama's love for music and song, along with her resilience, courage, perseverance and tremendous spirit—the traits that I felt so lucky she possessed—now had vanished. She took more refuge in her books.

This was a period when I hoped the extended family that I brought into the U.S. would jump in to help their brother's family. I kept my siblings, who continued to live with their newlywed spouses in our house in San Diego, informed about the dire and helpless situation my core family was facing. However, no offer to help was forthcoming from any of them. Understandably, they were preoccupied with their own lives. Family unity and their family ties to me and responsibility to my family's well-being did not seem to come to their mind. If this thought did cross their mind, did they simply conclude that their older brother and his family was invulnerable and did not need their help?

Rama and I wanted to discuss the predicament we were in with her Residency and the frequent health issues that our son was facing. We decided to discuss these problems over dinner. We left Nesh with the babysitter at our house and went to our favorite Chinese restaurant Cheng Du in Cincinnati. Rama was elegantly dressed in a beautiful saree. She mildly complained that she did not get to wear a saree ever since the start of her second year of Residency at the UC.

Over servings of Sichuan chicken, fried rice and spicy green beans, Rama explained how difficult it had become for her to face her fellow Residents at the Medical Center who were forced to put in extra hours at work when Rama took time off. Rama was concerned that she had not been keeping up with her training skills and her superiors were beginning to take notice.

I began to counsel her. "Rama, you need to hang in there. You are close to being over the hump in your Residency. Particularly if the Anesthesia Board were to give partial credit for the year you invested in the Physical Medicine Residency. You already earned your license to practice medicine, which was a marvelous accomplishment."

Rama dabbed at the tears trailing down her cheeks. "I don't think I can keep going," she said.

I reached for her hand and said, "Rama, I don't want you to give up. You are so close to reaching our goal. You know how difficult it was for you to get into this Residency. You are so close to reaching success. I can already sense the sweet smell of your success!"

However, my words of encouragement did not have the intended effect on her.

I could see that tears were building up in her eyes, which she was fighting. Moments later, Rama broke down in tears at the dinner table. She could not take a bite after that.

Before leaving the restaurant, we received fortune cookies. I cracked open the cookie I picked. It read, "*A golden egg of opportunity falls into your lap.*" The other, meant for Rama, read, "*One that would have the fruit must climb the tree.*" "How appropriate," I muttered under my breath.

I knew how serious a situation Rama was facing at the Medical Center. She was torn between the welfare of our precious son and the attainment of her professional success as an Anesthesiologist. I knew that she had become despondent. That night, I told myself that Rama would not be able to continue her Residency and may sooner or later terminate it.

I routinely checked with the tenant who rented our house in Kettering, now on a month-month basis, to see how his tenancy was going. I hinted to him that my family may move back into the house because of my potentially changed circumstances. I alerted my tenant that he may have to vacate the house on short notice, without specifying a deadline. He was very receptive.

In early January 1983, the thought crossed my mind that perhaps Rama needed a break from her intense training. Perhaps a move from the gloomy and eternally overcast skies of the Dayton and Cincinnati area to a sunnier place would be a welcome change for her. With this in mind, I started to explore new opportunities to embellish my own career.

Two attractive corporate counsel positions immediately

appeared on the horizon for me to consider. Both were arranged by Bob Piehl of the Patent & Legal Placement Agency in Carlsbad, California. Bob placed me with NCR in 1979.

The first was a position with Texas Instruments based in Dallas, Texas to handle enforcement of TI's semiconductor patents for licensing to other companies. In mid-January, the Chef Patent Counsel Mel Sharp invited me for a personal interview in Dallas.

As I was not in a position to burden Rama with our son, I audaciously suggested, "Mel, would you be able to travel to Cincinnati to meet me?"

Surprisingly, he accepted.

A few days later Mel made a trip to Cincinnati where I met him for dinner. Even though he was enjoying a gourmet dinner with several servings of fine wine during our conversation, I resisted the temptation to imbibe and also avoided any items on the dinner menu which might obstruct the clarity of my oral communication with him.

The conversation seemed to have gone well and Mel asked whether I would be able to meet his staff for a formal interview at TI's headquarters in Dallas, Texas. I accepted. The following week I made a quick dash to Dallas to meet with a team of five or six patent counsels and managing attorneys, including Rhys Merritt, Rich Donaldson and Mel who explained the imminent launch of an ambitious program of licensing TI's extensive semiconductor patent portfolio. Mel was extremely eager to hire me because of my extensive qualifications and strong background in Physics and my Asian heritage. He impressed upon me that the TI's launch would initially focus on the Japanese and Korean semiconductor companies who he said had been infringing TI's patents. After that TI would extend the licensing program to other companies in Asia, including in Taiwan, Singapore and Hong Kong. I was fascinated by the enthusiasm that the TI team displayed to establish TI as a potential benchmark for patent licensing.

That evening I was treated to an extravagant dinner in a prestigious restaurant in Dallas. Mel and Rhys wined and dined me in the hope that I would come to work for TI. By the end of the evening, Mel could not resist making me an oral offer of employment at TI, with a promise of a formal written offer to follow. The salary Mel offered was substantially more than what I was earning at NCR. Importantly, the nature of the job Mel offered was exciting. I felt happy that the entailed move of my family to the warm and sunny Dallas would be a welcome change for Rama.

Upon returning home, when I detailed my interview at TI and the job offer I had received, Rama was relieved. She saw the light at the end of the tunnel of her Residency. She was happy that I was advancing in my career, which would take away the immediate pressure on her Residency.

The second corporate counsel position was with IBM Corporation in Fishkill, New York. After my initial telephone inquiry in mid-January 1983 about this position with the IBM site Patent Counsel Joseph Redmond, I received a formal invitation for a personal interview scheduled for February 4 to meet with him and other IBM attorneys in Fishkill.

I flew to New York's LaGuardia Airport, rented a car and followed the written directions I had received. Fishkill appeared to be in the boonies, quite far away from New York City. Besides Joe Redmond, I met with John Jordan, who was the Managing

Attorney under Joe, and several other IBM staff attorneys. I toured the microelectronic facility where semiconductor chips were being fabricated. The job was a low-end attorney position, somewhat akin to my current job at NCR. However, I was impressed with IBM's worldwide organization of the Patent Department and the immense opportunities for advancement that it offered.

Upon returning home, I followed up with a letter of thanks to Joe for inviting me, sent back my filled-in IBM employment application and identified three personal references as requested by John. I expected to hear from Joe almost immediately as he seemed to be in a hurry to fill the open position. I awaited word about the result of my interview, but I received only absolute silence.

In the meanwhile, as promised, Mel Sharp formalized and mailed the job offer with TI that he had communicated to me in person in Dallas weeks earlier

I was under some pressure to make a decision on TI's offer, but I wanted to hear from IBM about their decision. Weeks passed by and still only dead silence from IBM. Upon making inquiries using the recruiter Bob Piehl, I found out that there had been an unexpected change of management at IBM-Fishkill from Joe Redmond to a new Manager Ed Brown. During this management shuffle, my employment application apparently fell through the cracks.

When I contacted Ed Brown, he was apologetic about this oversight. He invited me for a second interview with him and two Senior Patent Managers from IBM's Corporate Headquarters: Paul Carmichael and Murry Nanes. As I did not wish to further disrupt Rama's schedule at the Medical Center by saddling her with our son, I requested whether it was possible for the IBM management to meet with me on a Saturday when Rama normally stayed home and could attend to our son. Paul and Ed graciously agreed. We decided to meet on March 5 at the Roger Sherman Inn in Wilton, Connecticut.

As before, I flew to LaGuardia and drove from the airport to Wilton. The interview over lunch was very cordial. Paul did most of the talking. He was extremely gracious and amicable. From his body language I could tell that I was making a positive impression on him, particularly after he asked me about my expected starting date at IBM.

I quickly realized that Paul was the decision-maker on hiring me. I asked about the opportunities in Asia, as I was still pondering over TI's overture to engage me in patent licensing in Japan and Korea. Paul explained that an unlimited growth potential existed at IBM, particularly the opportunity to work at the IBM Asia Pacific Headquarters in Tokyo.

My conversation with Paul reinforced my sense that IBM presented by far a greater opportunity geographically, as well as the choice of work for a patent professional. I came away with the impression that as an attorney I could continue to be a patent prosecutor like I was now at NCR or handle transactions, non-patent work, licensing, legislation and litigation. The dual opportunity to advance either on the professional ladder or to climb the management ladder impressed me. The large IBM Patent Operations with over one-hundred patent attorneys and well-established guidelines and procedures, was a plus for working at IBM.

Days after my second interview, Ed Brown called me to extend an offer of employment at IBM, which he followed up with a written offer on March 22, 1983. The salary that IBM offered was comparable to that which TI previously had offered, with similar benefits. The letter expressed the hope that "you will be able to start your employment at IBM on April 25, 1983," the start date that I had proposed during my interview with Paul.

In late February, even before IBM extended a job offer to me, and as I was already sitting on a job offer from TI, Rama notified her Directors, Dr. Brian Robbins and Dr. Philip Bridenbaugh, of her intention to take leave effective immediately.

She left her hard-earned Residency position with a heavy heart and disappointment. In retrospect, perhaps we were too hasty to have brought our son back from India. Perhaps if we waited a little longer, Rama would not have been distracted from the health issues with our son. Perhaps if my mother-in-law had come to Cincinnati to take care of our son, he might not have had contracted bouts of pneumonia triggered from his exposure to the other children at daycare. If only Rama had had such support, she could have maintained her momentum and successfully completed her Residency and become a full-fledged Anesthesiologist. However, it was now water over the bridge.

"Nothing in life is certain," I told Rama.

I thought personal introspection might help Rama heal her broken spirit; there was nothing she could have done to reverse the bleak situation that she ended up with in her professional career.

Rama's abrupt decision to terminate her medical Residency brought about robust strains on each of us—manifested in depression, suicidal thoughts and family dysfunction. However, my newfound job at IBM took me away from a long-term dysfunction, but Rama did not have such an external professional outlet. Instead, she focused on our son Nesh, infused him with love and begun to shape him into a marvelous young boy devoted to his mother. Rama, in due course, slowly began to regain her resiliency on her own.

The ordeals, successes and failure that Rama was experiencing now were reminiscent of what I had endured when I did not find a job as a physicist immediately after earning my doctorate. Like before, the imposed challenge now provided a catalyst for change in our lives.

In the meanwhile, at my request, the tenant vacated our Kettering house. Because he had a large dog living there during his tenancy, I had to have the house thoroughly cleaned and disinfected before we could move back with our young son. In mid-March we vacated our Cincinnati home that we had rented and moved back to our owned home in Kettering.

We quickly settled back into our familiar house. Rama found a daycare center nearby where she arranged to have our son spend a couple of hours per day to interact with other children of his age. She also needed to recover herself from the profound change in her professional life and to regain her mental stability by having some needed free time. My commute to NCR was now a breeze.

With the IBM offer in hand, on April 1, 1983 I alerted my boss at NCR of my intension to resign effective May 1 and formalized it with a resignation letter. I promised that I would button up my unfinished NCR work items before I left.

Weeks earlier, I called Mel Sharp at TI and informed him that

I was unable to accept his generous employment offer. He was disappointed. When I told him that I was joining IBM instead, he felt even more disappointed.

He told me, "Your refusal is a loss to TI but a huge gain to IBM."

I felt guilty at my rejection as Mel had walked an extra mile to woo me to be on his team. I was convinced that he envisioned great expectations for my career at TI, although I also sensed that he had the ulterior motive of exploiting my teaming with the TI's patent licensing group to generate hundreds of millions of dollars of income for his company.

So my decision had been made to move to Fishkill, New York. IBM generously made a relocation offer to help me sell my house, either by picking up the sales commissions and costs associated with the sale or taking the house outright from my hands at the appraised value. We opted to spruce up the house with a fresh coat of paint, sell off furniture to unclutter the rooms, and add other nice small touches to maximize the appraisal value. Once we received the appraisal, by working with the IBM Relocation Agency, we put the house up for sale at a slightly higher price than our purchase price of four years earlier. Because of my preoccupation with the house appraisal, I made arrangement with Ed Brown to commence employment with IBM a couple of weeks later, on May 9, 1983.

During the first weekend of May 1983, I travelled to Fishkill alone and signed up for employment with IBM on Monday May 9, 1983. I received my employee number and the IBM badge. After going through the formalities with the Human Resources

Department, John Jordan, who was anointed as my immediate manager, ushered me into my private office. The office had large floor-to-ceiling windows on one side and was completely enclosed with a door. This was a dramatic improvement from the 5-foot-high open cubicles in which I worked at NCR. All of the other attorneys had similar offices, so did John and Ed who occupied corner offices with two continuous walls of glass.

As the first order of business, John and Ed encouraged me to focus on finding a house in the Fishkill area. I combed Duchess County, where IBM was located, for an apartment or house to rent. I lined up several dwellings with the expectation of inviting Rama to travel to Fishkill and make the final decision on the dwelling. Rama arrived with our son the following week. We decided to rent a two-bedroom apartment on a temporary basis on the beautiful Hudson River in Beacon, New York until we found a nice house to purchase. I signed a six-month lease. Rama returned with our son to Kettering.

However, while we were away, our house in Kettering had been burglarized. Rama was scared by this untoward incident when she returned home and discovered the burglary. By smashing the glass windows in one of the bedrooms, the burglars entered the house and stole our TV, stereo, jewelry and other belongings.

The next day I returned home to Kettering and we accelerated our move by accepting the IBM offer to purchase our house at the appraised value. I had the moving company arranged by IBM's Relocation Department. The deal was that they would pack up our household belongings and deliver them, along with one of our cars, to our apartment in Beacon, New York.

I drove our family to Fishkill. On the way, like Rama and I did six years earlier when we drove cross-country from Philadelphia to San Diego, we stopped in Pittsburg, Pennsylvania at the Lord *Venkateshwara* temple. I believed in making a pilgrimage to this temple, which we had soon after our son was born. While we did not really make a planned pilgrimage this time, as Pittsburg happened to be on our way to Fishkill, I felt compelled to stop.

I silently prayed for Lord *Venkateshwara* to grant me the serenity to accept the things I could not change. I prayed for the His blessings on my family who had gone through so much trial and tribulation over the past few months. Rama's recovery from the battering that she recently took was paramount in my prayers. I silently prayed for success in my career at IBM so my wife would not have to work ever again as a physician. I prayed for her resiliency and the restoration of her cheerful laughter. Perhaps, the Lord heard my prayer!

TRIUMPH AS INTELLECTUAL PROPERTY ATTORNEY

TOWARD THE END of May 1983, after the moving company arranged by the IBM Relocation Department delivered our household belongings, we moved into the rental unit in Beacon, New York on the Hudson River. Moving to a new place was intimidating and a lonely experience with potential isolation. Given the dark past that Rama had experienced with her Residency in Cincinnati and the burglary in Kettering, we did not miss our old homes in Ohio and felt no need to keep in touch with the friends and colleagues we left behind.

At the same time that the move was intimidating, it was also exciting. It was adventurous and opened up our curiosity to find out the new town's history, culture, social aspects, recreational facilities and other offerings. We explored the diverse and rich history of Duchess County, where Beacon and Fishkill were located. During the weekends, we crisscrossed the county and discovered the quaint and picturesque towns along the Hudson. This included historical sites in Ticonderoga, the Roosevelt Memorial in Hyde Park and the West Point military academy south of Newburg.

Life goes on, right? The change of place was a badly needed therapy for Rama, as it kept her fully occupied and brought about the sense of a new beginning in our lives. We did not start making lasting friendship with our neighbors in the rental complex as our stay there was expected to be short, pending the finding of a house we anticipated owning and settling down.

One of the perks that IBM extended exclusively to its employees was free access to the country clubs that the company owned. One such club was located in Poughkeepsie, which was less than ten miles away from Beacon. The club was sprawling with a golf course, tennis courts, racket ball courts, a bowling alley, cafeteria, and picnic grounds for children to play in. Spending our time at this club became a regular weekend event and opened up our social life in the IBM community.

We channeled much of our energy into finding a good house for our family based on our allowed budget. A house that I regularly drove by on my way to and from work intrigued me. The doors and windows of this house were fully boarded up. However, it was an English Tudor perched atop a small hill, with a curved and paved driveway leading to the house. The front yard, which sloped to the street level, had over-grown weeds. It was surrounded by many tall Canadian maple and spruce trees. Although located on a busy county road, the Tudor house was somewhat isolated except for a single neighbor whose ranch-style house was located across an active creek. I walked around the side of the house to the backyard. The back of the house had a neatly constructed stacked stone wall, and it was private with acres of wooded grounds. Adjacent to the house structure was a raised wooden deck with steps built for access to an above-ground pool, but the pool itself was dismantled. The house carried no sign for sale, and it looked abandoned.

I was intrigued by this house despite the fact that Rama and I had looked at dozens of nice houses for sale in the neighborhood yet did not settle on one to buy. By checking with local realtors, I came to know that the Tudor was now possessed by a local bank. Apparently, the previous owners of the house went through a divorce and walked away from meeting their mortgage obligations.

My inquiry to the bank prompted interest to sell. The quoted selling price was very attractive. However, the bank imposed the condition that the sale was "as is" at the offered selling price. I was not sure whether I could qualify for a mortgage without the benefit of Rama's salary for a typical normal house in Duchess County, which costed substantially higher than the Tudor. Besides, I was already burdened with a mortgage on my San Diego house. So I opted to take a huge risk and accept the bank's conditional offer.

After six weeks, in October 1983, my mortgage application to purchase the Tudor was approved, and we closed on it. Upon un-boarding the house, Rama and I did our first walk-through to inspect it. We were pleasantly surprised at the condition of the home. The entry door to the house, after the boards were removed, was made of solid mahogany wood with decorative carvings on the inside and outside. Right off the bat, we were impressed by the quality of construction of the house. Inside, it was well-constructed all around with solid visible wooden beams in excellent condition, a blue-tiled entryway, a nice kitchen, family, dining and formal living rooms on the first floor, which lead via an easy staircase to three well-laid-out bedrooms and a bath. The house was contemporary in style with large windows in every room, which filtered the sun from two or three directions. The carpets were of high quality and in excellent condition, except they needed a thorough cleaning. The refrigerator in the kitchen was smelly from abandoned food but in working condition.

Rama and I could not believe what an excellent find this house was. We had the house thoroughly scrubbed and quickly made it livable. What remained to be done was essentially outside the house in the front and back garden areas, as they were completely overtaken by weeds. I decided to take care of the weeds after we moved into the Tudor.

We made arrangement with a local firm to move our household belongings from our rental unit to the Tudor. However, an unforeseen tragedy involving our son Nesh befell us. The night before the firm was to move us I dismantled a queen-sized bed and let the wooden frame lean against a wall. Unbeknownst to Rama and me, Nesh—who was playing in the house—went to the leaning wooden frame and seems to have pushed it. It fell on him. His right leg was caught under the frame and he yelled in agony. We rushed him to the Vassar Hospital in Poughkeepsie. The X-rayed photos of his injured leg revealed that he suffered from a tibia fracture along the length of his bone, between the knee and ankle. A cast was applied on his fractured leg to have it reset. The Orthopedics specialist who applied the cast advised that the cast be left on for two to three months for complete healing.

Rama and I felt so remorseful for this grim happening. I felt very guilty for not being watchful of Nesh's moves and careless in leaving the bed frame dangerously leaning against the wall.

We moved into the Tudor house as planned the next day, despite the accident that saddened us and made our son suffer from the pain caused by his injury. As if Rama did not have enough on her hands, she now had to devote extra care to our son including physically carrying him everywhere.

I told Rama, "You have your hands full with Nesh. Please just focus on him. Don't worry about the house. I will attend to it and restore it with whatever time I need to invest during the weekends."

Rama put Nesh on the sofa and let him watch cartoons on TV. She got into sprucing up the inside of the house.

When I told my boss Ed Brown at IBM about my adventurous house purchase, he was bewildered. He could not believe that I would take such a huge risk with the purchase of a house unseen on the inside. He was happy with the outcome of my purchase and remarked about the house: "I am sure you are bound to make a silk purse out of a sow's ear."

From the first day, I was fascinated by IBM in every aspect. I was impressed by the IBM management and my fellow Patent Attorneys who were cordial, friendly and willing to share their work experiences. Some were so talkative that at times I had to politely escort them out of my office and shut the door so I could concentrate on my work.

Brilliant people worked at IBM, including mathematicians, physicists, chemists, computer scientists, etc. A few were Nobel Prize winners. They carved new frontiers in their fields of study bringing fame and fortune to themselves, to IBM and to America. The inventions they made were simply mind-boggling. To understand their breakthroughs required scientific knowledge. This was where my background in physics came in handy. In my capacity as a physicist and a patent attorney, I could speak their language, make intelligent conversation, and comprehend the breakthroughs they made. The combination of physics and law that I possessed rendered it easy to document their ideas for legal protection.

It seemed ironic that a decade earlier, fresh after earning my Ph.D., I dreamed of working at IBM and continuing my research in superconductivity. That avenue then was not foreordained. I could not get into IBM. However, by taking a new path I made my way into IBM in a different capacity—as a Patent Attorney. Also, my effort a decade earlier toward my doctoral thesis to find the high temperature superconductor was realized in 1986 by my fellow IBM'ers. Two physicists who worked in the IBM Research Labs in Zurich, Switzerland discovered such a superconductor. They won the Nobel Prize in Physics that year.

Even though I had the luxury of a dedicated clientele, namely the employees of IBM-Fishkill, I had to keep multiple balls in the air to fulfill my job responsibilities. This included staying on top of the technology to understand the inventions made by my clients, keeping abreast of the decisions of the federal, state and local courts, and also being linked to my specialty of Intellectual Property law to counsel my clients. This meant an up-to-date knowledge of patents, copyrights, trademarks, and trade secret laws. This demanded endless hours of reading technical, legal and IP literature. Writing patent applications, petitions and appeal briefs associated with patent prosecution and the handling of transactions and advising clients kept me productively occupied.

Being a glutton for punishment, I took interest in a brand-new law known as the U.S. Semiconductor Chip Protection Act that was enacted in 1984. I took the pioneering task of registering IBM semiconductor chips for protection in the U.S. Copyright

Office under the new law. My efforts in the SCPA culminated in penning and contributing a chapter on "Chip Protection, Licensing, Litigation and International Issues" to a legal treatise in 1988.

IBM, being a New York company, mandated its attorneys who aspired to climb the management ladder be admitted to the local bar. I had management aspirations. Accordingly, even though I had worked less than five years as a member of the state bar of Ohio and could not be automatically admitted into the New York bar, I studied the rules of the New York Supreme Court for gaining admission to the bar. Armed with this knowledge, I crafted a unique petition to the Court requesting admission without examination. Surprisingly, the Court agreed, and I gained admission to the New York bar. Ed Brown was astounded at my petition and the Court's approval. The New York bar membership opened up the horizon for my career advancement in IBM.

I never said no to work. I considered it a badge of honor to be asked to take on new and challenging assignments. In just four years after joining IBM, I was blessed to have made great strides in my career. IBM rewarded me with plum assignments, tons of responsibility, not to mention big raises. By any professional measure, I was succeeding.

Meanwhile, I continued my self-imposed goal to help my family. I never lost sight of my duty to help my father, one way or another, to meet the dowry demands placed on him. By now, there remained the matter of my two sisters Vitri and Mini in India.

I also wanted to check whether my parents would like to immigrate to the U.S., as I had the power to sponsor them for U.S. Green Cards. With this in mind, I wanted my parents to come to the U.S. on a visitor's visa and find out whether they would like the climate, food and other living conditions. I wanted them to experience the family environments in which their four children in the U.S. lived. My father outright refused my invitation without providing a reason. However, my mother expressed interest in coming to the U.S. to see her children and grandson.

Accordingly, on April 8, 1983 when my family lived in Kettering, I had sent her a Letter of Invitation. I designed the letter to assure the U.S. Consulate in Madras would grant my mother a visitor's visa. The letter read as follows:

My dear mother,

I am hereby inviting you to come to the United States. As you know, I asked you many times in the last seventeen years that I have been living here to come to the United States to spend some quality time with me and my immediate family, but hitherto circumstances in our family in Bangalore, India did not permit you to do so. I hope that you will be able to come now and spend a few months with us. Your grandson will be a source of great fun and joy when you come here. Coming to the United States will also enable you to see your other children and their spouses. In addition, your stay in the United States will give you much deserved rest and prove to be beneficial to your health.

Needless to say, I will make every effort to take full responsibility for bringing about an enjoyable stay for you.

On the basis of this letter and the enclosed Affidavit of Support, you should qualify for entering the United States on a tourist visa. Please take these documents to the U.S. Consulate in Madras and receive your nonimmigrant visa.

Yours fondly

TR Coca

However, my mother was unable to apply for the visitor's visa right away. There was an unexpected development involving my sister Mini, which delayed my mother's prospective travel to the U.S.

From what my mother wrote in a letter, a young Indian gentleman who was living in Houston, Texas sought a bride based in India. He discovered Mini through a matrimonial advertisement that my father had placed in the newspaper. He met Mini at my parents' house. Their interest in each other immediately clicked. The outgoing nature of Mini and her excellent communication abilities impressed this lad. The fact that four members of my family and their spouses immigrated to and were living in the U.S. on a permanent basis, and that my sister Mini was awaiting her Green Card to also immigrate encouraged this suitor to move forward and tie the wedding knot to Mini.

The young man had been living in the U.S as a permanent resident. He was sponsored years earlier by his older brother, who was a naturalized U.S. citizen. His family—consisting of two older brothers, their wives and children and his mother—were now living in Houston. He was employed with the Texas Welfare Department.

He proposed to marry Mini. Due to the pressures of time on his short visit to India, the couple decided to get married right away. My sister Mini refused to listen to her sister Jaya and brother-in-law Raj who lived in Bangalore, to not rush into the wedding until I verified the background of the groom in the U.S.

Without notifying me or waiting for me to check the background of the potential groom, Mini hastily moved forward. Their wedding was hurriedly arranged to take place in Bangalore. Mini apparently took full control of her wedding and had it celebrated per her whim.

There was no discussion of a dowry payment to the groom for accepting Mini as his wife, which was a positive outcome of this unexpected wedding. I admired the morality of the newlywed groom, now my fourth brother-in-law, for not demanding a dowry payment from my father.

After the wedding, the new groom filed a petition with the U.S. Consulate in Madras for a Green Card for his newly married wife. His petition, filed under the Second Preference category, reduced her waiting period for her visa number to three months, as opposed to the additional waiting on the petition I filed for her in 1982 under the slow-moving Fifth Preference category.

While the wedding of my fourth sister caught me by surprise, I was pleased with its outcome as it fully met my goal of having her married without straining my father by demands for a dowry. Moreover, this sudden matrimony accelerated the intended final outcome of her getting a Green Card.

In due course, my married sister Mini joined her husband in Houston. With her arrival, the number of my siblings who lived in the United States as Green Card holders had grown to four. The number of members of my family in the U.S. had grown to eleven, including the three in my nuclear family.

With the completion of the marriage of Mini, there remained only my third sister Vitri to get married. Finding a suitable husband for her definitely posed a continuing challenge. My well-conceived idea of sponsoring her for the U.S. Green Card and using it as currency for luring an alien spouse from India, which had worked like magic with the three siblings I sponsored earlier, might not work with Vitri.

Paying a dowry to get Vitri married seemed inevitable. Endowing the dowry bank for her benefit was now definitely needed. My sister Jaya reminded me that if my father found out about the dowry bank and had access to it, he might squander it for other purposes. Relying on this, I asked her to serve as the custodian of my endowment, which she agreed to do. The endowment that I had established for Vitri was massive. It was expected that we meet the prevailing dowry payment to attract a professional bridegroom for her. My father, however, was not made aware of this endowment. That was a huge mistake. Later, I regretted not letting him know about this endowment.

In the summer of 1984, there was a development with the status of my younger brother-in-law Rajen in Jamaica. He decided to get married to his girlfriend Sai who lived with him. The wedding took place hurriedly with neither of his sisters and their families living in the U.S. or parents living in India attending the event. I could only surmise that Rajen planned this wedding in order to have his new wife hitch onto the petition for permanent U.S. immigration that Rama filed for him in 1981. This action reinforced my observation that Sai seemed more eager to get into the United States to pursue her medical career and establish herself.

The next development with Rajen and Sai was that in the summer of 1985, a son was born to them in Jamaica. Because of the birth of this nephew of Rama, the 1981 petition for a Green

Card that she had filed for Rajen now needed to be expanded from one to three relatives who waited in Jamaica to enter the U.S. This was a classic chain migration benefit that an alien brother enjoyed by the mere biological relationship with his sister who was naturalized.

The Affidavits of Support that Rama filed five years earlier for her brothers in conjunction with the petitions for Green Cards were no longer valid. Rama no longer held a job providing the income which was the basis of her previous affidavit. I prepared two new Affidavits of Support for my brothers-in-law. My new affidavits attested to the salary that I earned from IBM, the savings in my bank account, and the details of the real estate that Rama and I jointly owned. As required, I had them executed, notarized and sent to my in-laws in Jamaica.

In early 1986 after a wait of more than five years, the U.S. Consulate in Jamaica approved the issuance of his Green Card to my brother-in-law Mali. He promptly arrived at the JFK Airport in New York where Rama and I greeted him to extend a hearty hand of welcome to the U.S. A surprising physical change that we noticed in Mali at the airport was that he was no longer bearded, unkempt and in dingy street clothes. That had been the image that he cultivated as a doctor when we saw him last in Jamaica. He now presented himself clean shaven, well kempt and dressed in a tailored grey suit, necktie and polished leather shoes.

It was an enjoyable reunion for Rama, and we were delighted to host him. Mali stayed with us in our Tudor for months while he sought a medical Residency opening.

My other brother-in-law Rajen, his wife and son, however, did not receive their authorization for approval for their Green

Cards from the U.S. Consulate in Jamaica. Rajen unfortunately failed to pass the mandatory health screening that was conducted by the Immigration Panel doctor at the direction of the Consulate. Rajen reportedly contracted tuberculosis for which he needed to be treated and cured. This failure set him and his family back. After he underwent treatment for the cure of his TB and successfully passed the health screening, he and his family eventually entered the U.S. and received their respective Green Cards to live in this country permanently. Rama and I did not have the opportunity to extend them the hand of welcome to America since they chose Detroit, Michigan as their first port of entry into the U.S.

With the new arrival of these relatives from Rama's side of the family, the count of our family relatives who received Green Cards either directly or indirectly through me now ebbed to eleven. Discounting my sponsorship of my sister Mini, which was preempted by sponsorship by her spouse, I directly sponsored Rama and three of my siblings in California which enabled them to bring their respective alien spouses into the U.S. totaling seven. Rama sponsored her two alien brothers, one a single individual and the other with three members in his family, with the net result of sponsoring four Green Card holders as members of her extended family. This was the net total of chain migration that I and Rama precipitated so far.

In mid-1986 my mother, who I previously had invited to America, finally indicated that she received her U.S. visitor's visa and was ready to visit us. I purchased a round-trip airline ticket, with an open leg for her return trip and sent it to her. She used it and landed first in Los Angeles to spend time with her children based in San Diego. She stayed for a couple of months with Ohan and his wife Shree, who by then had moved out of my house in San Diego and were living in a rental unit with their infant son. Later my mother stayed with Mala and her husband Shank, who also were living in another rental unit in San Diego.

My other sister Swati and her husband Subh, who were also living in their own rental unit in San Diego, however, were reticent to host my mother. They merely invited her for an occasional short visit to spend a couple of hours with them. This bizarre behavior insulted my mother. It certainly bothered me when I found out. I explained to my mother over the phone that "Perhaps your son-in-law Subh is stressed out from his inability to pass license examinations to establish himself as a veterinarian in California. He is continuing to depend on Swati's earnings to survive. Perhaps, Subh is feeling inadequate. Perhaps, he may have developed an inferiority complex. This may be precipitating the disharmony of Subh and Swati with the rest of our extended family in San Diego."

After my mother's visit with her children in San Diego, I flew to there and escorted her to our Tudor in Duchess County. My short stay in San Diego reinforced my sense of the disharmony among my siblings that my mother had also noticed. Rivalry among the siblings there, which was inflamed by their spouses, was not what I had expected.

Rama and I were by then in the throes of having a new house built in Hopewell Junction, New York closer to my IBM office. The new house was in a residential development with several other homes, which Rama and our son needed to have neighbors and children for Nesh to play with. My mother witnessed our move into our new house. Two local firms moved our household belongings.

Seeing them hard at work carrying our household goods in the slippery rain, my mother said to me, "Please pay the movers generously; the poor guys worked hard for you," which I did.

My mother graciously participated in a simple traditional Hindu housewarming ceremony (*gruhapravesam*) in our new house that we had asked her to facilitate. Her well wishes and blessings, participation in our move and her presence in our new home meant a great deal to me and Rama.

Besides my mom witnessing my family settling down in our new dwelling, which was a unique experience for my mother, Rama took her to see her new female Indian friends to socialize. During weekends when I was home, we made it a point to take her to surrounding places in New York's Duchess and Ulster counties, such as the Vanderbilt Mansion in Hyde Park. A place that she enjoyed visiting on a sunny afternoon in October 1986 was an apple orchard in Upstate New York. This was an orchard of trees with fully ripened golden apples, and it spread out over several hundred acres. The apples were free for picking. My mother and members of my family enjoyed picking the apples directly from the trees and eating them to their hearts' content.

Toward the end of a stay of couple of months with us, my mother witnessed the vibrant foliage of fall colors on the maple and other trees along the Hudson River and in our own large backyard. As it was beginning to turn frigid, it was my sister Mini's turn to take her to the warmer climate of Houston, Texas where Mini lived with her husband. Mini travelled to our new home in Hopewell Junction and escorted our mother to Houston. There my mother met relatives of Mini's husband, particularly his mother who she hadn't met before. My mother stayed with Mini and her relatives in Houston for a couple of months, after which she flew back home to Bangalore with a stopover at JFK in New York where Rama, Nesh and I went to see and bid her farewell.

Her visit to America was a wonderful opportunity for my mother to reunify with her children living in this country. However, witnessing firsthand her five children and the independent lives they were leading left an indelible mark on my mother. Certainly, she did not sense a strong family-focused unity among them, which she devoutly preached to practice when we were young. It appeared that the spouses who now joined her children in San Diego did not have the same sense of unity. They seemed to stretch the bond of unity beyond its limit. My mother sensed that her children in San Diego and their spouses had begun to become selfish, self-centered and had entered into a destructive race to make themselves financially better than their other siblings in America or the siblings who were left behind in India. Greed over money seemed to have taken precedence over family unity in their new homeland.

In 1987, about six months after my mother's visit, it was my father-in-law's turn to visit us. Rama's sister Arna arranged for his tourist visa to the U.S. and drove him to our house in Hopewell Junction. He wanted to spend time with his most favorite daughter Rama and his grandson. We showed him around New York City including riding up one of the Twin Towers of the World Trade Center. He and my family were thrilled with the view from the top. It was memorable.

My father-in-law, who always encouraged Rama to succeed in her career and was a force behind her, now became quiet on this matter. Perhaps he understood the ordeal that Rama had gone through at her last Residency in Cincinnati and he chose to not push her again. I was always fond of him. He was a simple man. Honest and true to himself. His letters to me asking for patience with Rama helped me to cope. Since the day I met him, I admired his goal to educate his four children to be doctors. All his children had by now moved to live permanently in the United States.

In addition to my sister Vitri, two of my brothers living in India still remained unmarried. My second younger brother Enku was employed as a clerk in the Bangalore High Court. My last brother Kash was employed as a well-paid officer in a prominent bank in Bangalore. Finding suitable matches for these eligible bachelors was relatively easy despite the fact that they did not hold U.S. Green Cards and remained in India. The clout that my family enjoyed with five members and their spouses now well-settled in the U.S., the other members who remained in India holding enviable jobs and being an established good family was very helpful. Even though these brides would not be promised an opportunity to immigrate to the U.S., perhaps they might expect such an opportunity for themselves and their future family by virtue of marrying into our family. It was unquestionable that the fact that one half of our large family now lived in the U.S. was a tempting attraction to potential brides for my unmarried brothers in India.

Sure enough, suitable matches for them were arranged and their weddings took place on different dates in succession per their age. I was never told, nor asked, whether my last brothers received a dowry. This fact remains shrouded in mystery. I only hoped that they did not take a dowry, which I always regarded as immoral and unethical and an undue financial burden on the bride's parents.

Having played an important role in helping several of his children find suitable spouses and getting them married, my father was emboldened to find a husband for his last unmarried daughter Vitri who continued to live in his household. I assumed that my other siblings in India, particularly my sister Jaya who was overseeing the large dowry account that I had established, also were on the lookout for a match for Vitri. If my father was not emboldened to match up his last unmarried daughter, he was at least desperate to complete this last act.

I was preoccupied with the lucrative promotions and fast-paced advancement that IBM offered, and which I embraced. In less than two years after we settled into our new house in Hopewell Junction, an assignment came up to work directly with Paul Carmichael at IBM Corporate Headquarters in Purchase, New York. I jumped at it. I commuted from home, 40 miles each way, for this assignment, which I successfully completed in just four months to Paul's complete satisfaction.

I looked up to Paul with admiration and appreciated the confidence he showed in me. Although he was an authoritarian figure in the IBM Patent Department and he seldom engaged in small talk, he inspired me as a leader and a workaholic. I started emulating him in my years at IBM, particularly to become a workaholic like him.

IBM rewarded me with a promotion and my first management position at the IBM Watson Research Lab in Yorktown, New

York. I was promoted to Assistant IP Counsel, overseeing a group of eight seasoned Patent Attorneys. I commuted to this new job without moving my family from Hopewell Junction.

The second promotion, which happened exactly six months after I was made the Assistant Counsel, was to a higher management position in Burlington, Vermont. I assumed the Site Patent Counsel position at the IBM operations there. Soon we sold our house in Hopewell Junction and moved to Burlington.

In Burlington, we ended up purchasing a beautiful brand-new house at the Summit at Spear in South Burlington. Rama and I loved this rambling house which had six bedrooms and two master bedroom suites. It was in a secluded setting with a manicured lawn and tall and slender Aspens, and just walking distance from a viewpoint at the summit on Spear Street.

The rolling hills of Burlington, with distant tall mountain ranges, offered a spectacular lush landscape. Lake Champlain which is the lake between the Green Mountains of Vermont and the Adirondack Mountains of New York was the main attraction of Burlington. We enjoyed watching the golden sunsets in the waters of Lake Champlain from the scenic viewpoint at the Summit at Spear. The sunsets reminded us of the gorgeous and glistening waves on Mission Bay in San Diego, when the water reflected the declining sun as it set on the distant horizon.

As we moved from place to place, Rama and I made sure that Nesh went to the best public schools as his education was paramount to us. We paid close attention to his education and ensured that he excelled in his grades. Rama instilled discipline in him to do his homework and be fully prepared and ready for school the next day. She participated in teacher-parent conferences to receive firsthand information of our son's progress in his classes.

We encouraged Nesh to participate in sports, such as soccer and baseball, which he did. I encouraged him to hit golf balls on the large manicured lawn in the front yard of our house by purchasing a set of golf clubs and balls, which he tried. Rama regularly took him to a local swim club, where he and she took private swimming lessons.

My son developed an interest in learning to play the violin in his primary school. He played the violin with passion and commitment. I listened to him with my eyes closed so I could concentrate on the melodious music he played. We encouraged him to master this musical skill by arranging a private violin tutor. My wife regularly took him to the tutor after school ended to learn more and practice this stringed instrument. He worked at it slavishly, practicing hours a day. Within a year of practicing under the teacher's tutelage, he was selected by Vermont's Youth Symphony Orchestra. We hoped someday in the future he might become a violin virtuoso because the way he played the violin was just outstanding.

I remembered a statement made in jest by a colleague at Abington a decade earlier when I revealed that I just had married a doctor. He said, "You will rake in the dough." Unfortunately, I never raked in the dough because I married a doctor. I continued to look back and think that Rama was so close to becoming a successful Anesthesiologist, but she was forced to give up after making a gallant try. The thought of Rama wasting away all that she invested in and achieved, especially earning her license to be a physician, haunted me from time to time. Perhaps, some unseen forces were shaping our lives. Why did this happen? I wanted to know, but the answer remained elusive.

I expressed my feelings to Rama, but she was unmoved. The scars of her failure left an indelible mark on her and she never spoke about returning to complete her unfinished Residency. Rama found inner strength in raising our son into a wonderful boy. It appeared that Rama had reached equilibrium—a universal balance—in her life.

It was difficult to control my irrepressible hope that Rama would be a working doctor. Instead, for my self-preservation, I started to believe that some matters were in the domain of God, like *karma*, or luck or some other force.

I marched forward focusing on my career at IBM, which I continued to enjoy both psychologically and materially. My career there saved me from dwelling on my disappointment with Rama's inability to become a practicing doctor.

I worked hard all my life in relative obscurity, often being someone with an unfulfilled dream, but that was about to change.

No sooner than we had settled into our brand-new house in South Burlington and just months after I was sworn in as a member to the Vermont Bar in Montpelier, Vermont (my fourth bar membership), Paul Carmichael from the IBM Headquarters called me. He made a new employment offer.

He asked, "Would you be interested in an International Assignment in IBM Asia Pacific Headquarters in Tokyo, Japan?"

I could not believe what a wonderful job just had fallen in my lap!

Paul elaborated on my duties in my new job in Tokyo. I attentively listened while controlling my glee.

He told me, "Think over the assignment, talk it over with Rama and get back to me with your decision."

I then realized Paul all along had been my mentor at IBM. During my earlier stint directly under Paul's tutelage that I completed in IBM Headquarters in Purchase, New York, I might have made an impression on him. I recalled pointedly asking Paul in my first job interview seven years earlier of attorney job opportunities that IBM might have in Asia, as I was then still considering accepting the job offer from Texas Instruments to handle patent licensing work in Japan, Korea and other Asian countries. Paul seemed to have captured my interest in working in Asia. After I joined IBM, he trained me and groomed me for this eventual international assignment in Japan.

I sometimes believed the hand of God brought me to IBM. He blessed me with Paul as my mentor. Perhaps Paul had all along been God in disguise. How else could I explain the fortune of such a wonderful job coming my way?

I was euphoric and immediately called Rama and posed this unusual question: "How would you like to live in Japan?"

Rama could not believe what she just heard. I explained the job offer that Paul just made to me.

She asked, "For how long?"

I responded, "It depends. It could be for up to two or three years." I added: "This is a once in a lifetime opportunity for me and us."

This was a plum job which most IBM managing attorneys craved for and waited for their entire IBM career. It entailed being based in Tokyo. The job required supervision of teams of IBM professionals located in Japan, South Korea, Taiwan, Hong

Kong, and Australia as well as developing and managing IBM's regional Intellectual Property portfolio. Another requirement of this assignment was licensing and enforcement of IBM Intellectual Property rights across the entire Asia Pacific region where IBM conducted its business.

That evening Rama and I had a long discussion of the wonderful promotion that Paul just had offered. We weighed the pros and cons of accepting the promotion. The con was disrupting our son's education that was going so well in school. He would not be able to play violin in the Vermont Youth Symphony. The pros were too many. The net was that the IBM job transfer and promotion was so attractive and such a once-in-a-lifetime opportunity that I could not pass it up. It opened an opportunity to rapidly advance and potentially be a candidate for the top job of Chief IP Counsel at IBM. We together decided to accept it.

The next morning, I informed Paul that I would accept the offer he made.

I told him: "Paul, I am so grateful to you for extending this generous promotion to me. I sincerely thank you for your confidence in my management abilities to take on this one-of-a-kind job in IBM. I promise, I will live up to your expectations in the international assignment in Tokyo you offered. It is truly an honor for you to have chosen me!"

After accepting, in the summer of 1990, I unceremoniously plucked my family and moved to Tokyo for the IBM international assignment. I anticipated a new set of experiences and monumental challenges involving new workers, new cultures, new languages and new legal systems to learn and practice. It was a thrilling move for Rama and our son, who were about to face many new experiences. A brand-new world was awaiting me in the Asia Pacific region with IBM.

I believed in the value of hard work, and it had paid off many times. My long-term goal of helping my father was also nearing completion. Only my fourth sister Vitri remained to be married.

While I was preoccupied with my hectic IBM career, my father looked for a suitable husband for Vitri. He generally placed matrimonial advertisements in the local newspaper. One such ad seemed to have put my father in contact with Anda, who was a high-school classmate of my brother Avi and me. In high school I had played soccer with him during lunch breaks. He did not display a high degree of intelligence in the classroom, except that he was good in math. In fact, Anda had attended my wedding reception in Bangalore in 1976.

I was reminded that Anda was now employed as an officer in a local state-controlled bank in Bangalore. Like my last brother Kash, who also was a bank officer, I concluded that Anda was probably paid well. I recalled him telling me at my wedding reception that he had earned a bachelor's degree in Commerce.

However, when I first found out from a letter my mother wrote that my father was considering Anda for a marriage alliance with Vitri, I was stunned and became unglued.

Anda came from a low class and low caste Hindu family. His father had passed away when he was very young, and he was raised by his mother who had additional children. I recalled Anda telling me in the past that his mother scrubbed clothes in a lake and made a living on that service for their family. He belonged to the Scheduled Caste, which was an Indian government's designated class to safeguard people in that class from atrocities committed by others belonging to a higher caste. People in the Scheduled Caste received special treatment in college admissions and consideration for government jobs when the minimum educational requirements were not met by them. I could not help presuming that he received lucky breaks to earn his bachelor's in Commerce and become a bank officer because of his classification as a member of the Scheduled Caste.

From seeing Anda at my wedding reception, I recalled that he was frail and bony and devoid of masculinity. He appeared meek. While Anda was courteous to me and Rama at the reception, I had no information as to his character, integrity and the type of person he grew up to be since I had lost touch with him after high school.

There was no doubt in my mind that Vitri deserved someone better than Anda to be her husband. I checked with my siblings in California about this proposed alliance. None of them knew much more about Anda. They did not want to second-guess my father's judgement. Jaya and Raj in India were ambivalent and did not have a high regard for Anda as a person or for his family. However, they did not protest my father's decision. My older brother Avi, who knew Anda better than I did, seemed to have acquiesced in my father's unilateral decision or he did not care.

I took a strong stand against this proposed alliance and communicated it to my father in no uncertain terms. I emphatically told him that he should not go forward with Anda. I told him that there exists a vast divide between the stature of our family and Anda's, without denigrating Anda's family. I explained that "A refined girl like Vitri would not be happy if she married into the unsophisticated family of Anda. She would not be happy with him or in his household. I know you are trying to do the right thing, but please do not do something this desperate without giving thought to Vitri's future."

Despite my strong objection, in another letter I received from my mother, I learnt that my father decided to move forward with the alliance and finalized it. My father did not have money to give as a dowry to Anda's family. He was not aware of the dowry account that I had established for Vitri's benefit. I did not know what promises he might have made to Anda. Perhaps, he enticed him by saying that after the wedding I would sponsor my sister Vitri and him for their Green Cards? Or did he promise that my sister would inherit the house that he owned? My father did not share with me any such promises he might have made to lure Anda to agree for the marriage to Vitri.

Was the decision my father made, which might negatively impact the future life and well-being of my Vitri, an act of desperation? I struggled to understand my father's dogged determination to have proceeded with the alliance. Perhaps, there was a dark past in Vitri's life that I was unaware of which compelled my father to settle for the meek and docile Anda to mask that past?

The wedding of my sister to Anda took place in Bangalore without any of her siblings living in the U.S. attending it. It was a low-key wedding, which was attended by my siblings who remained in India and their immediate families. Vitri moved into Anda's tiny house, which was occupied by his aged mother and his other siblings all under one roof.

Vitri's marriage to Anda left me with sadness and anger: sadness, because Vitri deserved better; anger, because my father acted in desperation for no apparent reason. I also was hard on myself that I withheld from my father knowledge of the existence of the dowry endowment I established. Had he known about the endowment, might he have used it to pay a dowry and arrange a better bridegroom for her? I regretted my decision. But for my silence, the matrimonial alliance between Vitri and Anda might have been avoided.

The endowment that I established to pay for the dowry of Vitri and alleviate the financial hardship on my father never was put to use. The dowry account remained unutilized and intact for her future benefit.

After what happened to Vitri, I asked myself: What were you feeling? It wasn't joy, for sure. It wasn't satisfaction. It was regret and remorse. I wished I could do it all over again. If I could, I would do it differently.

As indicated to me by Paul Carmichael, the assignment at the IBM Asia Pacific headquarters in Tokyo entailed that I supervise a seventy-five-person team and manage the foreign Intellectual Property portfolio, along with licensing and enforcing IBM IP rights. I supervised IBM law departments dispersed in Australia, China, Hong Kong, Japan, South Korea and Taiwan by studying, learning and adapting to the cultural differences of people and differences in laws. Based on the culture, I tailored different approaches in coaching my teams based in the different countries. By holding annual team gatherings in Tokyo, I established a strong sense of collaboration and a bond of common purpose among them under the IBM umbrella.

Enforcement of IBM's Intellectual Property in the Asian countries offered challenges. However, by coordinating with my IBM team on the ground, the local police and prosecutors, and by persuasive counselling, I successfully met IBM's expectations.

An enduring leadership role that I exercised in the Asia Pacific region was serving as an IP ambassador from America. By coordinating with the U.S. Trade Representative's Office, I pushed for IP legislation that the U.S. Government and IBM together desired. I invested time and energy by meeting one-on-one with Asian Pacific local officials in government, industry and academia to explain the U.S. IP laws with the expectation that they would emulate them. I gave talks to IP organizations in many Asian countries. I published articles on IP in Asian journals and presented at international conferences. Coaching and imparting knowledge on IP to the local communities was a part of my leadership repertoire.

While I was travelling on business, the bliss that came from knowing that Rama was with our son Nesh in Tokyo and looking after him and caring for him was extraordinary. Rama and Nesh were the best things that ever happened to me. Nesh attended a private school in Tokyo established for children from America and other foreign countries. It was St. Mary's International School. He took Japanese as a second language at the School. He made the Honor's roll consistently, every semester, and brought us happiness.

This international assignment normally was limited to two years. However, Paul Carmichael was generous to extend it for five years, which I attribute to my good cultural fit and job performance. I was promoted to the executive ranks during this assignment. One of the many perks that IBM provided during the assignment was to return our family to our home in Burlington, Vermont on yearly basis for home leave. This provided my family opportunities to travel around the world, shuttling between our homes in Tokyo and Burlington. On every home leave, we made it a point to stop in Bangalore to see my parents and siblings.

It was on one such stopover in Bangalore that I noticed that Vitri had moved back to live with my parents.

I asked her, "How long have you been living with Mom and Dad?"

She replied, "For almost a year." Vitri added, "The living conditions in Anda's home were deplorable. Many adults and children were crammed into a tiny house. Basic comforts were lacking."

She paused, and then said, "I never had any privacy in the house with Anda. We were married in name only."

I presumed this to mean no opportunity prevailed for a conjugal relationship between the married couple.

I asked, "What do you plan to do now?"

Though timid and sweet as she always had been, Vitri was prepared with her reply. She told me, "Brother, I cannot go back to Anda or his house, ever."

With Vitri's clear pronouncement of her unwillingness to live with Anda, divorce was the only solution I could envision. However, my father would not give up. While I was in Bangalore, he made many phone calls to Anda at the bank where he worked. Anda mostly evaded those calls.

During one such call, I overheard my father say, "Your friend from America is here." He pleaded with Anda to "please come and see him." Anda never came to see me.

My father pressured me to meet Anda at his bank. My father expected that I could talk sense into Anda to take back Vitri and live in his own house independent of the rest of his family and save his marriage. He believed that magically I would be able to bring the separated couple together.

I acquiesced and went to meet Anda at the bank on the pretext of converting U.S. dollar bills into rupees. At the bank, I requested the bank teller for a meeting with Anda. Although I could see Anda at a distance in his open office, he never showed interest in meeting me. This incident only reinforced my belief that he was meek and did not have the courage to face his marital problems.

Disappointed, I returned home to my father and advised him to have a petition for Vitri's divorce from Anda initiated in the Bangalore High Court. I advised that under the Hindu Marriage Act of 1955, the couple satisfied the requirement of living separately for a year. The petition should specify that the divorce was with consent and ask for no alimony or maintenance payment for Vitri as part of the annulment. I wanted the divorce to be quick and without complications.

My father asked that I should engage my friend Shiv to handle the divorce proceeding. I suggested that this was a small case for Shiv, who was known to handle exclusively large and complicated cases involving huge fees. Instead, I suggested that he should have Shank's father, who was still practicing law, to handle it.

I admonished, "Dad, let us keep this divorce matter within our family as much as we can, OK?"

That was the last time my father and I discussed the potential divorce between Vitri and Anda.

I was never told whether Vitri's divorce ever happened, but a year later I received in Tokyo a wonderful piece of news from my mother. She wrote that a new matrimonial alliance for Vitri had been agreed upon. She did not write how this alliance came about, but she filled me in other details. The new alliance partner for Vitri was a widower from near the town where I was born. He had a grown-up son and a daughter who was married. The daughter and her husband lived with him, while his son now lived somewhere in Tennessee. He alliance partner was ten years older than Vitri. He knew Vitri was married before and did not have children. He was gainfully employed. Being a widower, he did not expect a dowry to marry Vitri, but the stature of our well-established family in the U.S. and in India was a positive factor in agreeing to marry her.

I arranged to have the endowment that I had established for Vitri be transferred as a wedding gift, which Vitri was so thankful to receive. I heard that the groom was surprised with my generosity, although he never expressed it in words when I met with him as my brother-in-law years after he wedded Vitri.

With the completion of the second wedding of my sister Vitri, all of my siblings were now married. Some were married for over a decade. Were they all happily married? Only time would tell.

Was it fair to conclude that I had accomplished my original goal of helping my father avoid bankruptcy by removing the financial strain of paying for the dowries? Did I succeed in my mission to gift the U.S. Green Cards to my unmarried sisters for using the attendant benefits in exchange for their dowry money? No doubt, I succeeded in this mission with my sisters Swati and Mala. Certainly, I would have likewise succeeded in the mission I launched for my sister Mini as well, except she abruptly took a different path to achieve the same end result. My father benefitted from the Green Cards that I gifted to my sisters, as he did not have to pay a dowry for them. It was fortuitous that my father did not have to pay for his first daughter Jaya, despite the feared consequences of her elopement with the previously married Raj. It was a blessing that Vitri was now married—albeit for the second time. My father did not have to pay for dowry for Vitri, either.

Did the family reunification principle—which was the bedrock foundation of the U.S. Immigration System, and the basis on which my alien brother and sisters received their Green Cards and an eventual path to citizenship to our country—meet its intended goal?

In the short span of four years after I was naturalized, I exercised my right to kinship for at least a part of my family's reunification in the U.S. Under the spirit of the 1965 Immigration & Naturalization Act, family reunification was important. It was intended not just for the social and emotional well-being of the sponsor but also the economic well-being of the community in which the sponsor lived. My extended family remained in San Diego. My nuclear family, for the most part, was separated from them by thousands of miles within the country when we moved away to Dayton, Cincinnati, Fishkill and Burlington and then more when we moved overseas to Japan. Because of this physical separation, the family reunification did not seem to fully serve its intended purpose.

Also, since half of my immediate family had now immigrated to the U.S. and the other half remained in India, which of these two halves was enjoying better family unity and happier lives? These are questions that I continue to ponder.

The IBM international assignment gave me new insights. Living overseas as an American taught me cultural attitudes about life and money and changed my perceptions. I could see the world differently and that perspective helped me to forge stronger connections with those around me. I gained a better understanding of wide-ranging cultures as I travelled though the counties in Asia. It helped me engage in conversations, to become a better listener as I asked incisive questions and learned from them. For example, I appreciated the mentality of "seize the moment" by the Chinese and "here and now" mentality of the Australians. I felt that I was being in the zone in my IBM international assignment.

Following the international assignment, I repatriated to the IBM Microelectronics Division in Fishkill, New York as the Chief IP Counsel where a dozen years earlier I was the newly hired and lowest ranking attorney. It was a wonderful homecoming for me. As the Head Counsel, I had the responsibility to manage seventy employees including thirty Patent Attorneys dispersed across five sites in the U.S.: Fishkill, New York; Endicott, New York; Burlington, Vermont; Austin, Texas; and Rayleigh-Durham, North Carolina.

On the personal front, we built a beautiful home in Ridgefield, Connecticut surrounded by a myriad of maple and apple trees. Plus, a bubbling creek crossed our yard. I commuted to work in Fishkill, forty miles each way. Our teen-age son Nesh went to Ridgefield High School and continued to make the Honor's roll like he did at St. Mary's in Tokyo. Based on his scholastic achievement Nesh competed for and was awarded the prestigious Thomas J. Watson Memorial Scholarship designed for children of IBM employees to pursue higher education. He then moved on to Cornell University in Ithaca, New York where he additionally received the McMullen Dean's Scholarship which was the most prestigious merit award available from the College of Engineering at Cornell for scholastic accomplishment and personal character. Rama and I were thrilled at Nesh's academic accomplishments and personal growth.

It was a thrill to orchestrate the large microelectronics team under me to accomplish three critical annual objectives: file one-thousand new patent applications; issue one-thousand new patents to sustain IBM's top patent rank in the U.S.; and generate an income of $700 million to $850 million from patent licensing. Generating income was the most challenging part. It required commanding leadership and being fanatical about patent monetization. I assembled an A-team of workers who shared my fanaticism. I believed that when fanatics came together with other fanatics, the multiplicative effect was unstoppable. I distilled the complex art of patent licensing into simple components and delegated them to my team with set expectations and fostered creativity in closing deals.

Over a period of six years, my team consistently met all objectives and delivered over $5 billion of income to IBM through patent licenses, patent sales, and technology transfers. This was my tangible payback to IBM, which had treated me so well to triumph as a lawyer. I groomed many lawyers into successful professionals and managers.

I was at the peak of my performance as a lawyer. However, the stress of meeting incessant demands and the constant breathing down my neck by people from IBM's Finance Organization to raise more revenue from IP assets compelled me to seek a reprieve.

Rama also needed a change of venue. She was craving to get

away from the cold, snowy winters in the East. I asked IBM to move me to the more enjoyable climate of San Jose, California where IBM had offices and needed an experienced managing counsel. The company readily obliged. We moved back to California. However, it was not the same as returning to San Diego, which we continued to miss. We had sold the house that we owned in San Diego years earlier, after my three siblings and their spouses who had lived there decided to move into their apartments.

Under my new title of IP Research Counsel at the IBM Almaden Research Lab, I functionally managed Research Labs located in San Jose, Beijing, New Delhi and Tokyo. I directed the IP teams based in these locations by being stationed in San Jose. I was back working with brilliant scientists and marveled at the scientific breakthroughs they made in nanotechnology, new memory devices, quantum computing and artificial intelligence. My new goal was simple: safeguard their inventions for IBM's future monetization.

My mentor Paul Carmichael retired from IBM when I was in Tokyo. I kept in contact with Paul. He moved to Cupertino, California where he was counselling a young CEO Jensen Huang at Nvidia Corporation in Santa Clara, California. Soon after I moved to San Jose, Paul called me. He said "I just hired the first General Counsel at Nvidia. His name is David Shannon. David is looking to hire the Chief Patent Counsel under him. Are you interested?" The job interview followed, and I received an offer of employment for this position. However, I wanted to log in a few more years at IBM to enhance my retirement benefits and I provisionally declined the job.

Three years later, I called David to see whether he had a job opening under him. David responded "Fortuitously, I have an opening for a Senior Director of Litigation. Would you like to join?" I plunged into it after tendering my resignation to IBM. After twenty three years my rewarding and enjoyable career as a patent counsel at IBM came to an abrupt end.

In my career as a lawyer I never directly handled defensive patent litigation which was the responsibility I took on at Nvidia. Patent litigation had been the sport of kings because of the expense and complexity. I pushed as a hard-charging type-A lawyer until the wheels came off at Nvidia. I handled a dozen patent suits, as a defense counsel by engaging external litigators, in the Federal District Courts, Court of Appeals and the International Trade Commission. With the inherent unpredictability of litigation, the substantial costs of what would have been a long and complicated legal process and ongoing distraction to the business, I promoted that settlement was the best solution.

After four years of leading as a litigator at Nvidia, I was sought by an ex-IBM executive Robert Melendres who now the General Counsel at International Game Technology in Las Vegas, Nevada to work as the Vice President of Intellectual Property under him. I accepted and offered a sharply focused lens on monetizing the patent portfolio of this casino game-machine manufacturer. This job was the culmination of my long, enjoyable and rewarding law career.

My years of education in physics and law and the experience I gained at the prominent international companies where I worked gave me the essence of wisdom. It was akin to possessing a vast library and understanding how to use it. What I accomplished filled the canvas of my life. I finally reached the stage of life known in Hindu religion as *Sannyasi* in Sanskrit which means "into the forest". What was left now was to adjust my life to service and dedicate to the fruits of enlightenment.

TRIUMPH AS INTELLECTUAL PROPERTY ATTORNEY

Looking back, decades earlier I came to the United States because of a generous gesture of goodwill that Temple University had extended to me. By placing trust and confidence in me and the degrees I had earned from the University of Mysore, Temple gave me admission to enroll in their doctoral program, offered free tuition and a stipend. Based on this gesture, I obtained my student visa to come to this country. My performance in my coursework at Temple, which netted my second master's degree, and the advanced doctoral research I conducted enabled me to qualify, under a skill-based immigration preference, for my Green Card. My Green Card paved the way to my U.S. citizenship. I spent a decade to earn my three degrees, including my J.D. from Temple.

In monetary terms, Temple awarded me valuable free tuition and a paid stipend during a six-year period of my doctoral study. Importantly, Temple gave me the opportunity to be what I am today. It is said that "you haven't learned how to live until you learn how to give."

Accordingly, I established a fund titled "*T.R. Coca, M.A. (1968), Ph.D. (1972), J.D. (1979) Scholarship Fund.*" This fund would award an annual scholarship to a rising student at Temple School of Law who enrolled in courses in Intellectual Property Law and aspired to be a Patent Lawyer. The cash that I invested in this fund was more than the tuition and stipend I had received from Temple in my six years. The fund was irrevocable, and the scholarship was intended to continue in perpetuity. Perhaps, one day my protégé will emerge from this funding!

Is life not fair? Not so, in my case. It is foolish to expect fairness at least when it comes to matters outside the scope of law. One's life can be controlled to some extent, but it may need redesign and hard work to rebuild, as I did by switching from physicist to lawyer. Matters that cannot be controlled by human effort are in the domain of a Higher Being. Personally, I was dealt a good life with the grace of God. Looking back, I honor the life I led!

REFLECTIONS

I WAS RAISED with strong family values. My duty to help my parents and meet any burden they faced dawned upon me at an early age. When I was growing up in India, there was little pressure from my parents to achieve. All of the pressure I faced was self-imposed. I was driven by self-directed goals and found my own motivation to accomplish those goals. My values, outlook and my independence emerged early in my childhood. I felt gifted with a sound mind. I wanted to be an intellectual and had sights on the world beyond India.

I pondered what the calling was to my life? In the journal that I kept ever since I was in high school, I wrote this entry at age fifteen on August 25, 1958: *I feel helpless that my family continues to grow. We are ten siblings now. What is going to be my destiny? There is so much to think about my large family. What kind of life will each of my siblings have? What is my duty to my parents and my siblings? What exactly is the calling to my life? What do I believe in? Who really am I?*

Another entry in my journal from around this time reads: *My mother expects me to be a good role model to my younger siblings. How am I going to fulfill this huge responsibility?*

I made up my mind to make a difference in my family. The failed attempt by my father to have me join the Indian Army before I reached the age of fifteen jolted me in to action. I was awakened to the fact that my father needed wealth or else he might become destitute because of the heavy financial burden placed on him to pay huge dowries for my five unmarried sisters. My failure to qualify for the Army was a blessing in disguise. I developed a passion to excel in everything I did so I could earn money in a different way.

My determination led to new, nontraditional thinking. I forced myself to think big. The gospel I practiced was to invest in hard work today so I could reap the financial benefits tomorrow to help my family.

Obtaining the best possible education was my immediate goal. I believed that such an education would open the door for me to go to America. Going to America was a thought unheard of in my family and in the community in which I lived. Nevertheless, I plowed forward with this thought. I planned to gain admission to an American university along with financial aid, obtain my doctorate, earn money and help my father to pay for the dowries.

I earned an impeccable education with the bachelor's and master's degrees I obtained in India, which paved the way to higher studies at Temple University in Philadelphia, Pennsylvania. I arrived in the U.S. at the age of twenty-two with little money. I had little more than a dream of what might be. Yet America had taken me in. I continued to work hard and received my second master's degree and a doctorate in physics from Temple.

However, circumstances beyond my control diverted my goal to earn money as a physicist when I could not find such a position. I settled on becoming a physics instructor, a job that enabled me to survive for some time. I concluded that my teaching career was a detour and I strode with purpose to find a job for which I was trained.

My inability to develop a career as a physicist for five years after earning my doctorate was tough on me. It was stressful.

Even so, my gift of ambition and goal setting propelled me to overcome this setback and redesign my life, which is what I did.

At the ripe old age of thirty-one, I decided to embark on a new career path. I resolved to try a new profession which would give me full control of my destiny. I complemented my education in physics with a law degree, transitioning my career from teacher to lawyer. As I embarked on my law study, I was blessed with a wonderful job as a physicist with General Dynamics Corporation which I gladly accepted while continuing my study to be a lawyer on the side.

The sixteen years of time and effort that I invested in my higher education opened unexpected vistas for my career and enriched me in ways I never had envisioned. After I earned my J.D. and received admissions to various U.S. bars, I knew I had found my real calling as an American Intellectual property attorney.

My struggles to come to America, earn my degrees in physics, resort to being a physics instructor, go to law school, work as a physicist, and become a lawyer to help my father all made my life worthwhile. They say fortune favors the bold. My bold decision and stubborn streak to change my career into an incredibly different profession from the discipline of physics to the discipline of law paid off handsomely. I was now able to help my family.

To honor my parents and enrich my nuclear family, I settled for an arranged marriage with a physician from India who joined me in America. My wife has been my best partner who I cherish every day. She empowered my nuclear family and supported my duty to my father and generosity to our extended family. She made a gallant effort to establish herself as a licensed Anesthesiologist in America. She succeeded to an enormous extent, even earned her license to practice medicine in the U.S. Her efforts made her a stronger person. I joke these days that my wife changed her specialty to Family Practice. She now has three dedicated patients in my family to look after: our son, herself and me.

My diversion to a new career as an American lawyer altered my original plan to earn money and return to India and continue to financially help my father with the dowries. The new plan was to capitalize on my new legal status as a naturalized American citizen, an incredible honor I earned when I was in law school. My revised plan was to use the U.S. Green Card as a tool to rescue my father from paying the dowries. I sponsored my unmarried sisters in India for Green Cards and accommodated them to join in my household in the U.S. My sisters successfully used their Green Cards to interest eligible bachelors in India to marry them without my father paying a dowry. The quid-pro-quo for marrying without a dowry was the bride sponsored the 'groom for a Green Card of their own.

I served my father and helped lift the heavy burden of dowries placed on him by using the Green Card as a tool. The true and direct beneficiaries of the Green Cards that I orchestrated were the siblings that I sponsored. By gaining entry into America through my sponsorship, my siblings and their new-found spouses won life's lottery. I could confidently say that none of them would have gained entry without my sponsorship. Certainly, none would have gained a permanent visa to live and work in the U.S. By being born as my sibling, they and their spouses won this lottery the value of which is immeasurable.

Ultimately, I delivered something which improved the lives of my siblings and their spouses. I participated in a grand human drama by simply helping them with a new life in a new country.

The same applied to the two brothers of my wife who

obtained their Green Cards from their relationship to my nuclear family. Her younger brother triply benefitted by sweeping in Green Cards for his wife and son as well.

Did the immigrants that my wife and I sponsored work to preserve the family as a unit in our new country and stay united? The family reunification I devised certainly helped to alleviate the financial hardship of dowry payment on my father. It also enabled our migrated relatives to significantly enhance their financial potential. My nuclear family had been the bedrock of stability. I and my wife offered support to our migrated relatives. I encouraged my siblings to preserve our family's unity and stand together like my mother expected.

To borrow an analogy from physics, our nuclear family is tightly bound by the forces among the components of the nucleus. If you believe in Neils Bohr model of the atomic nucleus, my extended family is circling around us in various orbits. If you believe in the Erwin Schrödinger model, the extended family is in a quantum field surrounding us with the uncertainty principle of Werner Heisenberg in full effect.

Neither I nor my wife expected to get rich overnight by stumbling into some American El Dorado. We studied, worked hard, learned and attained our status. Because of our status, we were able to reunify our family in America. On balance, did the family reunification process bring in the right blend of immigrants to America and enrich it with cultural, intellectual and economic vibrancy? Only time will tell.

Personally, I was dealt a good life by the Creator. I lived a life that I was blessed with. I was able to do something for someone who I never expected to be able to repay.

Looking back at my life, I do not just remember it. I honor it.

Importantly, every day I cherish the incredible opportunity

that America gave me to achieve my dreams. Opportunity was not a guarantee of success as I quickly found out after earning my doctorate, but I could achieve my aspirations by starting a new course of action as a lawyer. Such change of course was possible only in America.

A lot has been written about American exceptionalism. What does it mean? It means that the American people have been extraordinary. They have made a global impact lifting millions out of poverty. Americans liberate, but not subjugate. Americans have been a unique force for the good of humanity.

I truly believe in these American ideals and subscribe to them wholeheartedly. No other country could come close to what America has done for humanity and will continue to do going forward. Many foreigners have taken advantage of the generosity of this country. The time has come for them to pay back to America and rejuvenate this great society to contribute even more to the humanity at large.

AUTHOR BIO

T.R. Coca

T.R. Coca has a rare combination of multi-disciplined education, a kaleidoscopic professional career and rich cultural background. His first love of Physics drove him to the pinnacle of leaning of Physics, as evidenced by the degrees he earned which include a B.S., M.S., M. A., and Ph.D. While working as a teacher and later as a Physicist at General Dynamics Corporation, T.R. pursued law to synergistically combine his rich technical background with knowledge of the U. S. laws and became an Intellectual Property attorney. T.R. has been admitted to practice in New York, Ohio, Vermont and the United States Patent Bar. He is admitted to practice before Federal Courts including the U. S. Supreme Court.

Before being appointed as the Vice President of Intellectual Property Law at IGT, he was a Sr. Director of Litigation and Licensing at NVIDIA Corporation. Prior to that, T.R. worked as a senior corporate counsel at IBM where, for a period of over two decades, he held many executive and management positions in many world locations including a five-year international assignment as the Assistant General Counsel in charge of IP in IBM's Asia Pacific Headquarters based in Tokyo.

Of Indian heritage, T.R. has synergistically combined his rich and disciplined Indian cultural upbringing with the consensus building of the Japanese tradition that he was exposed to while living in Japan and the competitive and innovative work ethic prevalent in the United States.

T.R. presented and published innumerable papers and talks in Physics and intellectual property, and corporate law matters, including contributing a chapter on the Semiconductor Chip Protection Laws to the legal treatise Intellectual Property Litigation & Licensing. He served on the Editorial Board of the AIPLA Quarterly Journal of the American Intellectual Property Law Association

T.R.'s varied experience has been as a teacher, physicist, software architect, lawyer, speaker, mentor and writer.

www.ingramcontent.com/pod-product-compliance
Lightning Source LLC
Chambersburg PA
CBHW071215080526
44587CB00013BA/1383